D0262504

Professional Parents

For
MARGARET
who stayed at home
and did the parenting
while her husband went abroad
and talked about it.

Professional Parents

Parent Participation In Four Western European Countries

NICHOLAS BEATTIE

The Falmer Press

(A member of the Taylor & Francis Group)
London and Philadelphia

UK   The Falmer Press, Falmer House, Barcombe, Lewes, East Sussex, BN8 5DL

USA   The Falmer Press, Taylor & Francis Inc., 242 Cherry Street, Philadelphia, PA 19106-1906

© N. Beattie 1985

First published 1985

Library of Congress Cataloging in Publication Data

Beattie, Nicholas.
  Professional parents.

  1. Home and school—Europe—Case studies. 2. Parents' advisory committees in education—Europe—Case studies. 3. Citizens' advisory committees in education—Europe— Case studies. 4. Comparative education. I. Title.
  LC225.33.E85B43   1985   370.19′31   85-16251
  ISBN 1-85000-077-8
  ISBN 1-85000-078-6 (pbk.)

Jacket design by Leonard Williams

Typeset in 11/13 Caledonia by
Imago Publishing Ltd, Thame, Oxon.

Printed in Great Britain by Taylor & Francis (Printers) Ltd, Basingstoke

Contents

Contents

Acknowledgments

Any book of this sort, assembled piecemeal over a decade, draws perforce on a wide range of human contacts. It would be invidious and impossible to list all colleagues, students, librarians, parent activists, teachers and administrators who have helped me in one way or another at one time or another. In all four countries, all sorts of busy people have been amazingly ready to talk to me, and offer food, drink, hospitality, good company and stimulating conversation. I can only thank them all and apologize that the book gives so feeble an impression of what to me so often appeared as a kaleidoscopic variety of human interaction and commitment.

I must also thank various institutions which at different times helped fund my visits: the French Ministry of Foreign Affairs, the German Academic Exchange Service (twice), the Italian Institute, the Sir Ernest Cassel Educational Trust and the University of Liverpool (repeatedly, by travel grants and two terms' study leave).

The book has been assembled and revised over a long period, so various typists have converted various versions into typescript: I thank them too. Particular gratitude is due to the staff of the University of Liverpool Education Library, and especially to Hazel Crebbin, who pursued with exemplary enterprise and resolution inter-library loans for obscure works in languages she did not understand.

Nicholas Beattie
Liverpool, January 1985

1 Introduction

1.1 Participation and Parent Participation

'I never see my parents — they're always fighting for school kids' rights at school governors' meetings,' says an English adolescent to his friend. 'In the old days dad had another job,' says a French counterpart, 'but now he's become a parent.'[1] These are captions from two cartoons independently conceived in two separate countries, and each makes the same point: that a new class of person has appeared on the educational scene, a 'parent governor' or 'parondélève' (written in the French cartoon as a single word as though it were a new washing-powder), and that this person devotes much time and energy to — what?

The question is surprisingly hard to answer. Parents as an orga nized body of people are nothing if not vociferous, and 'the parent movement' generates month by month a very large volume of words in its newsletters, reviews and magazines. Yet as a movement which sees itself as activist — making education more 'accountable' or 'democratic', establishing 'parents' rights', etc. — it has had neither the leisure nor the inclination to stand back and consider calmly the reasons for its existence or the direction in which it is going. This book is an attempt to begin a process of reflection about parent participation in decision-making about schools, and about the rapid growth of committees and councils on which parents sit. Its method is comparative. It attempts to promote reflection by concentrating on four Western European coun-tries since 1945, devoting special attention to the period since about 1965. Since that date all four countries have devoted considerable energy to legislation or decrees establishing or consolidating various structures to encourage parent involvement with schools.

Parent participation in this legal sense, even if its roots go back a long way, is relatively new in Western Europe. Phrases such as 'parents' rights', 'parent power', 'the parent movement' suggest a degree of awareness among parents of themselves as a distinct interest group; yet in most parts of Western Europe that consciousness seems to have been absent until quite recently. Until roughly the 1960s, interaction between parents and schools was usually based on assumptions delimiting traditional spheres of influence. Decisions about curriculum, resourcing of schools, etc. were reserved to professionals (administrators and teachers) with some more or less distant oversight from the political system, to which ultimately the schools were answerable. Parents on the other hand were responsible for sending their children to school on time, clean and adequately fed, clothed and equipped. They were also often seen as responsible for the moral and religious upbringing of their children. Communication between parent and teacher tended to be in one direction, from school to home: deliberate efforts to set up a more equal dialogue, though not unknown, were rare. In these circumstances organized parent activity was not absent, but it tended to be sporadic and unstable and aimed at supporting particular schools rather than at questioning or altering the system or conveying parent views to teachers or administrators.

In the background there was often some general normative legislation, some of it arising from concern felt after the 1939–45 war about the downgrading of the family by totalitarian regimes. The Universal Declaration of Human Rights (1948) mentioned parents who, it stated, 'have a prior right to choose' the kind of education that shall be given to their children.[2] Article 2 of the First Protocol of The European Convention of Human Rights (1952) elaborated this:

> In this exercise of any functions which it assumes in relation to education and to teaching, the state shall respect the rights of parents to ensure such education and teaching in conformity with their own religious and philosophical convictions.

The lengthy discussions which led to these statements, and the reservations expressed by many national delegations once the norms had been formulated, showed that the relationship between parents and the state as the provider of education was complex and controversial. They also showed that national governments had no intention of substantially altering their own legislation to conform with extremely general international declarations.[3] National legislation itself was equally full of loopholes and uncertainties. Perhaps the truth of the matter was that at least in western democracies the family had always seemed such a central social institution that no serious attempt had been made to define its limits. This meant that everywhere family law was an untidy amalgam of pragmatic detail and generalized and often conflicting statements of parental rights and duties.[4] There seemed no very obvious reason for tidying up this area, still less for extending parental rights or creating new institutional expressions of them.

In the late sixties and early seventies there was an apparently radical change in the position of parents as governments began to implement various schemes for increased citizen participation in decision-making. Parent participation in this sense was only one subset of much wider changes, affecting government, places of work and tertiary educational institutions as well as schools. These changes centred on the idea that democracy should be extended beyond the formal periodic elections of political assemblies. The vagueness and elasticity of the participatory ideal was part of its attractiveness, but in practice it usually involved attempts to transfer some aspects of decision-making to lower levels of the political and administrative hierarchy and to secure wider representation of workers, students, etc. on the resultant committees.

Most studies of participation have concentrated on 'workplace democracy', and most theoretical writing is based on factories, offices and businesses rather than schools or universities. This emphasis, combined with the vagueness of the concept of participation and its use as an exhortatory slogan, has tended to conceal the fact that participation in a school necessarily differs in one important respect from participation in a factory or a university: the majority of persons most immediately affected by a school's activities, the pupils, are minors. Their direct involvement in decision-making is therefore problematic, and it has seemed natural in working out the practicalities of participation to turn to those who are legally responsible for pupils — i.e., parents. Thus participation as applied to schools (especially primary and lower secondary schools) results in the creation of a new category of *indirect* representation. The indirectness lies in the fact that parent representatives have no day-to-day experience of schools other than what their child conveys to them. In addition parents form a relatively loose and heterogeneous constituency by comparison with workers on a shopfloor or students in a faculty, and their common interests may be quite difficult to define.

A further complication is that in contemporary societies the functions of parents — particularly the functions of parents *vis-à-vis* schools — are far from consensual; yet the idea of a generally accepted function is central to developed theories of participatory democracy which imply 'the constant participation of the ordinary man in the conduct of those parts of the structure of Society with which he is directly concerned, and which he has therefore the best chance of understanding.'[5] Parental concern differs considerably in strength, and in the degree to which it is informed about educational questions, and both these factors combine to make its application to school matters controversial and its functions unclear.

Behind these difficulties lies another. Parents are citizens and voters as well as parents. Traditionally state schools are established and maintained by legislation or ministerial decree so that ultimate accountability is through the *general* democratic process. If parents are then allocated some *particular* responsibility for schools without the general framework being altered at the same time, there will be obvious problems of overlapping or competing jurisdiction. Strain or controversy may then arise for various reasons. The sectional interests of a group of parents may be at odds with more general interests such as the equal sharing of resources. Some issues affecting schools may raise controversial issues of value. In these ways the decision to involve parents more closely in the running of schools may have consequences which were not foreseen or intended.

Over the past ten or fifteen years, such issues have provoked much rhetoric and polemic, but little sober analysis. 'With all the furor about participatory democracy,' writes Bell,[6] 'it is curious that few of its proponents have sought to think through, on the most elementary level, the meaning of these changes.' Yet as a real-life experiment in democracy, participation is of considerable general interest, partly because it seems to offer a way out of an impasse. Pateman, for example, points out the circularity of reasoning prevalent in much recent democratic theory, with the theory being modelled on a practice which is depressingly unambitious:

> In the contemporary theory of democracy it is the participation
> of the minority elite that is crucial and the non-participation
> of the apathetic, ordinary man, lacking in the feeling of politi-
> cal efficiency, that is regarded as the main bulwark against
> instability.[7]

The attempt to introduce an element of parent participation into the running of schools is at its best an attempt to actualize a more idealistic and dynamic notion of democracy. As such it repays analysis as an example of a theory translated, however tentatively, into action. At one level, therefore, this study is a collection of descriptions, similar to Pateman's account of workers' self-management in Yugoslavia, weighing aims against implementation, in order to consider how far the aims were practicable. It thus becomes necessary to have some general idea, or working model, of what participatory democracy is trying to achieve.

1.2   The Aims of Participation

Pateman points out the difficulty of defining participation, which she amplifies as 'participation in decision-making': the term is used, she says 'to cover almost any situation where some minimal amount of interaction takes place, often implying little more than that a particular individual was present at a group activity.'[8] Although this adequately describes many of the situations in which parent representatives frequently find themselves, it is plain that a more revealing analysis requires some definition of the *aims* of participation.

Pennock, summarizing the work of a number of recent theorists, lists four main reasons for the introduction or extension of participatory democracy:[9]

(i)   *responsiveness*: participation should improve governmental output by increasing flows of information and enabling a more flexible response to needs;

(ii)   *legitimacy*: participation should make governmental output more acceptable to the governed,

(iii)   *personal development*: individuals may achieve their full moral and intellectual development only if they have some responsibility for matters which affect them;

(iv)   *overcoming alienation*: participation should bring individuals together and thus enable them to understand more clearly the collective purposes of society.

Aims (i) and (ii) are predominantly institutional and *conservative* in character, being concerned above all with the smooth functioning and continuance of the machinery of state. By contrast, aims (iii) and (iv) correspond to the viewpoint of persons outside that machinery, and spring from a feeling of personal and/or collective powerlessness. Potentially therefore aims (iii) and (iv) are *reformist* — or even 'in some forms of aim (iv)' *revolutionary*.

These four broad aims appear repeatedly in the justifications for introducing parent participation in the running of schools. They also feature in criticisms of the way the policies are implemented, when they are used as criteria for judging the effectiveness or otherwise of different participatory schemes. Observers emphasize the differing aims to varying degrees. The aims take on a different colour according to the ideological, political or social context in which they appear. As this mirage-like or protean quality is one of the main characteristics of parent participation, Pennock's large-scale grouping of aims will be more useful in establishing types and trends than a more detailed breakdown would be.[10]

The problem with more rigorous definitions of participation is that they cover only part of what is attempted. Political theorists, for example, tend to highlight decision-making as the crux of the matter. The success or otherwise of participation is then judged by whether or not the participants' presence produced decisions which in their absence would have been different. Pateman, for example, distinguishes between

(i) pseudo-participation ('techniques used to persuade employees to accept decisions that have *already* been made by the management');

(ii) partial participation ('the final power of decision rests with the management, the workers ... being able only to influence that decision'); and

(iii) full participation ('each individual member of a decision making body has equal power to determine the outcome of decisions').[11]

These categories are useful provided that some decision can be clearly identified. A large part of the activity covered by 'parent participation' is, however, quite different from straightforward policy-making. Pennock's four aims reflect that underlying complexity quite well. In a similar spirit, and moving from aims to behaviours, Macbeth *et al.* list four main 'types of participatory action', of which only the first fits easily with most theoretical writing on participatory democracy:[12]

deciding
ensuring (i.e., checking on performance, accountability)
advising
communicating.

The fact is that the parental function in participatory democracy is less easily pigeonholed than the function of, e.g., a worker on the factory floor. The activities of ensuring, advising and communicating may amount only to 'pseudo-participation' in Pateman's rather strict terminology, but that does not mean that they are meaningless or useless in themselves. Even where decisions are involved, ensuring, deciding and communicating may be steps on the way to deciding, or preconditions for effective decisions.

A multiplicity of aims means then that there is no single yardstick by which participatory systems can be judged more or less successful. That is in a sense true of all complex political and social arrangements.

In the case of participation as a policy, an additional complication is the subjectivity which lies at its heart. Ultimately, participation is designed to affect what people think or feel.

> I would describe participation as satisfactory [writes Dahl] if every citizen who wished to could participate about as much as he wanted to, every viewpoint was pretty adequately represented in the process, no one who actively tried found decision makers inaccessible, and few if any citizens felt that people like themselves were denied adequate opportunities to participate.[13]

This stress on people's perceptions means that the new structures must be assessed in terms of their context: are they likely to result in different attitudes or opinions from those prevalent before they were instituted?

1.3   Two Interpretations of Parent Participation

Pennock's fourfold division of aims gives us a tool for placing parent participation as a policy innovation in some sort of historical context. The first two aims (responsiveness and legitimacy), and in some interpretations the third aim (personal development), are of a broadly 'liberal' or 'reformist' character — i.e., the political *status quo* is implicitly accepted but judged to be capable of gradual, piecemeal reform. The rationale for an increase in participation is not based on any analysis of economic pressures or class conflict but on psychological assumptions: people *learn* to be democratic by being given opportunities for democratic activity. As Pateman indicates, in summarizing Rousseau, 'Once the participatory system is established . . . it becomes self-sustaining because the very qualities that are required of individual citizens if the system is to work successfully are those that the process of participation itself develops and fosters . . . .'[14]

Participation as a policy adopted by a number of governments in the sixties and seventies was more than a pragmatic response to political problems (Pennock's second or 'legitimacy' aim), though it was that: it was also a statement of a world-view characteristic of its time. Maybe in the short term the legitimacy aspect was paramount, as governments tried to counter public disillusion and disaffection: the need for increased legitimacy provided the initial impetus necessary to overcome institutional inertia. The longer-term meaning of these changes could, however, be understood only in a more ambitious framework in which democracy was supposed to produce more democracy. At the end of the sixties political theorists like Dahl tried to formulate this broader vision:

> The old patterns are losing out, paradoxically, because old ideas about authority, particularly democratic authority, encourage demands for new systems of authority. The paradox vanishes if we realize that because democracy has never been fully achieved, it has always been and is now potentially a revolutionary doctrine. For every system purporting to be democratic is vulnerable to the charge that it is not democratic enough, or not 'really' or fully democratic. The charge is bound to be correct since no polity has ever been completely democratized. Even today, what one ordinarily calls democracies are, as we all know, a very long way from being fully democratized political systems.[15]

Now if this way of thinking, which links the democratic aims of political systems with people's capacity for developing those aims and learning from their own experience of them, is broadly correct, then two consequences should logically flow from it:

(i) other things being equal, participation should appear earlier and more easily in polities where citizens already have more experience of participation rather than less;

(ii) once established, participatory structures should see a gradual lessening of the importance of aim (ii) (legitimacy) and a corresponding upgrading of aims (i), (iii) and (iv) (responsiveness, personal development and overcoming alienation); or in Pateman's terms an increase in 'full participation', in Macbeth *et al*'s in 'deciding'.

These generalizations are in principle testable against what has actually happened over the last ten or fifteen years.

As indicated above, the policy of participation was a statement of a world-view. But there are other world-views than the liberal or reformist. A feature of the liberal viewpoint is that it does not question the system as a whole. It takes the political assumptions for granted and restricts its objectives to improvements within the system. In this perspective, a comparative approach is of interest but not of critical importance. The advent of similar changes in several states at roughly the same time is not seen as problematic: it means that useful alternative reform models are available, and may assist in more rational policy formation, but the coincidence itself calls for no particular explanation.

It may be viewed as merely coincidental, or as the result of the flow of information from one polity to another, or even as a sort of evolutionary process.

A broader focus — deliberately not labelled Marxist because it is not necessarily entangled with the apparatus of economic determinism, even if it is in practice associated mainly with Marxist or Marxian thinkers — would concentrate precisely on the coincidence of several states proceeding in a similar direction at a similar time. It would explore the question of whether these particular phenomena were evidence of some more general forces in action in western society at large. In this focus, comparison becomes central rather than incidental.

Habermas, for example, argues for a general 'legitimation crisis' in western societies.[16] To summarize adequately his dense and multifaceted arguments is impossible, but he maintains that as the underlying causes of strain are broadly economic, it is to be expected that societies operating in a single economic sphere will take similar steps at roughly the same time. Moves toward participation are in fact attempts to restore public support ('legitimation') which has been undermined by the need for more all embracing and rational planning. This is particularly critical in the 'cultural' area (including education),

> not only because the expansion of administratively processed matters makes necessary mass loyalty for new functions of state activity, but because the boundaries of the political system shift as a result of this expansion. In this situation cultural affairs that were taken for granted, and that were previously boundary conditions for the political system, fall into the administrative planning area. Thus, traditions withheld from the public problematic and all the more from practical discourses, are thematised. An example of such direct administrative processing of cultural tradition is educational planning, especially curriculum planning. Whereas school administrations formerly merely had to codify a canon that had taken shape in an unplanned nature-like manner, present curriculum *planning* is based on the premise that traditional patterns could as well be otherwise. Administrative planning produces a universal pressure for legitimation in a sphere that was once distinguished precisely by its power of self-legitimation.[17]

If this sort of thinking is closer to the truth, then parent participation in schools will originate and evolve in a different way from that suggested by the liberal model:

> (i)   it will appear sooner and in more elaborate forms in polities where the need for legitimation is greater;
>
> (ii) once the participatory machinery has been set up, aim (ii) (legitimacy) will retain its supremacy: aim (i) (responsiveness) will be limited to its bureaucratic or efficiency aspects ('pseudo-' or 'partial participation', with information flow largely from client to bureaucracy), and the aims of personal development and the overcoming of alienation will receive little or no attention in reality, however useful they may be in rhetoric.

To summarize, the first, or reformist paradigm (which was the model behind the adoption of participatory policies) would lead to an expectation of *development*, while the second, or general crisis paradigm would lead to an expectation of *stasis*. Thus one of the central questions in evaluating the two models concerns development or mobility. How would the observer know that it had in fact taken place?

A practical problem is that if the general crisis theory is correct, and participation is a way of shifting attention from the realities of existing power structures, frequent cosmetic change can be expected in order to remind the general population of the continuing benevolent activity of the state in consulting public opinion. Thus the mere fact that structures change or become more elaborate is not a clear index of development. Development means that the system becomes more responsive to opinion outside the governing elites, and therefore more flexible in its decision-making, more open to community pressures, a more rewarding area for the involvement of interested lay persons. In other words, development implies that movement proceeds in a certain direction over time. It implies that participation moves through a series of *stages*.

As participatory structures are initiated by governments for their own purposes, it is hypothesized that in the early stages the main purposes which participation is expected to fulfil will be those relating to legitimacy. There should then be evolution in the direction of responsiveness as politicians and administrators perceive the advantages of taking earlier and fuller cognisance of clients' perceptions, thus minimizing conflict and allowing more rational planning and more effective manipulation of opinion. When the public — in this case, parents or sections of parents — appreciates the greater responsiveness of the system it is more likely to band itself into associations and pursue collective aims, thus highlighting the aims grouped under 'overcoming alienation'. In this way the possibility of 'personal development' through operating the system becomes much more of a reality than it does when the system is preoccupied with achieving more legitimacy for its own operations.

It should be stressed that this is a model. In practice at any given stage all four sets of aims will be present. They will feature in differing proportions in different parts of the system, and according to the differing viewpoints of participants. For example, a minority of parents will always be heavily concerned with 'personal development': these will be activists who find much satisfaction in semi-political activity of a more or less idealistic kind, yet for the system in which they operate the encouragement of such activity may be a low priority. Or, to take another example, an education committee covering a local district may be concerned with all four aims together, e.g., (i) to legitimate decisions already taken by the bureaucracy; (ii) to increase responsiveness (e.g., by providing information which will permit the bureaucracy to adjust admission zones or other procedures with maximum efficiency and minimum fuss); (iii) to encourage the local community to formulate its own desires about the sort of schools it wants, and thus lessen alienation; and hence (iv) to provide concrete opportunities for local people to operate democratic structures in matters which are close to them. At any particular meeting all these aims may to some extent be realized.

The greatest difficulty in assessing the development of participatory structures lies in deciding which set of aims in any given period or situation is paramount. One problem is to disentangle realities from rhetoric, given that an elite preoccupied with increasing its own legitimacy tends not to state its preoccupations very clearly. Other problems arise from the structural and cultural differences between systems. For example, the absence of parent representation on a city education committee in England and Wales may be highly significant, because many decisions are taken in that forum, while a similar gap at municipal level in France would simply reflect a different pattern of decision-making.

As with the subjectivity problem discussed at the end of the preceding section, these difficulties mean that no straightforward tests can be applied to the data. Indicators such as proportion of parents voting in annual elections, proportion of parent representatives sitting on committees at various levels, number and range of committees open to parents have meaning only when viewed against the national and historical background. Obviously evaluation is based on fact, but in the last resort it must be impressionistic.

Parent participation is thus resistant to unambiguous 'litmus-paper' tests or evaluation. It is more complex and elusive than participation of workers in the running of their firms or workplaces. Workers in a factory are a clearly defined group, usually organized over a long period. They have experience and knowledge which constitute a *prima facie* case that they have a useful collective contribution to make to decisions required to run a factory smoothly and productively. Parents, on the other hand, as a quasi-political group or class, formally recognized as contributors to the running of schools and school systems, are rather different. They are a category in a sense created by authority to perform tasks whose nature is often as unclear as their qualifications for doing them. For that very reason, we may learn different things about participation by looking at parents rather than workers. Dahl has suggested that 'In a world with so many interdependencies, the hope for democracy cannot rest on total autonomy but ... on democratic systems constructed like Chinese boxes, the smaller nested in the larger.'[18] Parent participation provides examples of Chinese boxes rather different from those usually discussed by theorists of democracy. As we shall see, in some ways these boxes are empty. It is almost as though society had created an empty category of representation and said, 'Let's see what fills it.' The difficulty in conceptualizing this area is part and parcel of the origins and character of the idea: how the vacuum was filled may say quite a lot about the surrounding environment. This is still the case even if parents never come within 'sniffing distance' of Pateman's 'full participation' or Dahl's 'total autonomy'.

1.4 Testing Theory by Comparison

The preceding section has sketched two alternative hypotheses relating the emergence and development of parent participation in education to wider theories of social change. The aim of this study is to test those theories against events — to see how useful they are in ordering and explaining complex social and political interactions, and whether this process suggests that one hypothesis is more helpful, valid or 'correct' than the other. The obvious way of tackling this task is through *comparison.*

The emergence of comparative studies (of which comparative education is a subsection) as a distinct discipline or approach has been accompanied by much dispute[19] — often as a result of misunderstandings about the very different kinds of academic activity for which a comparative approach may properly be adopted. Twenty years of debate in comparative education have produced, not a single generally accepted recipe or approved approach (which would be absurd in view of the widely differing tasks attempted under this label), but at least a general agreement about the desirability of explicitness. If comparison is a way of exploring complex human situations which cannot be investigated by experimentation, then the terms of the comparison must be specified so that the comparison can if necessary be extended to other situations in a process analogous to the replication of an experiment.

Thus in spite of differences of emphasis, philosophical assumptions and practical approach, comparativists agree on the need to state clearly the aims of an enquiry: if the aims are unknown, then logically the enquiry cannot be evaluated. Clear aims imply a need to specify the sources and types of data available; they also suggest that hypotheses or clearly stated organizing theories are important even if opinions differ as to whether those hypotheses should appear at an early or late stage of a study. In addition it is generally thought that quantifiable data are desirable where appropriate.

The previous sections of this chapter have clarified some aspects of this enquiry into parent participation. Two broad alternative hypotheses have been stated. It has also been suggested that quantification is not appropriate as a basic method of validating this particular hypothesis because multiple imprecise aims are almost a defining feature of 'participation'. Thus this study differs both from the Beredayan model (where hypotheses are distilled at quite a late stage of analysis)[20] and from the model proposed by Noah and Eckstein, with their strong emphasis on quantification and relative distaste for 'messy' enquiries of a broadly historical kind.[21]

It is usual for writers in comparative education to give the impression that their study followed a smooth and predictable course from initial conceptualization to triumphant conclusion.[22] Sometimes this is no doubt true. However, studies conducted by a single person probably more often follow the pattern of this one: an initial interest in the topic aroused by personal experience (in this case as a parent and parent activist); observation and description of the way things were done in a few accessible foreign countries resulting in a sporadic output of descriptive reports; but growing realization of common patterns followed by attempts to relate the particular theme to broader issues and conceptualize that relationship more satisfactorily.[23]

That personal comment may be helpful if it assists the reader to read critically in the knowledge that the approach recorded here was not the only thinkable one, nor even perhaps the best one. In particular, the methodological justification should not disguise three shortcomings of this study.

   (i)   The choice of countries, though adequate to produce interesting insights into the topic, may not be ideal: it was in practice determined by proximity and by the fact that the author (a British citizen) speaks French, German and Italian. Scandinavian, North American, Marxist or Third World cases would probably have enriched the study. They would also have made it much more complicated.

   (ii)   Information was collected piecemeal over almost a decade. Over that period a wide range of documents were read and people interviewed, but obviously completeness of coverage was impossible and visits were made on a sampling basis, dependent on time and money being available. Thus there were periods, differing from country to country, when the study was inevitably dependent on second-hand information, e.g., correspondence or the relatively narrow range of foreign journals available in Britain.

   (iii)   More importantly, the organizing hypotheses emerged only towards the end of the study, so that information collected in the mid-1970s was assembled without a very clear idea of how it should be used. Perhaps the study is more Beredayan than it appears at first sight, with the case-studies — or at least the published articles which in several instances have been re-arranged to contribute to the case-studies — in part constituting Bereday's 'browsing' phase, and the hypothesis emerging later than its early placing in the book suggests.

Bearing these caveats in mind, let us now consider the overall shape of the book. This will be governed by the alternative hypotheses sketched in section 1.3, which direct attention to two broad aspects of parent participation:

   (i)   its *emergence* — whether the new structures arose sooner and with greater ease in polities which already have substantial experience in operating democratic structures; the extent to which aims (i), (iii) and (iv) featured, as revealed in the provisions made for parent participation;

   (ii)   its *development* — whether aims (i), (ii) and (iv) seem in the ascendant, while aim (ii) declines in importance.

One possible way of arranging the case-studies would therefore be in two sections, the first devoted to the emergence of parent participation with four illustrative case-studies, the second to development, presenting the second stage of the four cases. However, it seemed more satisfactory to present both aspects in complete national case-studies. This is partly because emergence and development form a single entity, with one flowing naturally from the other, partly because retention of the national focus makes for a more readable account, chronologically arranged. Each case-study will finish with a section in which its general interest is highlighted, and the overall conclusions will be discussed and developed in a final chapter organized in four sections drawing general conclusions from the particular cases presented:

(i) the emergence of parent participation;
(ii) the development of parent participation;
(iii) the relative merits of the two theories;
(iv) discussion: the implications for decision-making.

The focus on the origins of parent participation might suggest that the case-studies should be presented in order of appearance (German Federal Republic, France, Italy, England and Wales). The German case is, however, a complicated one to present both because it goes back a long way and because of the federal framework, with different areas evolving at different rates. The decision has therefore been made to start with France as a relatively simple case of participatory innovation in the classic centralized bureaucracy, to follow France with Italy as a variation on the Napoleonic theme, and then to present the Federal Republic and England and Wales.

Although, as has already been confessed, the selection of the four countries to be studied was determined initially by their accessibility to the author, they do jointly constitute a useful test-bed for the policy innovation under study, and not only because taken together they are the four largest members of the post-1973 European Community. Basically, France, Italy, the German Federal Republic and England and Wales are sufficiently similar for comparisons over time to be sustained without undue strain, and yet differ sufficiently to make comparisons instructive. They are all liberal democracies which

(i) have implemented some form of parent participation;
(ii) differ in the recency of introduction of the policy, and its style and completeness;
(iii) are roughly similar in size, ideology and level of economic advancement;
(iv) differ in political and administrative structure, this being one of the main determinants of the form of participation.

Table 1 indicates some of the broad parameters of similarity and difference which will, where appropriate, be refined and elucidated in the case-studies.

The figures on population density and *per capita* national income represent in a world context — compared, for example, with India or Zambia — a broad similarity of underlying economic and geographical conditions. However, the figures do differ considerably, and might suggest alternative hypotheses to those already proposed: that parent participation was related to economic growth, or to the degree of dispersion of population. The national figures hide substantial regional differences, so that it seems more sensible to discuss these possibilities in the final chapter after presenting more detailed national accounts.

The 'interest-groups' parameter divides the nations into two categories. On the one hand are France and Italy, where the historic divide between Right and Left has produced a system where many groups align themselves formally or informally with one or other of the great blocks of opinion, so that they operate largely by gaining credibility and

Table 1. Broad Parameters of Similarity and Difference[24]

	France	Italy	German Federal Republic	England and Wales
Estimated population 1979	53,478,000	56,919,000	61,337,000	49,177,000
Population density (persons/km^2)	98	189	247	325
Per capita national income 1977 (US $)	6410	3076	7456	3951 (UK)
Historical status	Old nation state	Unified mid-nineteenth century	Unified mid-nineteenth century; split post-1945	Old nation state
Political capital, also cultural and economic capital	Yes	No	No	Yes
Main locus of decision on education	Capital	Capital	Capitals of Länder	Dispersed: capital, local authority, school
Position of interest-groups	Part of polarized political structure	Part of polarized political structure	Substantially independent of political structure which aggregates IG inputs	Substantially independent of political structure which aggregates IG inputs
Date of original legislation on parent participation	1968	1973	Mainly 1946–9	1980

influence *within* those blocks. On the other hand interest-groups in West Germany and the United Kingdom tend to see and present themselves as independent of the political machine, which they influence from *outside* by various means. Again, this broad distinction will be refined and considerably qualified in the case-studies, but it has had very real effects on the movement for parent participation.

Obviously there are other relevant categories of comparison which are not so easily placed on a table of this sort, especially variables relating to attitude. The most ambitious comparative attempt to assess attitudes to government dates from the early 1960s; it omitted France and dealt with the United Kingdom as a whole rather than England and Wales only. It will, however, serve as an indicative baseline. Almond and Verba asked people in different countries whether they felt competent to affect government policies at local and national levels.[25] The resultant 'levels of subjective civic competence' must be treated with care but give some general idea of differences in attitude at that time between Italy, West Germany and the United Kingdom (see Table 2).

Perhaps it is also worth noting the absence from Table 1 of a category such as 'prevalent norms on parental responsibility'. The reason for this is that the position in all four countries seems very similar. Presumably the norms derive ultimately from common religious sources. While there are differences in emphasis between Roman Catholic, Lutheran and Anglican teaching on the family, they are too slight to affect perceptibly the ways in which different nations view the home-school relationship, and any differences there may be are effaced by the persistent refusal, already noted, to define parental responsibilities at all clearly. In any case, any such ideological differences pale into insignificance by comparison with long-term social and economic changes.[26] In the four countries under consideration, industrialization had already substantially altered the functions of the traditional family

Table 2. Respondents Expressing a Feeling of Civic Competence (percentages)

	Italy	GFR	UK
At national and local levels	25	33	57
At national level only	2	4	5
At local level only	26	29	21
No feeling of competence at either level	47	34	19

by 1945, so that with a few exceptions such as the Italian *Mezzogiorno*, cross-national difference between family structures and influence were not very marked. Everywhere there remained, however, a nostalgia for a supposedly more healthy and vital form of family life, sometimes but not always voiced by the churches, and often informing social and educational policy.[27] While a rejection of the conventional family had been one of the recurrent themes of the intelligentsia at least since the Romantic movement, it was still the case that democratic states repeatedly declared their support of the family and sometimes (in inaugurating family allowances, for example) backed up their opinions with hard cash. Even socialist or Marxist critiques of the family as the perpetuator of traditional beliefs and economic inequalities have usually been muted and ambivalent when translated into policy. In the Soviet Union, for example, the traditional family has in practice *co-existed* with generous nursery provision, state-sponsored youth groups and boarding-schools, not been replaced by them. Certainly in Western Europe, writers such as Musgrave, prepared to state baldly that 'family interference is inimical to educational health' and to condemn 'the sentimental hankering for maximum parental participation',[28] have always been a tiny minority. The norms remain overwhelmingly bland, somewhat conservative in their general approval of parental authority, but above all ill-defined. Thus they would become a significant factor in distinguishing between the societies compared only if a nation were included with markedly different norms — perhaps a communist or Muslim nation, or one in which tribal or extended family responsibilities were much more dominant than is the case in predominantly urban, liberal democracies standing broadly in the Judaeo-Christian tradition.

1.5 Definitions and Arrangement

If, as indicated in the previous section, the central hypotheses about the emergence and development of parent participation determine the overall shape of the book, that will also be true of the individual case-studies, and it is at that level that the definition of terms becomes crucial as complex reality is matched against simpler, because more abstract, theoretical frameworks. Thus this section is intended as a link between the general discussion of the previous sections and the particular examples which follow. It

> (i)   restates the two competing hypotheses in tabular form (see Table 3);

(ii)   defines the key terms of those hypotheses briefly and as concretely as possible;

(iii) maps out the field of parent participation in terms of the system within which the new policy has to fit, the levels of the educational machine at which parent participation may happen, and the areas of decision or policy which parent participation may affect;

(iv)   specifies in tabular form the pattern of the case-study chapters, indicating how the broad questions raised by the theoretical discussion are related to the concrete reality of particular places and times.

Initial working definitions of the main terms of these hypotheses follow. Whereas the discussion in section 1.3 above concentrated on presenting a broad and rather abstract picture, the underlying question highlighted in these definitions is: how in practice would you recognize the presence of this concept in the jumble of events, institutions and opinions?

Parent participation: the legally required association of parents with the schools their children attend through systems of elected representatives and committees.

The central idea here is 'legal requirement'. Obviously parents are 'associated' with schools whether or not this is legally recognized. This study differs from others in that it does not in the first instance try to

Table 3.   *Alternative Hypotheses on the Emergence and Development of Parent Participation*

PARENT PARTICIPATION . . .	is the product of	is established earlier and more easily in polities	subsequently develops
('Reformist' theory)	experience of and commitment to *democratic involvement*	offering more experience of *democratic involvement*	away from a preoccupation with *legitimation* towards genuine increases in *responsiveness, personal development* and the *overcoming of alienation*
('General crisis' theory)	attempts by the *ruling elite* to achieve greater levels of *legitimation*	where the *threat to the ruling elite* is most urgent	only in a cosmetic sense, with *legitimation* remaining as an overriding consideration

Note: Concepts defined and discussed in the text are italicized.

assess types and degrees of participation as they exist at a particular moment, though obviously those will be described. It concentrates instead on why democratic states in the second half of the twentieth century should see parent activity as appropriate for legal recognition and regulation.

Ruling elite: 'a relatively small, homogeneous and permanent group exercising effective power'.[29]

Descriptions of all four polities under consideration generally agree that much or most power is exercised by such elites, often categorized in socio-economic terms (the middle classes, the bourgeoisie, etc.) Although observers disagree strongly as to whether such elites are necessary or desirable, the whole thrust of participatory democracy, and thus ultimately of parent participation, is, at least in terms of its rhetoric, in favour of altering this state of affairs. This is, therefore, a central term of the argument.

In modern conditions ruling elites are not clearly identifiable (as an aristocracy was). They exist in the perception of themselves or of others — perhaps especially of others — and thus what constitutes an elite is often uncertain in particular circumstances. Thus much of this discussion has a slippery and elusive character, revealed in the 'relatively' of Pennock's definition, quoted above.

In some democracies, a ruling elite may also be in overt political control because it is clearly associated with a dominant political party or other grouping. Another arrangement is a two-party or multi-party system in which the ruling elite dominates in all parties irrespective of their overt ideologies. This reminds us that elites are only *relatively* homogeneous in the opinions they hold.

Democratic involvement: the more citizens contribute to the collective institutions of society, the more opportunities for such contributions exist, the more 'democratically involved' a society can be said to be.

Such opportunities exist in national and local politics, but also in the wide range of interest-groups which are characteristic of modern societies. Almond and Verba, on whose pioneering comparative research much of this line of argument is based, suggest that membership of such groups in a given society is one of the key indicators of what is here called 'democratic involvement'.[30]

Threat to ruling elite: the threat to remove or substantially dilute their power, i.e., basically a political threat.

Such threats may be highly visible — carried by the political system (e.g., the threat of electoral defeat or even of the collapse of the system itself in revolution or *coup d'état*). But they may also be much more subtle, especially in systems where the ruling elite is not identified with a single party. From the standpoint of the elite itself, a threat has to be perceived as dangerous before it provokes policy change. Such perception may depend not on the objective menace of the threat but on debates within the elite itself.

Legitimation: the achievement of increased support for the existing political system by evolving new forms of citizen activity which will distract attention from the fundamental distribution of power.

Democracy must, according to Habermas, remain formal and limited to periodic elections because

> Genuine participation of citizens in the processes of political will-formation, that is, substantive democracy, would bring to consciousness the contradiction between administratively socialized production and the continued private appropriation and use of surplus value.[31]

If this is so, then participation will be essentially a diversionary technique. Its rhetoric will be radical but its practice will be rigidly limited. Whether or not one accepts the economic underpinning, Habermas's formulation highlights the general importance of assessing the character and extent of parent participation as a subset of legitimation procedures. It was suggested above that this can usefully be done by looking at aims and trying to assess the relative dominance of four broad aims. This means trying to specify what would indicate their 'relative dominance'. Table 4 suggests a rough pattern based on Pennock's aims.

The case-studies will explore how these concepts are realized in particular places and times. The descriptions will be organized in terms of systemic context, levels and functions. By *systemic context* is meant the area crudely represented in Table 1 by historical status, functions of capital, locus of decision-making, functions of interest-groups, etc. Normally this is comprehensible only in historical terms. It is necessary next to consider the *levels* at which participatory activity may occur. Broadly speaking, participation in schools may occur at four levels: class; school; local or political subregion; political centre. The political centre will normally be the national capital but may be a lesser centre if responsibility is carried by regions.[32] Finally we must consider the *functions* of school systems which the presence of parents might be expected to affect. A very elaborate grid might be worked out,[33] but for

Table 4.   Types of Parent Participation According to Aims Stressed
AIM (see section 1.2)

Legitimacy	Responsiveness	Overcoming alienation	Personal development
Characteristics of system			
Elaborate centrally determined rules	More stress on pragmatically assembled working parties, etc. less on formal representation. Political and community allegiances overlooked rather than discouraged	Parents seen as part of wider community. Emphasis on mass meetings and similar collective events to underpin formal representation	Maximizing variety of structures at all levels
Frequent cosmetic changes of rule			Political allegiance overlooked or discouraged, representation not only through parent groups. Parent representatives as leaders. Two-way communication, but some stress on informed communication and influence from parental side
Parents seen as individuals: political allegiances discouraged			
Divide and rule tactics — discouragement of broader groupings, gaps in ladder of representation	Attempts to work out distinct functional areas of responsibility/ (parents/teachers/ administrators/ politicians)	Contribution of broader groupings (including political) encouraged at all levels. Stress on community accountability	
Parents removed from real loci of decision, recipients of one-way communication (i.e., from experts)	Parents advise on decisions at various levels	Two-way communication — little attempt to limit areas of debate	
	Stress on two-way communication, though administration determines what is appropriate to be communicated		
Results desired			
Reduction in controversy, avoidance of crises	Reduction in controversy, avoidance of crises; more efficient management	Increased community support for individual schools	More democratic involvement in society at large
Possible unintended results			
Increased controversy as the gap between rhetoric and reality becomes clearer to more people. Politicization. Incremental change slowed down by need to consult	Inequality, differential rates and directions of development, class divisions	As in first two columns, but also incoherence and inefficient management	As in first three columns, but also dominance of parent elite

the purposes of this study a fairly broad set of categories based on commonsense perceptions of areas of school activity which parents might expect to influence seems more useful. Possible headings are as follows:

(i)   *progress of individual pupils*: e.g., promotion from one class to another, allocation to secondary school, discipline;

(ii)   *curriculum, internal organization of the school and school-related extra-curricular activity*: e.g., subjects or other facilities available within school time; grouping (mixed-ability or otherwise); peripheral activities of the curriculum such as outings, extra sports clubs, or sex education out of school time;

(iii) *appointment and control of personnel*;

(iv)   *resourcing*: decisions about whatever funds are available; applications for increases in funding; fund-raising;

(v)   *planning of school provision* (local, regional, national), including decisions about going comprehensive;

(vi)   *Improvements of school-community relations*.

Combining all these questions and concepts, we can see that the case-studies will be arranged typically as in Table 5.

Table 5.   *Arrangement of Case-Studies*

---

1 *Systemic context.* The political system. Historical background and nature of ruling elites. Interest-group activity in general: its value as an index of 'democratic involvement'. Parents and their traditional relationship to the education system. Parent interest-group activity prior to legislation on parent participation.
2 *The achievement of legally required parent participation.* Descriptive narrative. Underlying question: why was legislation achieved when it was?
3 *The nature of the first legislation.* Levels and functions. Underlying question: what do the arrangements reveal about the basic aims of the system?
4 *Subsequent developments.* Normally a chronological account: Underlying question: is a trend over time observable?
5 *Discussion of the emergence of legislation.* How closely do the origins of this example correspond to the two theories?
6 *Discussion of the trends of subsequent developments.* Can the direction of development be specified? How closely do events correspond to what the two theories would lead one to expect?

Notes

1 WHEELER, COLIN (1979) *A Thousand Lines: Cartoons from 'The Teacher'*, Kettering, The Teacher Publishing Company, p. 37; CORNEC, JEAN (1972) *La Fédération des Conseils de Parents d'élèves*, Paris, Epi, p. 6.
2 Article 26.
3 See BANNWART-MAURER, ELENA (1975) *Das Recht auf Bildung und das Elternrecht, Artikel 2 des Ersten Zusatzprotokolls zur Europäischen Menschenrechtskonvention*, Bern/Frankfurt am Main, Peter Lang, *passim*.
4 For example, Articles 6.2 and 7.1 of the West German Basic Law, or Section 76 of the British Education Act of 1944, discussed in Chapters 4 and 5.
5 G.D.H. COLE, quoted in PATEMAN, CAROLE (1970) *Participation and Democratic Theory*, London, Cambridge University Press, p. 37.

6 BELL, DANIEL (1976) *The Cultural Contradictions of Capitalism*, London, Heinemann, p. 204.

7 PATEMAN, *op. cit.*, p. 104.

8 *Ibid.*, p. 68.

9 PENNOCK, J. ROLAND (1979) *Democratic Political Theory*, Princeton, N.J., Princeton University Press, especially Ch. 11, pp. 438–69.

10 A good example of such a detailed breakdown is MACBETH, ALASTAIR *et al.* (1980) *Scottish School Councils: Policy-Making, Participation or Irrelevance?* Edinburgh, Scottish Education Department/HMSO, especially Ch. 2, 'Purposes for school councils', pp. 14–24. However, the Scottish team's aims were rather different: 'One valuable approach to research presents hypotheses and seeks evidence related to them. That presupposes enough established knowledge of the field to generate credible hypotheses, but school councils are both new and evolving, so that our aims were broader. . . .' By 'broader' they mean more concerned with the practical detail than with more general theory. The Scottish team's approach is interestingly applied to a comparative enquiry in Macbeth, A (1981) *The Child Between: A Report on School-Family Relations in the Countries of the European Community*, Brussels, Commissions of the European Community. Although the purposes of this nine-country survey were very different from those of this book, there is some overlap.

11 PATEMAN, *op.cit.*, pp. 68–71.

12 MACBETH *et al.*, *op. cit.*, pp. 23–4

13 DAHL, ROBERT A. (1970) *After the Revolution? Authority in a Good Society*, New Haven and London, Yale University Press, p. 161.

14 PATEMAN, *op.cit.*, p. 25.

15 DAHL, *op.cit.*, p. 4.

16 HABERMAS, JÜRGEN (1976) *Legitimation Crisis* (trans. by T. MCCARTHY), London, Heinemann.

17 *Ibid.*, p. 71

18 DAHL, *op. cit.*, p. 146.

19 For two recent overviews, British but from rather different perspectives, see HOLMES, BRIAN (1981) *Comparative Education: Some Considerations of Method*, London, George Allen and Unwin, especially Ch. 3, 'The positivist debate in comparative education — an Anglo-Saxon perspective', pp. 57–75; and McDADE, D.F. (1982) 'The things that interest mankind: A commentary on thirty years of comparative education' *British Journal of Educational Studies*, 30/1, pp. 72–84.

20 BEREDAY, GEORGE Z.F. (1964) *Comparative Method in Education*, New York, Holt, Rinehart and Winston.

21 NOAH, HAROLD J. and ECKSTEIN, MAX A. (1969) *Toward a Science of Comparative Education*, London, Macmillan, especially pp. 99–103 — or consider their brave attempt to quantify 'otherworldliness' (pp. 132 ff).

22 Notable exceptions are HALSALL, ELIZABETH (1968) *French as a Second Language: Levels of Attainment in Three Countries*, Hull, University of

Hull Institute of Education, and KING, EDMUND J. *et al*. (1974) *Post-Compulsory-Education: A New Analysis in Western Europe*, London and Beverly Hills, Sage, especially pp. 8–11.

23 See BEATTIE, NICHOLAS (1978) 'Formalized parent participation in education: A comparative perspective (France, German Federal Republic, England and Wales)', *Comparative Education*, 14/1, pp. 41–8. The 'descriptive reports' mentioned are listed in the footnotes to the individual case-studies.

24 The figures are from UNITED NATIONS, DEPARTMENT OF INTERNATIONAL ECONOMIC AND SOCIAL AFFAIRS (1981) *Statistical Yearbook, 1979–80*, New York, United Nations. The other categories obviously call for much explanation and qualification, which will be found in the individual case-studies.

25 ALMOND, GABRIEL A. and VERBA, SIDNEY (1963) *The Civic Culture: Political Attitudes and Democracy in Five Nations*, Princeton, N.J., Princeton University Press. The table is adapted from p. 186.

26 Described comparatively, at least for Central Europe, by MITTERAUER, MICHAEL and SIEDER, REINHARD, (1982) *The European Family: Patriarchy to Partnership from the Middle Ages to the Present*, (trans. K. OASTERVEEN and M. HÖRZINGER), Oxford, Basil Blackwell. Compare, for France, ARIES, Philippe (1973) *L'Enfant et la Vie Familiale sous L'Ancien Régime*, Paris, Senil, for Germany, EVANS, RICHARD J. and LEE W.R. (Eds.) (1981) *The German Family: Essays on the Social History of the Family in 19th and 20th Century Germany*, London, Croom Helm.

27 See COHEN, DAVID K. (1976) 'Loss as a theme in social policy', *Harvard Educational Revew*, 46/4, pp. 553–71 — a stimulating article relating the family myth with education, drawing on nineteenth-century New England for illustrations.

28 MUSGROVE, F. (1960) 'The decline of the educative family', *Universities Quarterly*, 14, pp. 377–404; here p 391.

29 PENNOCK, *op. cit.*, p. 162.

30 ALMOND and VERBA, *op. cit.*; see, e.g., Ch. 11, 'Organizational membership and civic competence', pp. 300–22.

31 HABERMAS, *op. cit.*, p. 36.

32 E.g., in the German Federal Republic a 'subregion' will not be a *Land* but a section of it such as a *Kreis*.

33 E.g., the one presented in MACBETH *et al.*, *op. cit.*, Ch. 3, 'Functions of school councils', pp. 25–54. Their six groups of issues (p. 25) correspond in some ways to the following six headings, but my (iv) and (v) are not brought out very clearly in their list, probably because their categories relate in the first place to a particular system in which budgeting and organization were not salient issues.

2   *France*

2.1   Background

'To all of you, I said this morning: here we stand in year one of a
new history. Therefore my friends, let us be the soldiers of the
year two of a new school.[1]

The occasion for this peroration, with its deliberate evocation of *les
soldats de l'an II* who defended the infant first French republic against
the forces of reaction, was the annual congress of a large parents'
association held at Saint-Etienne in early June 1981. This was exactly a
month after the election of Francois Mitterrand as the first socialist
president of the fifth French republic. The 'new history' was thus a new
socialist history: the rhetorical exaggeration is pardonable in the light of
the long exclusion from national power of the French left. Less
understandable to many foreign observers is why *parents* should serve
as soldiers in defence of a new (socialist?) school. To try to answer that
question requires some knowledge of French history — of the meanings
and controversies focused on the central authority of the state, and of
how the state relates to schools.

At the height of the French Revolution, in 1792–3 (*l'an II*), an
absolute monarchy buttressed by the ideology of a rigidly traditionalist
church was replaced by a radical republican regime which was a sort of
mirror image of its predecessor — equally committed to total central
control of the national territory, but for a brief moment able and willing
to sweep away the antique inconsistencies and local traditions of the
ancien régime, and replace them with a more rational and coherent
machinery of state administration. This was to prove a durable
framework on which to build a new and improved state bureaucracy,
essentially the achievement of the Napoleonic era. If imitation is the

sincerest form of flattery, then the nineteenth-century bureaucracies of Prussia, Bavaria or Italy were evidence of the success of the French original. In that historic sense, France produced the prototype of a centralized bureacracy, so that the machinery of formal parent participation, viewed as a way of mitigating some of the shortcomings of centralized administration, is also a kind of model of processes happening elsewhere.

The Napoleonic administrative and legal system proved immensely durable. It was, if anything, strengthened by the constitutional see-sawing, punctuated by periodic revolutions, which characterized the French state throughout the nineteenth century.[2] This political instability has marked deeply the institutions and thought-patterns of contemporary France. Opinion remains intensely polarized. People are highly conscious of belonging to a historic 'Left' or 'Right', each with its own ideological apparatus: on the Left, secularism (*laïcité*) and Marxism of various brands; on the Right, traditional Catholicism. Although these ancient patterns have been breaking down fast, especially since the 1960s, some of their power remains, so that the rhetoric of political and educational discussion is frequently the rhetoric of class warfare, defence of republican legitimacy, etc. Pressure-groups (certainly in education) tend to amplify the rhetoric and to fall into one or other of these two camps. Groups which are weak or uncertain of their objectives often derive support and purpose from their adherence to these larger groupings. Their actions then become better informed and more coordinated than in polities where the grass-roots are less ideologically aware — but by the same token more closely controlled by more or less politicized central pressure-group bureaucracies whose structures reflect those of the central state.

To some extent the rhetoric of struggle and resistance, in which parents are seen as soldiers, retains its power because both 'Right' and 'Left' continue to feel insecure. Changes of regime are not only a nineteenth-century phenomenon. Many Frenchmen can still recall the traumas of 1940 and 1944, the shame (as they now see it) of the collaborationist Vichy government and the unsuccessful attempt to create a new political legitimacy out of the Resistance. Many more remember the ignominious demise of the Fourth Republic in 1958 under threat of military intervention from Algiers. Until the socialist victory of 1981, the Fifth Republic seemed to have been set up to guarantee a permanent hegemony of the Right, with a large and lively Left forced into a shrill and frustrated opposition. As seemed to be happening for a brief period in May 1968, the only prospect of substantial change appeared to be by extra-legal means. This basic insecurity reinforced the Right's instinctive reliance on firm control through the centralized administrative machine, and its reluctance to devolve power from Paris. It was perhaps symbolic that it was on this issue that President de Gaulle eventually resigned.

Against this background, the education service must be seen as the largest and most impressive sector of a centralized administration.[3] Teachers are civil servants, and may be posted to any part of the country. They work to quite detailed syllabuses and specifications published in the weekly *Bulletin Officiel*, and their work is controlled and evaluated by a national corps of inspectors. Although the conformity of teachers to this imposing machine is less than it appears, teachers' loyalties to a particular locality or an individual school are less strong than, for example, in Britain. Secondary teachers in particular often see themselves as lecturers teaching a defined number of hours. Although teachers may deride or ignore circulars from Paris urging them, for example, to increase consumption of fish in school dining rooms,[4] the centralized system still provides the essential framework within which they think and work. As Forquin points out rather maliciously:

> The administrative centralization of the French education system derives its strength and durability from a tacit consensus which at a deep level, runs directly counter to the protests and proposals periodically made by the partisans of innovation.[5]

Centralization is, he suggests, a sort of shelter against the psychological strain of arguing one's case in a political and social culture where consensus is largely absent.

It is certainly the case that throughout French history, and as a result in particular of the internal stresses which came to light in the Revolutionary period, French schools have been the focus of long and bitter controversy. How should a state school be controlled in a republic whose motto is 'Liberty, equality, fraternity', with all the potential for conflict which 'liberty' and 'equality' contain? What should it teach? Should a church which for long periods has been explicitly anti-republican be allowed to run its own schools or to propagate its views in state schools? Throughout the nineteenth century and into the twentieth, the schools have repeatedly served as a sort of restricted battle area for the conduct of noisy and bitter ideological struggle. *Laïcité* (secularism) is really short-hand for the unstable compromise eventually arrived at. The practical effect of secularism has been to remove from schools (in intention at least) anything which might arouse controversy; in French terms, to concentrate on *instruction* rather than *éducation*.[6] What Legrand calls 'the primacy of the cognitive' means that the civil servant teacher delivers defined skills and information and does not see 'pastoral care' as a central part of his or her work.[7] Attitudes, ethics, personal behaviour are seen as falling into the realm of the family. The dividing line between teacher and parent is relatively clear, and the traditional system seems intrinsically hostile to the blurring of lines and sharing of roles which is implicit in parent participation. 'The isolation of the school from the world of parents,' concludes Legrand in his important recent diagnosis of the sickness of French education, 'is one of the most striking structural features of the French school.'[8]

2.2 The Parent Movement before 1968

In the light of all this, it is not surprising that for many years the parent movement in France evolved in almost total dissociation from the official machinery of the education system, nor that its characteristic tone of voice was oppositional and politicized.[9]

Parent organizations reflect the perceived locus of power. The traditional form of French parent activity is the *national federation* with its headquarters in Paris. Parents' associations for individual schools had first sprung up in the early years of the twentieth century; the associations of a number of *lycées* came together in 1910 to form a 'Federation of parents' associations for *lycées* and *collèges*'. At that time, *lycées* and *collèges* were academic, middle-class institutions, so that the federation was not unduly alarming to the authorities: indeed, Jean Zay, the *Front Populaire* minister who first seriously advanced the idea of the *école unique* or comprehensive school, described its members as 'adversaries of any democratization of education'.[10] The *lycée* parents' federation gradually assumed a representative function at national level: by the early 1930s, it was represented on the *Conseil Supérieur de l'Enseignement Public*.[11] As it was restricted to the *lycée* sector there was no competition either from a small federation which was founded in 1932 with particular interest in technical education, or from a Catholic federation founded in the same year and necessarily operating outside the state sector.[12]

The present picture, of parent federations in competition with one another, did not begin to take shape until after the Liberation.[13] The huge federation which has for long been known as the *Fédération Cornec*, after Jean Cornec, its president from 1956 to 1980, was established in 1947 as a parents' *and teachers'* association.[14] It was an offshoot of the large, communist-dominated primary teachers' trade union (SNI), and carried from the start the blessing and support of the

Ligue française de l'Enseignement, a long-standing grouping of secularist organizations. The federation was formed quite specifically to strengthen the teachers' struggle against the Catholic menace. At the time many militants of the Left felt that the church had improved its position quite disgracefully as a result of the favour shown to it by the discredited Vichy regime. Discontent among secularists was reinforced by the *loi Barangé* of 28 September 1951 which sanctioned the payment of limited sums of public money to the Catholic sector of education. No doubt partly as a result of encouragement and support from the primary teachers' union, which gave it access to its excellent channels of communication, the newly founded federation grew very fast. By 1958 it was the sole national organization for parents in the primary sector. In numbers it was considerably larger than the *lycée* federation, with which, of course, it was not in competition. In political sympathies, it was explicitly left-oriented, and more boisterous and radical in style than the *lycée* federation.

The fall of the Fourth Republic in 1958, and the ensuing moves of the new government to incorporate Catholic schools into the national system by offering them public subsidy in exchange for undertaking to achieve and maintain national standards, precipitated fundamental changes in the parent movement. By late 1959 it was clear that the mass struggle of the Left against the new measures, involving among other protest activities a petition signed by nearly eleven million citizens, had failed. The *Loi Debré* passed into law on 31 December 1959.[15] In 1960 the primary school federation made approaches to the other non-Catholic federations with a view to amalgamating as a single parents' federation for the entire republic. When negotiations proved largely fruitless, militants of the Left began to form their own parents' associations in individual secondary schools, and in 1961 the primary federation was reformed as a general body with three sections: secondary, primary and technical. Thus the events of the first year or two of the Fifth Republic had not only increased the overt politicization of the existing parent federations, they had also had the unintended result of forcing them for the first time into competition with each other for members. Given the distinct class and ideological backgrounds from which the *lycée* parents' federation and that of Jean Cornec sprang, it was thus predictable that the 1960s would see a sharpening and clarification of conflict between these two groups of parents.

Now that the two principal federations could no longer rely on their monopoly position in separate sectors of the system to justify their existence, they had to appeal to their constituency, parents, both by improving the services offered and by campaigning for changes in an education system which was generally admitted to be outdated and under-resourced. For the *Fédération Cornec*, the objectives were plain. Still formally allied to the primary teachers' union, it had many teachers in its membership and objected in principle to parents' associations confined only to parents. The federation's general thinking was thus closely allied to that of SNI. This connection with the teaching profession gave the federation not only a consistent policy and practical support in organizing parents at school level, but also an *élan* and militancy which appealed to many in the mid-sixties, as disillusion with Gaullist paternalism grew more widespread. The federation consolidated its near-total dominance of the primary sector, and convincingly broke the monopoly hitherto held by its rival in the secondary sector.

The former *lycée* federation had a less firm ideological base. It was partly because of this, partly because links with the teaching profession were less strong, that policy began to evolve in the direction of parent participation in the early sixties. With hindsight, the evolution appears natural, even inevitable; yet it is worth reminding ourselves of how visionary in some ways the whole concept seemed in the France of the early 1960s. The Ministry remained as hermetically sealed from outside influences as ever. Its traditional resistance to lay pressure was reinforced by the sometimes almost pathological Gaullist mistrust of interest groups as sinister disrupters of the allegedly simple relationship between government and governed. The more successful of the two mass parent federations was heavily penetrated by teachers and committed to parent influence through cooperation; above all, 1968 had not happened.

In spite of these discouraging factors the former *lycée* federation did commit itself to working out detailed forms of parent participation, probably reflecting three factors. One was the genuine idealism of some members of the leadership. Another was the federation's need to find a unifying policy which would appeal to, or at least not be distasteful to, a heterogeneous membership containing substantial elements who supported the government. The third was the need to present a responsible and constructive face to that government. While Cornec's federation found itself in natural opposition, the rival federation tended more naturally to seek accommodation with the powers that be, to accept what had been done (notably in the matter of subsidies for Catholic schools) and to attempt to build on that.

The participatory structures which were adopted by the federation as its official policy in 1962 were not of course simply plucked from the air. They were based on a plan worked out by Jean Védrine at the independent *Centre d'Études et de Documentation*, and originally published in 1958. The basic mechanism of elected school councils, of various types and operating within various frameworks, had already been submitted to the 1959 government commission on church-state relations in education as a device for persuading the lion and the lamb to lie down together.[16] Although this element of conciliation between church and state was not the central purpose of Védrine's plan, nor the main motive of the former *lycée* federation in adopting it as policy, it was certainly uppermost in people's minds at the time that the rigid and politicized character of French education would be reduced by allocating more responsibility to local committees or councils. Schools, it was argued, should be removed from the stylized confrontations inevitable on the national political stage. To give some sort of power to parents and teachers in particular schools or districts would not only make schools more adaptable to the wishes of their customers, it would also encourage pragmatic, non-political decision-making. The child's welfare, rather than abstract ideology, would become the central consideration in a new depoliticized education system. This line of thought merged naturally with a strand of progressive educational opinion which went back at least to Roger Gal in the immediate post-war years and which surfaced from time to time in the *Comité de Liaison des Associations pédagogiques* and publications associated with it:[17] the view roughly that French schools should attempt to educate the whole man, not just the intellectual parts of him, and that this naturally involved much closer relations between teachers and parents. By 1967 Lobrot was able to furnish extensive intellectual underpinning for a more open, 'self-managed' school. His basic idea was that as real change in society can occur only if attitudes change, the school, in which attitudes are shaped, is the key to change throughout society.

> Without self-management at least in embryo in the school, without pupils taking some responsibility for themselves, without at least a partial sweeping away of educational bureaucracy, no real training can be expected, and therefore no change in the attitudes of individuals.... We must begin through the school. The society of tomorrow will come about through the school or it will not come about at all.[18]

This global and idealistic emphasis was very characteristic of French thinking about parent involvement in the sixties. Although here and there enterprising individuals were already experimenting with various more or less participatory or consultative schemes,[19] most such thinking remained of necessity theoretical and exhortatory.

The device of elected councils struck a chord in other more overtly political quarters, too. It was attractive to parts of the libertarian Left which now began to grow after the long trauma of Stalinism. Opinion on the Left was extremely various, ranging from a liberal or centrist desire to take politics out of schools, indistinguishable from the stance of the moderate-right former *lycée* federation, to a wish to restore power to the people in a highly politicized sense — a return to the short-lived Commune of 1871. Perceptions differed enormously, both in spirit and detail; the elected council remained as a common denominator, and was taken up by the Communist Party in 1967.[20]

For the Catholics, too, parents' committees neatly solved two problems, one practical, the other ideological. As Catholic parents have to opt into their system, the degree of parental commitment and the homogeneity of parental attitudes is naturally greater than in the state sector. In addition, most Catholic schools were, until the 1960s, locked in a permanent financial crisis. Schools naturally looked to their parents for support, and in fact a 'National Union' of Catholic parents' associations (UNAPEL) had existed since 1932. At the local level, indeed, the 'AEP' (*Association d'Éducation Populaire*) was a kind of governing body, responsible for the finances and legal existence of the school and backed up by an 'APEL' (parents' association) which had among its major activities the raising of funds. Thus when in the early sixties the church authorities became increasingly anxious to promote lay leadership and a new openness within the Christian community, in the education sector at least the tools lay to hand.[21] By 1967, 96 per cent of church schools had parent representatives on their management committees. The official slogan of the 1967 annual congress of the Catholic parents' federation was 'the educative community': families, schools and church were supposed to be collaborating in the single venture of educating the next generation. Thus, in part because of its relative freedom from Ministry control, in part because of its own internal dynamics, the Catholic sector of education, held by many on the Left to be arch-reactionary, was the only part of the system which had actually implemented a more open form of school government before 1968. Of course, in the sense that the parents of children in Catholic schools tended to agree on the ultimate objectives of the system they had chosen for their children, school government there remained relatively uncontroversial and apolitical. As UNAPEL was the only parents' federation operating in the Catholic sector, elections too were based more on personalities than policies. The fact remains that a working model of parental involvement already existed in the Catholic sector before 1968.

Thus when a great national 'colloquium' to discuss the problems of

French education was convened at Amiens in March 1968, two months *before* the explosion of May, participation was already on the agenda as a likely solution to some parts of the problem. Jean Védrine himself was one of the 620 participants, as were representatives of the moderate-Right parents' federation and of the Catholic sector.[22] The commission on school structures recommended 'a growing participation of families at all levels of the French system'[23] and suggested 'co-management' through a three-tier system of councils: an internal school council, a school management council carrying financial responsibilities and a district council.[24] The district was to evolve as an organic unit corresponding to the zone served by a *lycée*, or upper secondary school, with its two tiers of feeder schools — the primary schools and the 11–15 CES. These proposals were seen as a necessary precondition for any genuine decentralization, whether financial or pedagogical. While such a change would have obvious advantages in making the system more 'supple', the more important justifications stressed the need to 'liberate the potential for activity and creativity ... among teachers, parents and pupils.'[25] Sociology was held to demonstrate that

> The school does not simply contain individuals. It is the place where a community grows up.... Although the spirit of association has long been developed in some countries, it is not until now that the transformation of French Society seems to be accompanied by a certain reduction of individualism and the evolution of attitudes.... This general evolution ought to favour transformations in the life and management of educational establishments.[26]

In other words, the Amiens colloquium, which brought together on the eve of 'the May events' any French educationalist with a claim to be considered progressive, already saw participation as an obvious step forward, but stressed in the first place the aspects of 'personal development' and 'overcoming alienation', and then 'responsiveness'; 'legitimation' featured in its thinking not at all. Yet when two months after Amiens the real action began, it was 'legitimation' that was the dominant concern.

2.3 The Emergence of a Legal Framework

We have seen that in the state sector there already existed by 1968 a substantial and well-organized movement, anxious to involve parents more closely with the schools, quite closely engaged with professional educationalists and provided with blueprints of how this might be done. The working model of the Catholic sector and the rationale available through the progressive movement were further encouragements. Yet the Ministry of Education, and almost all schools, continued to operate as though parents were simply the biological producers of the schools' raw material. One of the achievements of the political crisis of May and June 1968 was for the first time to bring these two orders of reality into effective contact.

The government acted only under the most urgent of all political pressures: the threat of its own dissolution.[27] In late April and early May of 1968 the mishandling of student unrest in Paris sparked off a general strike and the virtual collapse, for a period of two or three weeks, of the authority and structures of the Gaullist state. At the end of June central authority was reasserted by the calling of an election. The result was a crushing victory for the Right; yet the events of May had been so traumatic that simple reaction was an obviously inappropriate response, for the task of the new government was above all to re-establish trust in the structure of the state. The revulsion from the centralized and authoritarian character of the Fifth Republic had been so widespread that it was necessary to steal the rebels' clothes — to give the impression that the government was doing what the student Left had been too divided or irresponsible to do. 'Participation' was de Gaulle's slogan: but an ordered and rational participation, not (to use the antique rudery unearthed by de Gaulle as his label for anarchy) *la chienlit*.

The May events had begun within the fief of the Ministry of Education. Public discontent with education was wide and deep. Some way must be found of conferring legitimacy upon these discredited outposts of the bureaucracy, schools and universities. When Edgar Faure took over the Ministry in July 1968, the universities, as the original seat of the unrest and the most likely source of further threats to the regime, were his main preoccupation. A radical *loi d'orientation* was rapidly drafted and passed through parliament, setting up a network of elected councils. The management of schools was, politically, a less urgent priority. Nonetheless, the May events had had a considerable impact on schools, especially secondary schools. Although it is difficult to generalize about so local and spontaneous a movement, many schools had experienced a period when the normal (i.e., bureaucratic) relationship between administrators, teachers, pupils and parents had simply collapsed, to be replaced, if only for a brief spell, by a feeling of openness and liberty, of the potential of education breaking through into actuality. A fair proportion of schools had institutionalized the moment of release by setting up action committees (*comités d'action lycéens* — CALs). For teachers, pupils and parents who had experienced this radical break in relationships, a mere return to the *status quo ante* was unthinkable, and many action committees survived into the autumn of 1968, claiming to be the legitimate repositories of power in their school. That claim did not go unchallenged, even at the local level, as teachers who had remained silent in the summer began to realize that the immediate threat of a takeover by the extreme libertarian Left was past. The most radical pupils of May had by September moved on to university, and less exciting problems — resitting the examinations which had vanished in the euphoria of May, starting up another school year — tended to be at the forefront of teachers' minds.

Edgar Faure had in mind an overall *loi-cadre* for the schools which would do for them what he hoped the university law would achieve for the tertiary sector. In the event, the preoccupation with higher education meant that the new structures of school government were worked out piecemeal and never knitted into a coherent whole, as Faure himself was removed from office before he could achieve that ambition.

Thus the structures of school government which were set up in the decree of 8 November 1968 were not the result of considered and careful reflection about the complex ways in which a school system interlocks with the community it serves. Rather, they appear as a relatively hasty and incomplete grafting on to the existing system of formal representative structures. The tripartite model provided for higher education (professors, lecturers, students) was adapted for secondary schools without any real questioning of its appropriateness. The radical decentralization to districts and schools recommended by the Amiens colloquium simply did not happen. As there was no redistribution of functions between Paris and local districts, or between the Ministry and the school, the actual work expected of the new school councils remained hazy. Primary schools were not included in the new system. Thus the new decree setting up a hierarchy of school councils bore all the marks of a device hastily drafted to meet a short-term problem: the irregular and potentially explosive situation in secondary schools.

The basic new institution, the *conseil d'administration* or school management council had existed in theory since 1944. They were set up in the euphoria of Liberation as 'a guarantee of liberty restored'.[28] Yet although these school councils had emerged from the democratic enthusiasm of the Liberation, they never in practice amounted to more than an official mechanism for approving school budgets, which were determined in essentials by the administration of the Ministry. Their membership consisted of appointed administrators and local notables with some elected teacher representation. Most people were unaware that these phantom bodies existed, and the school management councils of 1968, although similar in name to their predecessors, were intended to be a new departure. In the initial decree the powers of the school council were not clearly defined but subsequent ministerial orders specified an impressive array of duties:

> The management council exercises its functions in all areas which affect the educational, moral, financial and material life of the establishment or its impact within the wider community. In this task, and working within the general provisions of planning and zoning arrangements and other regulations, it determines the general rules governing the recruitment of pupils. It establishes the internal organization of the establishment.[29]

The problem with normative statements of this sort is that they tend to be meaningless. For example, 'the recruitment of pupils' or 'the internal organization of the establishment' are matters over which in France a school council 'working within the general provisions of planning and zoning arrangements and other regulations' can make no decisions other than trivially administrative ones. In other words, formal structures of participation were set up in 1968 without any real attempt to extend the autonomy of schools by lessening the influence of the Ministry. Thus the more realistic parts of the official texts are those which specify the council's consultative role in relatively peripheral areas of school life: spreading information, extra-curricular activities, school transport, etc.

The actual membership of the management council — the clearest part of the November decree — was to be mainly elected. A sixth of the council was to be co-opted members representing the local community, and a further sixth (elected) would represent the school administration and non-teaching staff. A third of the representatives would be elected members of the teaching staff. Elected representatives of parents and of the older pupils would each take a further sixth. The size of the council varied according to the size of the school between thirty and thirty-six.

Subordinate to the management council were several other councils or sub-committees. The discipline council and class councils, which had a potentially important assessment and counselling function in discussing pupils' progress and recommending promotion, were remodellings of institutions which already existed on paper. The standing committee of the management council was an executive body responsible for carrying out the orders of the management council. Another potentially important committee was that formed to run extra-curricular activities, societies, etc.: *l'association socio-éducative* or *foyer des élèves*. This had a majority of pupils.

To describe the system as a whole is to bestow upon it a unity which it did not seem to have at the time, as different decrees, orders and circulars came out on different aspects of school government. From the standpoint of the parent movement, however, the official recognition and incorporation of parents into the machinery of the state was a dramatic shift, even though the shortcomings of the new apparatus were apparent. For the drafters of the November decree, parents were a relatively peripheral consideration, allocated a sixth of the management council's seats for no very obvious reason and given no very obvious responsibility in the new structures. The failure of the Ministry to take seriously the educational case for parent-teacher cooperation was evident in the neglect of the primary sector, where the educational arguments were, if anything, stronger than at secondary level; clearly the crucial consideration was that secondary schools were more restive and troublesome. In addition, many parent activists, especially on the Left, were highly suspicious of the motives behind the new arrangements, believing participation to be a trick to emasculate the opposition by incorporating it into the Gaullist state. Yet when all was said and done, the pressure to make the new system work was irresistible. Although the special conference of the *Fédération Cornec* held at Nice in September 1968 was for the first time in twenty years deeply split on the issue of whether to collaborate with the government, it decided by a narrow majority to do so. It was apparently swayed by a speech from the Minister himself, who in his final sentence confessed disarmingly: 'I tell you quite simply — I need you.'[30] The political motivation behind the new arrangements was obvious; but what was much less clear was whether they would, as many hoped, lead to a new spirit in French education, a new relationship between society and its schools, and even a new vision of a 'self-managed participatory society'.[31]

2.4   Parent Participation in Action

The practical consequences of the original circular in mid-November 1968 naturally differed from school to school. Schools in which the events of the previous summer had had little lasting impact viewed these new-fangled councils at best with a weary scepticism — yet another Ministry fad to be implemented by a harassed local administration — at worst with suspicion and hostility. Teachers who regard parent and pupil participation as an instrusion on their professional domain have many ways of rendering parent representation ineffective. In France the commonest complaints were of councils being held at times (e.g., during the working day) when many parents could not attend; of meetings being conducted in a highly formal style which inhibited parent and pupil contributions; and of class councils resolving to exclude parents from consideration of individual cases, thus reducing their function to a nullity. Naturally enough, absenteeism among parent representatives soon declared itself as a problem, and there was often difficulty in recruiting parents to sit on class councils.

Even schools strongly favourable to the May upheaval had almost equal problems with the November circular, which required them to dismantle the council which already existed (CAL) and replace it with a more obviously bureaucratic mechanism. The spontaneous commitments of many individuals to their own local participatory arena inevitably withered when faced with the requirements of bureaucracy, the need to proceed to new elections, the obvious implication that the post-November councils could hardly have any impact upon schools before Easter — by which time the first school year of *l'après-mai* would be virtually over.

Nationally, the omens were in some ways more favourable to the new participatory structures. If the new management councils were to be seen as anything more than pseudo-participation, it was essential to secure the commitment of the huge left-wing parents' federation, the *Fédération Cornec*, whose assent to the new system had, as we have seen, been far from a formality. The new arrangements meant that approved parent associations had to be groupings of parents only. For the *Fédération Cornec*, which had always included both parents and teachers and had a close relationship with the teacher unions of the Left, this was a real stumbling-block. It was certainly a sign that a new spirit was abroad when the federation embarked upon the major constitutional change of separating itself from the teachers and establishing itself as a parents' federation pure and simple. This move was justified partly on the grounds that teachers would have their own representatives on school councils, partly that informal links would remain strong — as indeed they have.

Although the parent federations dominated the formal electoral processes which are the focus of this study, there were other groups with a more general interest in promoting parent-teacher interaction. The oldest and most prestigious of these associations was probably the *Ecole des Parents et des Éducateurs* founded in 1929.[32] It has never seen its work in a political context at all, and its main concern was with forming and training parents for their task. More openly combative and politicized were syndical organizations such as the *Confédération Syndicale des Familles* and the *Confédération Syndicale du Cadre de Vie*.[33] There were even occasional school-based parent-teacher associations based primarily on the activities clustering round a school, but these were very rare;[34] the centralized federations were the obvious framework within which local activities would naturally proceed, in spite of sporadic grumblings about political dominance, and in spite of the fact that only a minority of parents (probably between a quarter and a third in the 1970s[35]) were paid-up members.

Thus it was within that framework with its political resonances that all sectors of opinion took part in the elections of parent representatives for school councils, which were held, in secondary schools only, in early 1969. Voting was by proportional representation, so that most parents found themselves choosing between three or four lists prepared by the federations. By the end of 1968 four national federations were competing in the state sector: a large left-wing federation, a smaller but still very substantial moderate-right federation, a small federation of rather indeterminate left-wing character specializing in technical education, and a small, new, right-wing, anti-1968 grouping.

One of the problems in describing school government in France is that brief labels of this sort give an exaggerated idea of the politicized character of the system in its day-to-day operation. Two distinctions must in practice be made. One is between the small and the large federations. The right-wing federation (UNAAPE, often referred to as *'les autonomes'*) is ideologically homogeneous in a way that the left-wing and moderate-right federations are not. The moderate-right, or former *lycée* federation in particular, is a hotch-potch of differing opinions of a broadly middle-class, liberal to conservative character. The apparently greater ideological consistency of the left-wing federation, with its strong links with the political Left in general, is offset by its very large, and therefore heterogeneous membership. This brings us to the second crucial distinction: that between leadership and mass. If the leaders (or 'militants', as they are often called) are often very politically aware, parents at local level often have only the dimmest ideas of the supposed ideological colouring of the federation for which they vote or of which they are members. Many belong to federations in rather the same spirit that motorists belong to motoring organizations — as an insurance policy or for information, rather than because of their lobbying activities, of which indeed many members may be entirely ignorant. For most members, the main visible part of a federation's activity is informational, through meetings but perhaps mainly through well-produced monthly reviews, most of whose articles are not political in character at all. The federations also organize insurance schemes for children and parents. Even militants are often more pragmatic than they sound in public debate. It soon became normal practice for the two main federations each to take one of the two parents' places on the standing committee, irrespective of the overall school election results; and even across the Catholic-secular divide there may be local cooperation in, for example, pressurizing deputies or government for increased funds for local schools.

Thus, in spite of the relative infrequency in the late 1960s and early 1970s of independent candidates, the electoral process itself was less politicized than it appears if one restricts one's view to the public statements of the federations' leaders and spokesmen or the minority of overtly political articles in the magazines of the federations. In any case, the imperatives of the first two or three years of the new structures of school government — say from 1968 to 1971 — placed a premium on activity of a more or less consensual character. It was necessary to get the new structures to work. The federations had to consult with government about the stream of regulations which emerged in the year or so after the decree of November 8 1968 and which was intended to extend and clarify the notion of participation. It was also necessary to communicate to parents the potential of the new structures, and the journals of the federations in this period are full of information and advice about how to make the new structures work in the schools. For parents themselves, being involved in a management council or class council was in itself a learning experience. Often what was learnt was mere frustration, engendered by the resistance of professional teachers or the pointlessness of the tasks allocated to the new councils; a minority began, however, to accumulate both information and skills of negotiation and communication which in some cases led to some genuine evolution of attitudes among both teachers and parents. In the learning process, many were helped by the support and information provided by the federations, whose existence was undoubtedly a facilitating factor in launching so quickly such a large exercise in participation.

As the new structures began to function, two yawning gaps in this framework of school government became increasingly apparent.[36] The first was that primary and nursery schools were excluded from the participatory system. In the hasty decision-making of 1968, the educational importance of involving the parents of younger children in the management of schools was overlooked. Even when in the summer of 1969 this omission was repaired, *conseils d'école* (school councils) in primary schools were permitted, not required as in the secondary sector, and were to be set up only when requested by head teachers backed by their staff. The result was predictable: very few primary schools acquired a council. Gloton reports that one area of Paris with 'a flattering reputation for educational innovation' and a supportive local inspector had still failed to produce a single primary school council by 1973.[37]

The second gap was the failure to grasp the nettle of decentralization. Apart from one bold decision to allocate 10 per cent of the school timetable for school choice, almost all curricular and financial questions continued to be resolved in Paris. The autonomy of the local school remained a fiction, or restricted to peripheral matters (*le péri et postscolaire* — school buses, school clubs, etc.) or to administrative tinkerings. Thus although in theory the management council controlled 10 per cent of the school's running costs, councils which rejected the budget submitted to them by the administration found that a budget was simply imposed by administrative fiat — and was usually a lower budget than the one rejected.[38] This failure to redefine areas of responsibility was understandable in view of the complex and centralized nature of the French education system; it was also a recipe for frustration at school level, and a guarantee that the next phase of development would see a polarization of views, and hence an increased politicization of the debate on school government.

As the new councils gradually became a more accepted part of the French educational scene, it was the left-wing federation which began to focus this debate — and again, it is difficult to disentangle the school government issue from other, more overtly political controversies. The régime was beginning to recover its confidence after the *grande peur* of 1968: the political pressures towards consensus dwindled. The internal dynamics of the Left, and of the left-wing parents' federation within it, meant that it felt increasingly obliged to define itself, and bid for public support, by striking oppositional stances. The moderate-right former *lycée* federation found itself to some extent more in tune with the government in adopting the classic liberal position that education should be separated from politics. The Left criticized the moderate-Right as stooges. The moderate-Right retorted that its rivals were mere creatures of political extremism, and owed their conspicuous success in recruitment only to illegitimate support from leftist teachers and their unions. The quarrel was sharpened by the fact that in some schools, especially in the Paris area, left-wing parents and teachers were very successful in dominating school councils in a highly politicized way, and using them to pass resolutions on issues other than educational ones : for example, American involvement in Vietnam.

It is tempting to characterize this sort of argument between the federations as 'bickering' because it is predictable and fruitless and swells to a crescendo when external pressures are removed — in this case the very real political pressures summed up in the shorthand *'les Evénements'*. It is not bickering, however, in the sense that the issues are real and serious. To what extent should schools reflect the opposing value-systems present in society at large? Debates between parent groupings could ventilate such issues, though often in a somewhat confused way; they could not resolve them. At this point government again began to play an active part.

2.5   The Remodelling of the System

Government action in setting up school and class councils in 1968–9 had been reactive rather than principled and considered. From about 1973, however, successive Ministers of Education began to take initiatives to change the participatory system. By now, participation had ceased to be a slogan or a device for meeting an urgent political need. It had become an established institution, a complex network of vested interests. At a time when the entire education system was being rethought, it seemed natural to remodel and streamline it. These changes were planned in a well-publicized series of novel forms of consultation, starting with an opinion poll in July 1973 and moving on to a national colloquium (November 1973), a draft plan for secondary reform (March 1974), a series of working parties (autumn 1974) and a fifty-page discussion document (February 1975). A draft bill was published in May, debated in June and passed into law in July 1975 as the *Loi Haby*.[39] The participatory provisions of the new Act were quite a small subsection. They were extended and clarified in a series of decrees and circulars issued mainly in 1976 and 1977 and came into force at the beginning of the 1977–8 school year. What were these new arrangements? More importantly, what did they mean?

The structures were not unduly complicated. A basic distinction was drawn between secondary schools (*collèges* and *lycées*) and nursery and primary schools (*écoles maternelles* and *écoles élémentaires*). In the secondary sector, the school was to be governed by a *conseil d'établissement* consisting of five members of the administration (head teacher, etc.) five rather ill-defined co-opted 'personalities' representing the locality, five elected teacher representatives and five elected parent representatives. There were also elected pupil representatives — five for the *lycée*, or upper secondary school; two for the *collège*, or lower secondary school, where they represented only the older pupils in the top two years of the school. Dependent upon the school council, and reporting to it, was a discipline council responsible for serious matters such as suspensions. Councils were also provided at class level: each class had attached to it both a teachers' council consisting of all those teaching it, and a class council consisting of the teachers' council sitting with two parent delegates, two pupil delegates, and various pastoral and medical personnel. The class council, whose main function was to discuss progress and promotions, was to be chaired by the head teacher.

Nursery and primary schools were each provided with a *conseil d'école*, or school council. This consisted of a teachers' council and a parents' committee in joint session, chaired by the head teacher. The parents' committee consisted of five elected representatives, or less if the school contained less than five classes. The local *maire*, or other representative of local government, had a right to attend though not to vote. The parents' committee must meet every term. The school council was to decide for itself how frequently it should meet, though the circular recommended termly meetings.

The motivation behind these new arrangements was various. The run-up to the 1975 Act was very much the period of 'advanced liberalism' — President Giscard d'Estaing's slogan for modernizing, technocratic, consensual reforms which were supposed at one and the same time to reflect and promote attitudes appropriate to an advanced industrial society and to generate a new consensus, a new feeling of community among the various components of the nation, and a decline in class consciousness and unproductive controversy.

In this context, the style of consultation adopted (and already embarked upon before the death of President Pompidou in 1974) was in itself attractive to Giscard's administration as an earnest of a new openness between government and governed. Surprisingly, however, there was a total failure to consult through the channels established in 1968–9, the national network of school councils. This reflected in part the distrust and irritation felt by both bureaucracy and government for the polarized and restless system of parent federations which in effect ran parent participation in France.

Thus the post-1977 system of school councils reflected three desires on the part of central government: (i) to present visible reforms and to appear to consult with the people; (ii) to tidy up the rather messy arrangements arrived at in 1968–9, especially by including the primary sector; (iii) to promote a consensual, depoliticized, essentially supportive style of consultation. In the words of the final sentence of the 1978 circular on the functioning of primary school councils:

> There is no need to add that the exchanges which will be sparked off in all areas lying within the competence of these new institutions, both between families, and between families and school administrations, will be all the more fruitful if they are inspired only by concern for the children's welfare and by a common determination to seek out in all things an area of understanding within a framework of mutual respect.[40]

In other words, central authority still saw participation as a device for supporting rather than questioning, for harmonizing ideologies rather than facing confrontation. As any real shift of power from the centre would inevitably produce controversy and unevenness of provision, it was still unthinkable that decisions might be devolved in any meaningful way from Paris to either local authorities or schools. The unmentioned non-decisions spoke louder than the proclaimed decisions.[41]

Consequently the function of the school council remained uncertain, and its concerns were defined by the circulars in evasive generalities ('the whole life of the pupil') or with sweeping qualifications ('the internal organization of the school, which must be drawn up to conform to the type of organization adopted for the *département*') or in terms of more or less peripheral activities ('mutual information between families and teachers, nature study visits, school transport, supervision of children ... outside school hours, canteens, extra-curricular activities, safety and health').[42] At secondary level, the head teacher's position was strengthened by comparison with the post-1968 machinery by the abolition of the standing committee, which meant that the head was to carry executive responsibility between meetings. The head was also required to call the primary school parents' committee, and to chair the school council. The formal separation of a parents' committee in the primary sector was seen by many as a divide-and-rule tactic, whose real purpose was to foment disputes with teaching staff and thus reduce the potential power of both groups. By the autumn of 1979 the two main parent federations had come to a tacit agreement that parents' committees would not normally meet independently, only as part of the broader school council, thus reducing this part of the regulations to a dead letter.

The view that the unspoken aim of the new system was to side-track effective devolution of power over decisions to parents or local committees was borne out in the events after October 1977 when the first delegates were elected under the new scheme. Here it is again difficult to dissociate the general political scene from the narrower front of school government. The strategy of President Giscard d'Estaing was to bid for the supposedly consensual middle ground. In terms of schools, that meant sapping the existing parent federations, and especially the dominant *Fédération Cornec* with its strong ties with the Left. The extension of the electoral process to primary schools gave that aim a new impetus and reality. The last elections under the 1968 regulations, held in October 1976, had, as usual, produced insignificant numbers of votes for candidates operating outside the federations: 2.5 per cent for 'union' lists (i.e., local agreements between federations) and 6 per cent for 'various' candidates.[43] The primary schools swelled these 'non-political' candidates quite dramatically: in 1977 'union lists and independents' accounted for 43 per cent of all primary school votes. This compared with 45 per cent for Jean Cornec's federation and 7.6 per cent for its main opponent, the *Fédération Lagarde*.[44] The performance of the independents is all the more striking when one considers that the Ministry's original intention had been to adopt a simple 'first past the post' voting system for the primary sector. The parents' federations felt this would handicap them, and after some pressure, especially from the *Fédération Lagarde*, the more usual proportional representation system was used.[45]

The Ministry of Education immediately proclaimed the breaking of the 'quasi-monopoly of Cornec's federation'. The triumph of the independents shows, said a spokesman, 'that parents have often voted for candidates who were judged to be mainly interested in their children's school, independently of any federation membership.'[46] The two main federations saw things rather differently: both claimed that the new independents were at heart supporters of their views, and moved into increasingly sharp controversy, each claiming that the other was merely a political front organization. This polarization was exacerbated by the lengthy run-up to the National Assembly elections of March 1978.[47] The considerable success registered by President Giscard d'Estaing's majority then produced a certain amount of internecine political strife in the *Fédération Cornec* between those favouring an explicitly Marxist policy and the majority who supported a more broadly based movement designed to appeal to critical parents of all shades of political opinion. A further complication was a dispute with the teachers' union SNI, which in late 1977 refused to allow the new primary school councils to function unless the government reduced the teacher-pupil ratio; this action forced many parent militants to choose between political solidarity with the teachers and a more generalized commitment to parent participation. These underlying differences were still present in the Brest congress of 2–4 June 1979.[48]

Parent activists tend to be idealistic and also impatient, being aware through their own experience that a child only has one bite at the educational apple. Disputes of this sort, in the context of an apparently permanent right-wing monopoly of power, were enervating and frustrating. It is not surprising that at the end of the seventies, Jean Cornec was expressing deep disillusion: 'For ten years we have gone from disappointment to disappointment. Participation as Aladdin's lamp (which only gives you three wishes), participation as an excuse, participation as an alibi, participation as a trap for dupes: those are some of the expressions used by our activists. . . .'[49]

Although the complaints of the other federations were usually less combatively expressed, there was general agreement between them that the 1977 changes had strengthened the position of the head teacher and his or her role as an agent of central administration; that school councils rarely discussed important issues, and that the curriculum remained the sole preserve of teachers and administrators; that parental attendance at meetings remained difficult for workers who had no right to time off work or to reimbursement for wages lost; that class councils were usually a simple rubber-stamping of grades already allotted; and that consequently it was often difficult to persuade parents to take much interest in school and class councils or to volunteer for office on them.[50]

This consensus reflected a kind of three-way stalemate which by about 1980 had become institutionalized. The federations agreed, albeit with differences of emphasis, on what was wrong; the government refused to do more than tinker with the participatory system; and at the same time parents continued to vote and join the federations in sufficiently large numbers to legitimate both government complacency and federation demands for change.[51] In the space of a decade institutions which had been introduced ostensibly as the motors of change had become part of the system itself. The criticisms they made of the system were real enough, yet because they had no effect they became a kind of paradoxical support for it. The federations were like court jesters: that the king could be mocked was a sign of his strength and authority. The only way things could alter fundamentally would be for the king to be deposed.

2.6   The System under Socialism

The King's deposition — i.e., the victory of the Left in the presidential and legislative elections of May and June 1981 — was among many other things a test of this institutionalized parent participation. The first reaction on the Left — from the leadership of the *Fédération Andrieu*, as the *Fédération Cornec* had become known since Cornec's retirement in 1980 — was euphoria; the opening quotation of this chapter is only one example. The moment of rapture was prolonged as the new government symbolically restored 'national' to the title of the Ministry of National Education and created more than 11,000 new jobs in education to start in September 1981. 'Better already' was the title of Jean Andrieu's editorial in the September issue of *Pour l'Enfant . . . vers l'Homme*.[52] The reaction of Andrieu's predecessor, Jean Cornec, is particularly revealing of the deep feelings stirred by the change. The elder statesman of the left-wing parents' federation was invited to the ceremony at the Pantheon on the 21 May when President Mitterrand first solemnly and ceremoniously addressed the nation. Cornec had no sooner started to walk up the Rue Soufflot, he said, than 'the crowd, recognizing me, applauded, not me but the Federation, saying "long live the secular school, it's the *Fédération Cornec*, long live the Federation" all the way as I climbed the slope, and then, a few moments later, the President of the Republic, in office since that morning, arrived in the *place du Panthéon*, with his rose in his hand. . . . I thought of all that history, two centuries of it, and of Victor Hugo . . . and I thought that we had truly renewed contact with our history.'[53]

The other federations were naturally less enthusiastic. They reasserted their political independence and proclaimed their readiness to work with the new authorities. Jean-Marie Schléret, president of what had until 1980 been the moderate-right *Fédération Lagarde* (PEEP), said acidly on 28 May:

> I'll reply now to the president of the FCPE [Andrieu], claiming some time ago that his federation would never be the PEEP of a left government, I'll reply to him that the PEEP will take good care not to become this government's FCPE, it will refuse to practise mere sterile obstruction.[54]

The transition was made easier by the decision of new Minister Alain Savary to declare his early commitment to parent-teacher co-operation, and his promise to find resources to fund parent attendance at school and class councils.[55] In July and August delegations from all the parents' federations were received by the Minister. He saw them, of course, separately.

Yet in spite of their jealousies and reservations, even the smaller parents' federations found themselves part of a general climate of expectancy. The editorial of *L'Éducation* on 21 May was not exaggerating when it said: 'The world of teachers, youth movements and adult education, and of most parents through their unions, organizations and

49

federations, display on this occasion an almost unanimous attitude of support and hope.'[56]

In the aftermath of the elections, the parent federations had two main preoccupations: the operation of the education system, and participation itself. It was difficult to disentangle these two concerns. However emotive the rhetoric of struggle and victory, the analysis of the educational problem which prevailed in May 1981 was much more sophisticated than that of May 1968 when the participatory system was first seriously mooted. It was able to draw on, for example, Louis Legrand's 1977 diagnostic study which synthesized much research, especially of a sociological kind,[57] and on a detailed socialist blueprint of 1978.[58] Before 1981 there was in fact a considerable measure of agreement between the informed leaderships of the three main secular parent federations (Andrieu, Schléret, Démaret)[59] and UNAPEL, the Catholic federation, about what should be done. If change was to be real, it must not be decreed from on high, as had been the case with the Haby reforms flowing from the 1975 Act. But change could grow organically from below only if individuals could be entrusted with meaningful responsibilities at local level. In his very first interview as Minister, Alain Savary stressed his awareness 'that nothing fundamental is achieved in education unless it's for the long term.'[60] A plurality of values, he continued, could be sensibly accommodated only in a decentralized system. This was the only way in which value questions could be usefully debated between teachers and parents: only decentralization could sidestep the striking of rigid national attitudes and lead to curricular compromise. Although parents should not control schools, their presence was essential to any real change:

> On strictly educational questions, parents cannot have an overall vision.... But parents must be fully associated with the life of the school, and with the entire range of its pastoral activity (*action éducative*), of which the school is one important focus even if not the only one.[61]

In the same spirit, *Cahiers pédagogiques* of June 1981, bearing on its cover the triumphant message 'Victory at last!', sketched this more sober message in its leading article:

> But is it a question of replacing the normative curricula of the right by no less normative curricula of the left? ... Or should we ask the question in another and more wide-ranging way, in terms of the work load of pupils and teachers, the division of time into lessons and subjects, of curricula sketched in only

broad terms so that teachers, regarded as adult enough and honest enough to decide for themselves, would be working only towards very general objectives? ... We need to give people the freedom and responsibility to take their share in the working of the institution. Not through purely formal councils which lack both powers of decision and access to information....[62]

This meant that if schools were to be seriously 'open' to the needs and values of the communities they served, the curriculum must be much less tightly defined and controlled from the centre and must be seen as a proper topic for discussion and decision in school and class councils. This in turn required some degree of local financial control. Thus a concern to make the curriculum more flexible necessarily led to a renewed stress on genuine participation as opposed to the shadow-participation of 1968–81.

This fundamental link between the opening up of the curriculum and the shifting of responsibility from the centre to the school was not a new idea to the parents' federations, who had worked it over in congresses and working parties for at least a decade. Yet even for the *Fédération Andrieu*, with its close links with the progressive movement and the teachers' organizations of the Left, readjusting to the 'new history' was not always easy. The organized parent federations grew up in a kind of symbiotic relationship with the structures of the French state. In the words of Jean Andrieu:

Confined as we have been for almost a quarter of a century in deliberate opposition to the education policies carried out by successive governments of the conservative right, it has been essentially in terms of struggle, confrontation, strategy, mobilization and action that we have had to define our federal orientation.[63]

Later in the same speech he talked of the clenched fist of struggle opening to greet 'a new alliance of reconciled youth'.

The difficulties for the left-wing federation were partly those of moderating its externally combative image, but also those of shifting much more internal responsibility to its local membership. The structure of the federations, dominated by well-informed central leaderships served by excellent Paris-based information networks, reflected that of the state.[64] That was not a mark of bad faith, but an unavoidable feature of any association attempting to engage seriously with the centralized state machine; it meant however that like the Ministry itself, the federations had to learn to be tolerant of much greater local diversity and dissent. The *Fédération Andrieu*, for example, has moved more energetically since 1981 to encourage 'local councils' — i.e., informal *ad hoc* voluntary bodies at school level, holding regular meetings rather along the lines of the time-honoured non-political *écoles de parents*, and quite distinct from the statutory councils.[65] Some of the strains are revealed in the fussy advice in the federation magazine about avoiding politicization or trespassing on teachers' territory: 'Thus it behoves all parents on a local council to be careful and to maintain respect for these rules firmly laid down by the federation.'[66] Behind this central nervousness lay considerable recent experience in this particular federation of trying to contain a minority of activists considerably to the left of the national leadership and far from happy in a mass organization whose line they sometimes found too compromising or too authoritarian.[67] Yet the risks of local radicalism and controversy were likely to grow as the emphasis moved more to local initiative and as the unifying force of being in permanent opposition receded.

One other consequence of the socialist victory was that the Catholic schools once again moved into the limelight: a limelight fortuitously intensified by the fact that 1982 was the centenary of Jules Ferry's original hard-line secularist legislation. As the state parent federations were historically distinguished from each other by their attitudes to secularism, and as Védrine's original proposals for parent participation were partly motivated by a desire to integrate Catholic schools into the state system, *laïcité* was naturally very much on the parent agenda.

The Catholic parents' association, UNAPEL, reacted to uncertainty and apprehension over the new government's intentions towards the private sector by preparing a great mobilization of opinion ('Mobapel') through its 850,000 members.[68] A telephone network was set up through which massive local demonstrations could be quickly organized. Yet by the summer of 1982 the government's intentions were still far from clear. Addressing a large rally held in Paris in May 1982 to commemorate the centenary of the secular school (and drowning through his microphone shouted protests from parts of the crowd), Prime Minister Pierre Mauroy guaranteed the private schools' right to exist, then continued, characteristically combining a rhetorical style with non-committal matter:

> But are we going to maintain as they stand the present formulae which link private establishments to the public service without requiring them to respect all the obligations of that service? The answer is No.

Are we going, from one day to the next, and in an authoritarian way, to change that situation? The answer is No.[69]

It is fairly plain that the answer will be linked to decentralization and participation. Since the private system was rescued from bankruptcy by the 1959 Act, one of its main attractions has been school autonomy: a Catholic head differs crucially from his state counterpart in being able to recruit his own staff and thus build up a team and a school ethos. Here, as in 1968 with parent representation, the Catholic sector has been able to provide a working model envied by many observers who dissent profoundly from its ideology. There is some talk, e.g., among the Jesuits, of Catholic schools integrating into the state system.[70] Radical ideas of this sort are easier to contemplate if the state provision is more flexible, various and locally autonomous — and that is the stated intention of the government and most teachers' associations and parent federations. Even so, the provision of state funds for Catholic schools remains a real stumbling-block for many, and in the Prime Minister's words, change will certainly not come about 'from one day to the next'.

In spite of doubts and controversy about the private sector, the federations and the entire apparatus of school and class councils continued to tick over much as they did before May 1981. The appeals for a new spirit of cooperation between parents and teachers were frequent but sober, and by year two of France's 'new history' no dramatic outward changes in parent participation seemed likely. The government was emphasizing long-term organic grass-roots change, slow changes of attitudes and habits rather than instant legislation. Whether they overestimated the maturity of the electorate and underestimated the difficulty of overcoming a long historical process only time will tell. At least the parent federations, themselves a part of that historical process, had helped to formulate and propagate the new approach to educational change, and would over the years assist in conveying its meaning through local participatory activity to many ordinary people. For all their imperfections, the French parent federations appeared overall to constitute an asset in the difficult attempt to shift decision-making power from central elites to the people. Yet many thought otherwise.

2.7 Balance-Sheet

One of the early initiatives of the new socialist government was to set up an enquiry into the *collège*, or lower secondary school, under Louis

Legrand. In due course opinions were sought through local committees of teachers and others, including parents. In June 1982 *Cahiers pédagogiques* published a cartoon showing one of these local committees in session, with representatives of various unions parrotting their jargon and failing entirely to listen to each other.[71] At the extreme edge of the picture appeared a bald head repeating pathetically: 'I am a parent and I'm wondering what I'm doing here.'

The implied judgment on parent participation in France — that it is peripheral and ineffective — is widespread. An evening's conversation with a group of *'militants'* will produce many similar judgments from people who are deeply involved with the parent movement, and whose opinions command respect.[72] It is indeed the case that in terms of Pateman's categories parent participation is at best 'pseudo-participation'; and that according to Macbeth *et al.*'s four 'types of participatory action', there is almost nothing for French school councils to 'decide', 'ensure' or 'advise' on, so that 'communicating' or 'informing' is really their sole activity. As for the six broad functions listed towards the end of section 1.5, functions (iii), (iv) and (v) (appointment and control or personnel, resourcing and planning) still remain firmly in the hands of the bureaucracy, with participation remaining at best a rubber-stamping operation; function (i) (progress of individual pupils) still lies in reality with the teachers alone, as does (ii) (curriculum) — with the exception of a few marginal areas like sex education outside the regular curriculum.[73] The only area left for participation to affect is vi) — 'improvement of school-community relations' — to which ought perhaps to be added some readiness, at least among progressive teachers and parents, to discuss broad curriculum issues in school and class councils. The balance-sheet after a decade and a half is disappointing and negative judgments from parents are entirely understandable.

What is less often said, however, is that these negative judgments are usually made by people who are inclined to place a high value on 'personal development' and 'overcoming alienation' as controlling aims of the participatory system: people who responded intuitively to Jean Védrine's vision of class councils as 'a hundred thousand centres of citizenship',[74] or to the rhetoric of Edgar Faure: 'Participation is the antithesis of alienation . . . in the sense that it tends to restore to man control over himself. . . . Participation means becoming human again.'[75]

But participation has other aims. Chapter 1 attempted to clear the ground for a more differentiated evaluation by sketching four such aims and by trying to relate them to two alternative hypotheses. We must now consider in relation to the origins and subsequent evolution of parent participation which of those two theoretical positions offers a more adequate account of events in France.

To the question on the origins of parent participation the answer is agreeably clear. The appearance of school and class councils in 1968–9 was manifestly *not* the product of 'experience of and commitment to democratic involvement' (Table 3). The government's conversion to the ideals of participation was pragmatic, not principled; it was a hasty attempt to plaster over the cracks revealed in May and June 1968. The new structures were not clearly thought out, were applied initially only to those sectors of the education system where central control was most at risk, and were not accompanied by any real effort to decentralize power. The whole exercise was very obviously an attempt by 'the ruling elite' to 'achieve greater levels of legitimation'. The aim of legitimacy was paramount, even if the rhetoric (like Edgar Faure's, quoted above) gave a different impression. The 'general crisis' theory clearly offers a more satisfactory model in terms of the French case; and according to Emmy Tedesco's study of a group of parents at the bottom of the social ladder, in terms of that theory participation has been a success: 'That's what "reproduction" is about: managing to obtain from the victims a partial justification of the system.'[76] Patrick Boumard interestingly illustrates this 'success' by analyzing the proceedings of a single class council which is controlled totally by the head.[77]

Thus in considering the subsequent development of the 1968 structures we have a firm base-line from which to start, with legitimacy as the predominant aim. From 1968 to 1981 the picture became more complex and difficult to characterize, but at least from the point of view of the ruling elite which remained in effective central control throughout that time, legitimacy remained the most important concern (see Table 4). The rules governing participation grew more elaborate and the initial utopian impulse was bureaucratized and routinized. Rules changed — most notably at the time of the Haby reforms — but the distribution of power in terms of decision-making was hardly altered. The critical local or 'district' level, whose importance had been stressed by the 1968 Amiens colloquium, was entirely ignored in these changes. There was clear central preference for a depoliticized individualistic style of parent participation concentrated at school level. Parents continued to be distanced from decisions reached at national level where their representation was virtually nil, and neutered on class councils by the insistence on professional confidentiality. The less well-informed parents were frozen out: 'in parents' meetings the talk is always directed at parents who already *understand*; the debate goes on between parents who already *know*.'[78]

After the change of regime in 1981 the situation became more fluid. At the time of writing (1982) it is too soon to state categorically whether changes will be real rather than cosmetic, but there are signs of increasing emphasis on 'responsiveness'. While the Legrand Commission on the *collège* is in some ways reminiscent of the consultative devices used in the pre-1975 period, the recent use of school councils to prepare, discuss and monitor individual school plans, including curriculum development at school level, is a substantial step forward in making the system more flexible, though in an administrative rather than a radical sense, i.e., within the constraints of bureaucratic propriety, financial accountability, etc. The new government has made its first tentative steps towards the statutory funding of parent representatives. In the background is the move towards regional assemblies; how effective these will be in breaking attitudes which go back for centuries is unclear, as is their ultimate relationship with schools.

The Left claims that the elites which governed France from 1958 to 1981 have been replaced by quite different forces. One of the many tests of that claim will be whether 'legitimacy' recedes in importance as an objective in the machinery of parent participation. As for the moment the verdict must be 'not proven' then the 'general crisis' theory still remains more satisfactory than the 'reformist' alternative in accounting for the evolution of parent participation as well as its origins.

So far the discussion has focused on the initiatives taken by the ruling elite. However, that perspective oversimplifies the picture as the main decisions were the product of *interaction* between government and parent federations. The usefulness of thinking about this process in terms of four broad aims is that this throws up the highly divergent purposes of governments and parents in espousing participation as a national policy. For Jean Védrine in the late fifties, 'personal development', i.e., the moulding of a new responsible citizenry, was the most important concern, and to that the spontaneous soviets of May 1968 added a strong element of 'overcoming alienation'. Both strands of thought saw the 'responsiveness' of the system as desirable and likely to increase through participation, but this was more a by-product or a selling-point than a prime aim. As for legitimizing a regime which many of them held in contempt, this did not feature in their thinking at all. When subsequently the federations decided to operate the new system, they tended to shift towards an emphasis on 'responsiveness', as an aim which represented some sort of common ground between government and federations, and which justified the *de facto* jettisoning of 'personal development' and 'the overcoming of alienation' as achievable objectives. One of the interesting questions about the post-1981 situation is whether 'the overcoming of alienation' will be rehabilitated as a parent concern. There are certainly many signs of a desire to relate schools more organically to the communities they serve,[79] but again it is too soon to judge the long-term outcome.[80]

From the parents' point of view, therefore — or at least from the point of view of the federations as a sort of articulate vanguard of parent opinion — the picture is more complex than it was for the government. Neither the 'reformist' nor the 'general crisis' theory seems to fit the federations very well, or at least not as expressed in Table 3. It seems more helpful to see the federations as networks within which ideas are produced and publicized, and then modified by experience — both the experience of 'marketing' them and that of making them work. In France, the development seems to have been roughly as follows:

Pre-1968: Original ideas developed in federations — stress on 'personal development'.

1968: Crisis adds element of 'overcoming alienation'. Government takes over some of these ideas, in partial and distorted form because its preoccupation is 'legitimacy'.

1968–81: Continuing government emphasis on 'legitimacy' results in federations emphasizing 'responsiveness'. ('Personal development' and 'overcoming alienation' still used in rhetoric and by critics harking back to 1968.) This 'dialogue' leads in turn to a more subtle and complex picture of how schools and parents might/should relate to each other.

1981: Government shift towards 'responsiveness'? (Tests: statutory financing of parent representatives; some financial control moved to local and/or school level; curriculum opened up for school decision.) Federations shift towards 'personal development' and 'overcoming alienation'? (Tests: more emphasis on community involvement — other forces in addition to parents.)

All this suggests that the most helpful way of using the two theories might be to combine them, perhaps as follows:

The 'general crisis' theory provides the better explanation of the origins of parent participation, and of some of the factors (especially on the government side) controlling its subsequent development. However, a variant of the 'reformist' theory which views parent groups as information networks within which plans originate and evolve, should be grafted on to this if the full complexity of reality is to be reflected. The mismatch between the aims of government and parent groups provides part of the dynamic for development.

The adequacy of this revised model can now be tested in the three remaining case-studies.

Notes

1 ANDRIEU, JEAN (1981) 'Rapport introductif au débat sur l'orientation', *La Famille et l'École*, 214, pp. 18–20; here, p. 20.
2 For the historical background, see PONTEIL, FELIX (1966) *Histoire de l'Enseignement 1789–1965: Les Étapes*, Paris, Sirey; PROST, ANTOINE (1968) *L'Enseignement en France 1800–1967*, Paris, Armand Colin; MOODY, JOSEPH N. (1978) *French Education since Napoleon*, Syracuse, N.Y., Syracuse University Press.
3 The best description is still MINOT, J. (1970) *L'Entreprise Education Nationale*, Paris, Armand Colin.
4 Circular 75–316, 17 September 1975, 'Consommation du poisson dans les Etablissements publics scolaires'.
5 FORQUIN, JEAN-CLAUDE (1980) 'L'école française et sa difficile insertion communautaire', *International Review of Education*, 26/3, pp. 289–300; here, p. 295.
6 This matter is discussed in greater depth in BEATTIE, NICHOLAS (1979) 'The meaning of secularism in contemporary French education', *Journal of Moral Education*, 8/2, pp. 81–91.
7 LEGRAND, LOUIS (1977) *Pour une Politique démocratique de l'Education*, Paris, Presses Universitaires Françaises, p. 220.
8 *Ibid*. p. 14.
9 Most of the chronological account (up to and including 2.5) which follows has been reported in English in BEATTIE, NICHOLAS (1976) 'Parents' associations in France: Their growth and character up to 1968', *Irish Journal of Education*, 10/2, pp. 81–92; (1978) 'Parent participation in French education, 1968–1975', *British Journal of Educational Studies*, 26/1, pp. 40–53; (1981) 'The politicization of school government: The French example', in BARON, GEORGE (Ed.) *The Politics of School Government*, Oxford, Pergamon, pp. 181–203. More detailed references to the documentary base can be found in those articles. The best single source in French up to about 1970 is VEDRINE, JEAN (1971) *Les Parents, l'École*, Paris, Casterman.
10 ZAY, JEAN (1938) *La Réforme de l'Enseignement*, Paris, Editions Rationalistes, p. 109.
11 For a rather euphoric account, see STURGISS, BEATRICE E.S. (1937) 'A study of the respective places and contributions of parent and teacher in child education, with special reference to the parent and parent-teacher organisations in France and England', MA thesis, University of Bristol.
12 See TALBOTT, JOHN E. (1969) *The Politics of Educational Reform in France 1918–1940*, Princeton, N.J. Princeton University Press, p. 182, on the

origins of UNAPEL, the Catholic federation; and LE PINCHON, JEAN (n.d., 1970?) *Les Parents dans l'École*, Paris, UNAPEL, pp. 49 ff. for subsequent developments.

13 The summary account which follows is based mainly on information in contemporary parents' federation reviews, listed in BEATTIE, (1976) *op. cit.*, p. 91, and on more widely based journals such as *Education et Développement, Pédagogie, Parents et Mâitres*, and some of the teachers' union journals.

14 For Cornec's own account, see CORNEC, JEAN (1972) *La Fédération des Conseils de Parents d'Élèves*, Paris, Epi.

15 See COUTROT, ALINE (1963) 'La loi Scolaire de decembre 1959', *Revue françaisi de Science poletique*, 13, pp. 352–88; also FRASER, W.R. (1963) *Education and Society in Modern France*, London, Routledge and Kegan Paul.

16 COMMISSION CHARGÉE DE L'ÉTUDE DES RAPPORTS ENTRE L'ÉTAT ET L'EN-SEIGNEMENT PRIVÉ, 5 Juin–29 Octobre 1959 (1959) *Rapport Général*, Paris, Ministère de L'Éducation Nationale. On Védrine's plans, see VÉDRINE, *op. cit.* and VÉDRINE, JEAN (1968) 'Un project de structure de participation dans les lycées', *Education et Developpement*, 40, pp. 13–43.

17 Especially *Cahiers pédagogiques*. Number 55 (September/October 1965) contains a full discussion of 'school democracy' which is a useful summary of the progressive achievement shortly before 1968.

18 LOBROT, MICHEL (1972) *La Pédagogie institutionnelle. L'école vers l'Autogestion*, Paris, Gauthier-Villars, (1st ed. 1967), p. 277.

19 See, e.g., RAOUX, P. (1968) 'Vers un lycée possible, ou la participation dans un lycée', *Education et Developpement*, 41, pp. 10–27.

20 See JUQUIN, PIERRE (Ed.) (1973) *Propositions pour Reconstruire l'École*, Paris, Éditions Sociales, esp. pp. 35 ff.

21 Mention should be made of the *Centre d'études pedagogiques*, run by Jesuits and a longstanding source of progressive ideas in Catholic education. A monthly review of high calibre, *Parents et Mâitres*, had been promoting more open relations between schools and families since 1953. See the special number of *Parents et Mâitres*, 21/1, 1974.

22 ASSOCIATION D'ETUDE POUR L'EXPANSION DE LA RECHERCHE SCIENTIFIQUE (1969) *Pour une École nouvelle: Formation des Mâitres et Recherche en Education. Actes du Colloque d'Amiens, Mars 1968*, Paris, Dunod, The list of participants (pp. 449–70) reads like a roll-call of all that is progressive in French education.

23 *Ibid.*, p. 182.

24 *Ibid.*, p. 187. The district idea is expounded more fully on pp. 198 ff.

25 *Ibid.*, p. 180. The adjective 'supple' appears frequently, e.g., pp. 214–16.

26 *Ibid.* p. 179.

27 For basic references for the narrative which follows, see BEATTIE *op. cit.* (1978).

28 *Arrêté* of 2 May 1945; see also *arrêtés* of 21 September and 28 November

1944. By the Circular of 16 July 1948 ('Activités des associations de parents d' élèves') this early libertarianism had evaporated. LEGRAND, *op. cit.*, pp. 99–100, contains an account of the 1944 councils in their eventual emasculated form.

29 Decree of 16 September 1969.

30 FARGIER, MARIE-ODILE (1968) 'Approbation et réticences', *L'Éducation*, 24/4, 10 October, p. 26.

31 For contemporary opinions, see VÉDRINE, JEAN (1969) 'Les parents et la vie de l'école', *L'Education*, 36, 19 June, pp. 8–10; VOISIN,, ANNE-MARIE and GUILLOT, MAURICE 'A propos des conseils d' établissements', *loc. cit.*, pp. 11–12.

32 See ISAMBERT, A. (1962) 'Tendances actuelles de l'éducation des parents en France', *International Review of Educaiton*, 8, pp. 175–87.

33 For their views, see *Cahiers pédagogiques*, 177, 1979, pp. 14–15. While these *syndicats* pursue a work of agitation and propaganda among the workers, they rarely present candidates for election. The CSF issues a 'Bulletin — écoles et familles'.

34 For an example which the author admits to be unique, see BEAU, J.D. (1979) 'Organiser ensemble la vie scolaire', *Cahiers pédagogiques*, 177, pp. 17–19.

35 25 per cent was the figure in Le Havre in 1978 (see *Cahiers pédagogiques*, 177, 1979, 10). JEAN VEDRINE's estimate of a third for the state sector dates from 1970 and relates to a time when the electoral process was restricted to secondary schools (VEDRINE, JEAN (1971) *Les Parents, l'École*, Paris, Casterman, p. 99). The membership figures issued by the federations may err on the side of generosity.

36 For useful early attempts at a balance-sheet, see MONTAGNIER, CHARLES (1970) 'Bilan de la participation', in ACKERMANN, P. *et al.*, *Changer l'École*, Paris, Editions de l'Epi, pp. 221–39; also VÉDRINE, *op. cit.*, which is also the best (indeed the only) attempt at a 'history'.

37 GLOTON, ROBERT (Ed.) (1977) *L'Établissement scolaire, Unité éducative*, Paris, Casterman, p. 90.

38 GOVER, A.S. and PARKES, D.L. (1973) 'Academic government in France (the government and management of French educational institutions)', in PARKES, D.L. (Ed.), *College Management Readings and Cases, Vol.4*, Blagdon, Bristol, F.E. Staff College, Coombe Lodge, mimeo, pp. 119 ff.

39 René Haby was the then Minister. Technically, the Act is known as the Law of 11 July 1975. The main enabling decrees and circulars affecting the participatory system were those of 28 December 1976, 18 July 1977 and 26 January 1978.

40 Circular 78.004, 26 January 1978.

41 This view was not confined to Marxists — e.g., consider a careful account of the Haby reforms by a Jesuit: VANDERMEERSCH, EDMOND (1975) 'L'éducation dans la société giscardienne', *Pédagogie*, 30/7, pp. 1–16.

42 Circular 78.004, 26 January 1978.

43 ANON. (1976) 'Les parents aux C.A.', *L'Éducation*, 277, p. 11.

44 ANON. (1978) 'Elections scolaires', *L'Éducation*, 338, p. 6.

45 GUIGON, C. (1977) 'L'an I de la réforme — 3'. *L'Éducation*, 304, pp. 12–15.

46 ANON. (1978) 'Elections scolaires', *L'Éducation*, 338, p. 6.

47 BOBASCH, MICHAELA (1977) 'La guerre des Fédérations de parents', *L'Éducation*, 327, pp. 8–9.

48 BOBASCH, MICHAELA (1979) 'FCPE: entre le pédagogique et le politique', *L'Éducation*, 391, pp. 2–4; ANON. (1979) 'Le congrès à travers la presse', *Pour l'Enfant ... vers l'Homme*, 167, pp. 8–9.

49 BOBASCH, MICHAELA (1979) 'Participation: au delà des blocages', *L'Education*, 401–2, pp. 38–41; here, p. 41. 'Aladdin's lamp' is a free rendering of *peau de chagrin*, a reference to Balzac's 'wild ass's skin', which is less known to English speakers. For a less personal statement of parent disillusion, see DHONTE, N. (1977) 'Les parents et la participation, la grande désillusion', *Le Monde de l'Éducation*, 33.

50 For confirmation of this broad agreement, see for *Andrieu* ROCHE, JEAN-PIERRE (1982) 'Donner les moyens aux parents', *Pour l'Ènfant ... vers l'Homme*, 190, p. 6; for *Schléret*, FÉDÉRATION DES PARENTS D'ELÉVES DE L'ENSEIGNEMENT PUBLIC (1981) *Rapport d'Activité du Conseil d'Administration, 1980–81*, (Supplement to *Voix des Parents*, 209, 1981), pp. 25–6; for *Démaret*, duplicated leaflet: 'Congrès de Montelimar 1981'.

51 By the autumn of 1982, five years after the inception of the new system, the proportions of seats won by the federations and others seemed to have settled down into a fairly stable pattern: in the primary sector ANDRIEU took about half, SCHLÉRET 8.2 per cent, the other two small federations (Démaret and the '*Autonomes*') 11.8 per cent and 'various' 30 per cent (mainly rural); in the secondary sector ANDRIEU nearly two-thirds, SCHLÉRET about a quarter, and the smaller federations about an eighth. (ROCHE, JEAN PIERRE (1982) 'Elections aux conseils d'école et conseils d'etablissement', *Pour l'Enfant ... vers l'Homme*, 188, p. 6).

52 ANDRIEU, JEAN (1981) 'Déjà mieux', *Pour l'Enfant ... vers l'Homme*, 184, pp. 4–5.

53 ANDRIEU, JEAN and CORNEC, JEAN, (1981) 'Allocution prononceé par J. Andrieu pour le départ de J. Cornec; Réponse de J. Cornec'. *La Famille et l'École*, 214, pp. 32–3; here, p. 33.

54 SCHLÉRET, JEAN-MARIE (1981) 'Discours inaugural', *PEEP Info*, 83, pp. 8–13; here, p. 9.

55 See GRACIA, ÉMILE (1981) 'Complément au rapport d'activité', *La Famille et l'École*, 214, pp. 1–9; esp. p. 8.

56 GUILLOT, MAURICE (1981) 'Changement de ton', *L'éducation*, 457, 21 mai, p. 2.

57 LEGRAND, *op. cit*. Ch. 6 (Les faux-semblants de la 'participation'), pp. 91–121, is particularly relevant to the theme of this chapter.

58 MEXANDEAU, LOUIS and QUILLIOT, ROGER (1978) *Libérer l'École. Plan socialiste pour l'Education Nationale*, Paris, Flammarion. See pp. 161 ff. on

the proposals for participation by parents and others.

59 The Fédération Démaret was a small federation with particular technical and agricultural concerns. It seems to have survived the post–1960 polarization as a separate entity mainly because of the independent personality of its then president, M. Raymond Démaret (president 1955– 70); the presidency came in due course to his son Jacques (1979–   ).

60 GUILLOT, MAURICE (1981) 'Un mot-clé: décentraliser', *L'Éducation*; 461, 18 juin, pp. 4–6.

61 *Ibid.*

62 DELANNOY, CÉCILE and GEORGE, JACQUES (1981) 'Par delà l'euphorie, reposer nos "questions à la gauche"', *Cahiers pédagogiques*, 195, pp. 1–2.

63 ANDRIEU, JEAN (1981) 'Rapport introductif au débat sur l'orientation', *La Famille et l'École*, 214, pp. 18–20; here, p. 19.

64 LEGRAND, *op. cit.*, makes this point on pp. 16 and 223. For a broader context see BROWN, B.E. (1963) 'Pressure politics in the Fifth Republic', *Journal of Politics*, 25, pp. 509-25, or MEYNAUD, JEAN (1962) *Nouvelles Etudes sur les Groupes de Pression en France*, Paris, Armand Colin.

65 By 1980–1 there were reported to be 17,680 of these: the total had been growing for some years (ANON (1981) 'Rapport d'activité', *La Famille et l'École*, 212, pp. 1–27; here, p. 19). There are also councils in each *département* which coordinate actions against school closures, etc. — see VARIOUS (1981) 'Les parents agissent pour les enfants d'abord', *Pour l'Enfant . . . vers l'Homme*, 181, pp. 10–11.

66 ANON (1981) 'Un conseil local de parents d'élèves c'est . . . .', *Pour l'Enfant . . . . vers l'Homme*, 184, pp. 18–19; here, p. 18.

67 See, for example, statements made by two members of the national committee·who voted against the annual report in 1981 (VARIOUS (1981) 'Explications de vote', *La Famille et l'École*, 212, pp. 28–9). The voting figures at the Saint-Etienne congress show that the main centres of opposition are Paris and Marseille (*La Famille et l'École*, 214, 1981, pp. 16–17). For a recent external comment, see GAUTHIER, NICOLE (1982) 'Impatience et idées nouvelles', *L'Éducation*, 494, 3 juin pp. 2–5.

68 FALLOT, EVELYNE (1982) 'Ecole privée:pourquoi la guerre', *L'Express*, 1600, 12 mars, pp. 56–61. See also JULLIEN, CLAUDE-FRANÇOIS (1982) 'Ecole: pourquoi la guerre se rallume', *Le Nouvel Observateur*, 911, 24–30 avril, pp. 70–2.

69 GAUTHIER, NICOLE (1982) 'Une nouvelle laïcité', *L'Éducation*, 491, 13 mai, pp. 2–5; here, p. 5.

70 FALLOT, *op. cit.*

71 *Cahiers pédagogiques*, 205, 1982, p. 12.

72 A good example of grass-roots depression is BRIOLET, M. (1979) 'Huit ans de présence aux conseils de classe (1ᵉʳ et 2ᵉ cycles)', *Cahiers pédagogiques*, 177, pp. 25–7.

73 BEATTIE, NICHOLAS (1976) 'Sex education in France: A case-study in curriculum change', *Comparative Education*, 12/2, pp. 115–28. This issue

will be further discussed in Chapter 6.

74 VÉDRINE, JEAN (1969) '100,000 centres de civisme = les Conseils de classe', *Education et Développement*, 52, pp. 29–51.

75 FAURE, EDGAR (1970) *L'Âme du Combat*, Paris, Fayard, pp. 244–5.

76 TEDESCO, EMMY (1979) *Des Familles Parlent à l'École*, Paris, Casterman, p. 89.

77 BOUMARD, PATRICK (1978) *Un Conseil de Classe très ordinaire*, Paris, Stock.

78 TEDESCO, *op. cit.*, p. 161.

79 Consider, for example, the two schools described at length in GLOTON, *op. cit.*, pp. 143 ff. These have experimented with various kinds of committees and open meetings in a style which seems more common in Italy. Will this *local* experimentation become more common?

80 Since this chapter was written, an interesting study of 'educational consumers' has been published, which includes much information about the system from the parent-pupil angle: Ballion, R. (1982) *Les Consommateurs D'École: Stratégies Educatives des Familles*, Paris, Stock/L. Pernoud. For an up to date journalistic account of the debate on the form of participatory structures, see Betbeder, M-C, (1984) 'Conseil de classe: Crever l'abcès', *Le Monde de L'Education*, 110, pp. 28–34. The Legrand report on the lower secondary school (Legrand, L. (1982) *Pour Un Collège Démocratique*, Paris, Documentation Francaise) plans a renewed school council (pp. 118–120) but the suggestions remain fairly general. For parents' reactions, see *Ibid*, pp. 359–66.

3　*Italy*

3.1　Background

At a first glance, parent participation in Italy looks similar to its counterpart in France. The centralized and bureaucratic character of both systems, and the historic division between Left and Right, communists and Catholics, have tended to produce participatory systems with a certain family resemblance. Yet this likeness must not be allowed to cloak what is unlike in these two countries; indeed, it should make it easier to pinpoint the particularities of each, so that what is common in the participatory structures stands out more clearly.

Perhaps the crucial difference between France and Italy is that while France has been unified roughly within its present frontiers since the sixteenth century, Italy achieved unity as a nation-state little more than a century ago after centuries of fragmentation and exploitation. The problems faced by the new Kingdom of Italy were daunting: the creation of a united, stable and prosperous nation from a collection of small states at different, but generally early stages of economic and cultural development. The 1861 census of those parts of the kingdom which were united by then reflects the educational challenge very clearly: 65 per cent of the entire population over 5 was illiterate; the figure in rural areas was 80 per cent — greater in parts of the south and among women. Provision varied wildly from place to place. While in Piedmont 93 per cent of children between 6 and 12 were in school in 1863–4, the equivalent for Sicily was only 14 per cent.[1] Italian itself was spoken as a first language only by a small minority of the population: the peasant masses spoke local dialects which were often mutually unintelligible.

In these circumstances the northern liberal elite shrank from any form of cultural federalism, which seemed to them messy and unprogressive, because liable to play into the hands of a reactionary church. Piedmont imposed upon all parts of the new Kingdom its own central- ized and bureaucratic system of educational administration, modelled in part on that of Prussia. Compulsory education was thus introduced to large areas of Italy as a more or less artificial importation, operating in a language which was unknown to its peasant *clientèle*. The state school was, in Aymone's vivid phrase, a sort of mosque: children 'leave by the door the shoes they wear on their daily business'.[2] Local authorities had little opportunity to affect this situation. Even the small part they originally played in the financing of elementary schools was reduced as the years passed, and a rigid and unimaginative centralization was later strengthened by over twenty years of Fascist rule.

Thus for many Italians the school became much more than in France the local manifestation of an alien and distant *régime*. In Italian, the very phrase 'the state' (*lo Stato* — uttered with a malevolent hiss on the initial 's') carries *unfavourable* connotations — sometimes of actual corruption, usually of incompetence, discourtesy, irrelevance and time- serving, and always of centrality and remoteness. This contrasts with the warm feelings evoked by a person's native town or province, with its familiar dialect and cooking, its local politics, personalities and festivals. Even as an industrial society, with the large population movements that industrialism entails, Italy remains a country where people feel they belong to a particular place and where the distinctions between places are still substantial.

This local diversity, which at the personal level is what makes travel in Italy so pleasurable, has at the economic level less attractive aspects. The south remains, relative to the rest of the country, disadvantaged and poverty-stricken, a continuing source of massive internal and external migration, a complex mass of interwoven economic, political, social and educational problems. More than a century after its incor- poration into a united Italy, *il Mezzogiorno* still lags conspicuously behind the rest of the country on all indicators, including educational ones.

Yet the south is only an extreme instance of a more general Italian problem: the relative poverty of resourcing, especially of infrastructure. While the extent of absolute poverty is greater in the south than elsewhere, all regions have suffered from a persistent failure to evolve adequate sources of local revenue. For long periods, even current expenditure was not covered, and capital outlay remained extremely difficult. Against the background of a nineteenth-century provision similar in many ways to that of the present 'Third World', Italian education today represents tangible progress. Even so, school buildings are still quite often inadequate and ill-equipped, compared to those of Italy's European neighbours; there are still schools where separate shifts are worked mornings and afternoons; games-fields and gymnasia are the exception rather than the rule. Illiteracy is still relatively high. One example of the difference between Italy and Britain is that while in the latter local public libraries were established and consolidated in the last century, in Italy local libraries are at present being introduced by many communist and socialist administrations as an exciting and progressive innovation. No wonder that one of the features of Italian rail travel is the number of adult passengers unashamedly reading comics.

The ubiquity of the comic strip points up another revealing contrast, between, on the one hand, the ignorance and superstition of substantial sectors of the population, and, on the other, the vivacity and sophistication of the all-pervasive political debate. That contrast lies behind so much of the argument about parental participation in schools that it is worth stressing at the outset of this account. By British standards, Italians read very little. The press remains essentially local, overmanned and undercapitalized, with poor distribution facilities.[3] Yet the general quality of political discussion in Italian newspapers is surprisingly high. That discussion is perhaps given bite and depth by the worked-out Marxist analysis of current events which is permanently available to be supported, refined or refuted. Italians of all political opinions are often aware of the links between society, the economy, politics and education to an extent which makes much British political discussion appear superficial and naive. Yet the concrete results of this outward political sophistication are few and elusive. The political system remains notoriously ineffective in achieving change, and has been paralyzed since the earliest years of the Republic by the inconclusive struggle between the two largest groupings (Christian Democracy and Communism — DC and PCI). To some extent, the political debate remains shadow-boxing; or, to use a phrase which constantly recurs in Italian conversations, it lacks 'concreteness'. Yet this apparently sclerotic democracy commands considerable public support, if measured only in regular massive voting turn-outs: even in local elections, 90 per cent is not infrequent. Furthermore, an important minority of Italians clearly does not regard democracy as a mere apparatus of formal periodic votes, but is prepared to work and argue in grass-roots associations and pressure-groups, and if necessary to take to the streets to demonstrate the force of their opinions. The Resistance is often invoked by the powers that be as a sort of sacred myth — yet it would be excessively cynical to view that myth as merely a fiction, for a surprising number of people try to incorporate its values into their daily lives.

Behind the entire debate lies the historic communist-Catholic split. In this sense the Italian scene is similar to the French. There are, however, significant differences. The papal presence in the national capital, the papacy's history as the ruler of large tracts of central Italy, papal intransigence and political interference since 1870, the Italian Constitution's acceptance of Catholicism as in effect a state religion — all these facts of Italian history mean that hostility to the church is often shriller, livelier and more justified than in secular France.

Italian Catholicism's great post-war political success has been the launching of Christian Democracy, which has governed Italy uninterruptedly since 1946. Christian Democracy is, however, more a loose assemblage of viewpoints, more or less 'christian' or 'democratic', than a tightly controlled unitary party. Even the Italian Communist Party (PCI), by contrast with its French counterpart, seems relatively tolerant of individual views and local autonomies. Thus one of the perils of this study will be to avoid using labels like DC and PCI, or even 'Right' and 'Left', as though we know exactly what they mean.

Another danger is to assume too readily that the traditional Catholic-communist confrontation (which, as we shall see, dominates the structures of parent participation) is all it appears to be. Acquaviva and Santuccio suggest that a third 'culture' is forming as Italy is rapidly incorporated into the economic structures of Western Europe:

> 'A new culture is taking shape, a different code of behaviour, a fresh value-system, and Christianity and Marxism alike are coming to terms with the radically new life-styles that are emerging as sub-cultures within the context of Italy's wider and more diversified way of life.'[4]

The solidity and coherence of the traditional alternative cultures may blind us to the realities of a new 'consumer society' whose ideological underpinning is still tentative and pragmatic. Thus one of the central questions about parent participation in Italy is: does it represent a genuinely new reality, a new relationship between families and schools, which happens to have been colonized by Catholics and communists? Or, is it yet another institutional manifestation of the old ideological struggle? Does it look to the past or the future? And what concrete indicators could we find to help us to answer that question in one way or another?

3.2   Parent Participation Before 1968

Prior to the 1960s, there was little formal involvement of Italian parents in the school system. The introduction in 1877 of school-based welfare associations (*patronati scolastici*) for the distribution of subsidies to poor children did not flower, as it might have done in more favourable circumstances, into any wider network of governing bodies or parent-teacher associations;[5] a circular of 1910 urging the formation of school parent committees was oriented largely towards seeking the support of fathers in maintaining good discipline, and remained in any case a dead letter.[6] Fascist legislation restricted itself to general statements of solidarity between family and school.[7]

The written norms of the new post-war Republic also remained at the level of general aspirations, this time of a broadly Catholic colouring. For example, article 30 of the Italian constitution reads: 'It is the duty and the right of parents to maintain, instruct and educate their children' — a phrase which, as in France, maintains a characteristic distinction, between 'instruction' (the formal teaching of skills and information) and 'education' (the more elusive and controversial imparting of values and attitudes). Similarly, article 155 of the Civil Code states that 'whatever the person to whom their children may be entrusted, the father and mother retain the right to oversee (*vigilare*) their education.' In practice, like many other constitutional provisions, these norms had few observable consequences in the way teachers or parents behaved.

The 1950s were not, however, entirely a dead period. Although the edgy orthodoxy of Christian Democracy in the era of the Cold War was unlikely to experiment with unpredictable forms of grass-roots participation, its broad Catholic base gave it a genuine interest in the family, which it saw as the fundamental institution of a democratic society and wished to strengthen. It was partly in response to pressures from Catholic organizations such as the 'Family Front' that the Ministry of Public Instruction set up in March 1953 a national centre in Rome for the study of school-family relations,[8] which can now in retrospect be seen as the first substantial move in the direction of the participatory system which began to function twenty-two years later. Yet the politicians who set up the centre in the early fifties almost certainly expected no concrete policy changes to flow from their decision. Italy is littered with similar study centres, many of them mere fossils originally established simply to give an air of government interest in, or action upon, some temporary political problem. The Rome centre for the study of school-family relations was only one of several such 'Didactic Centres' set up at this time under legislation originally passed during the Fascist period, and intended to cover all aspects of the education system. Their origins, and the fact that their directors were Christian Democrat nominees, gravely reduced the potential of these centres as foci for educational innovation. In the case of the centre for the study of school-family relations, this meant a relatively individualistic approach to parental relations with schools, as opposed to the wider social orientation of some socialist and communist thinkers.[9] In spite of this, for over two decades the centre for school-family relations managed to nurture the sometimes sickly seedling of parental involvement with a regular flow of information through correspondence, conferences and regular publications.[10] Its influence over a long period has been unspectacular but surely genuine.

The fifties also saw the appearance of two parent journals. *Genitori* ('Parents') came out for the first time in February 1954. 'Always independent of everybody', it claimed proudly twenty years later,[11] 'never identified with anyone, we have never received a single lira from any minister, party or public body.' The editor then went on to list the assorted good works promoted by *Genitori* over twenty years, ranging from sex education in Italy to schools for poor blacks in Brazil. *Genitori* is explicitly Catholic in message and tone and quite acceptable for monthly sale through the parish network from which it derives a good deal of its support.

Five years later, on May Day 1959, appeared a left-wing counterpart, the *Giornale dei Genitori* ('Parents' Newspaper'). The five-year gap is significant. The forces of the Left had been relatively slow after the war to take up education as a central issue in the politics of the working class: the turning-point came in the mid-fifties.[12] The *Giornale dei Genitori* grew originally from the enthusiasms of Ada Marchesini Gobetti, a communist intellectual who had fought in the Resistance. In 1958 she published a book of advice for parents based on secular rather than Catholic norms and attempting to place the family against its broader social background. In addressing meetings of parents about these issues she came to realize that working-class parents needed advice and support which at the time were offered only by the church. Already a frequent contributor to the PCI's educational journal, *Riforma della Scuola* (founded in 1955), she decided to devote the profits of her book to launching the *Giornale*. After a number of initial financial and organizational problems, this had established itself by the mid-sixties as an attractive and thoughtful monthly publication.[13]

Thus by the end of the fifties the incipient Italian parent movement already differed in several ways from its French counterpart. In Rome, a national centre was disseminating information about parent activity in Italy and abroad. Parent journals existed which from their inception formed part of the extensive competing information networks of Left and Right. Small groups of intellectuals and specially committed activists were at work to propagate a shift towards a more open and democratic style of interaction between parents and schools. Yet actual parent activity remained, by comparison with France, small, localized and unstable. The national centre reckoned in 1959 that there were only about 300 'school-family associations and committees' throughout Italy,[14] and to read the parents' journals is to get an impression of small numbers of the righteous striving manfully to leaven the solid lump of ignorance, indifference and hostility. This impression is as valid for Catholics as for communists or socialists. The contrast with France is instructive. French parents' magazines emerged from parents' associations which *already existed* at a national level. In Italy they were launched as part of more general ideological groupings with the express intention of *provoking* parent groupings which in the 1950s hardly existed at all.

It is not surprising that *Genitori* and the *Giornale dei Genitori* not infrequently carried letters and articles which expressed the despair and frustration of intelligent parents faced with a rigid bureaucracy and an indifferent public opinion. Yet the sixties saw a slow and undramatic consolidation of parent interest. The national centre experimented over several years with 'schools for parents' on the model of the French *écoles de parents*. Local councils, committees and associations were set up in many parts of Italy, and if many were shortlived and unstable and suffered from their ill-defined functions and their dependence on official favour, some survived. At the level of planning and ideas, the evident problems of centralization and excessive bureaucracy were beginning to generate tentative answers worked out in terms of institutional change. In July 1963 a commission of enquiry on the present conditions and future development of education recommended a shift of power from the central ministry which, had it been implemented, would have made schools to some extent locally autonomous and governed by democratically elected boards.[15] In 1964 Lombardy and Veneto produced plans for what would have been community schools, serving local people and integrated with the local environment in a way quite unknown in Italy. At the same time, a small but growing number of teachers was becoming aware of more progressive approaches to teaching and learning, and this necessarily led some of them to reconsider their attitude to parents and the whole issue of democracy in schools. Typical of this new strand in teachers' thinking was the MCE (*Movimento Cooperazione Educativa*), based originally on the ideas and practices of the French educationalist Freinet.[16]

One can trace in the journal *Cooperazione Educativa* a growing realization that educational problems cannot be solved simply by improved pedagogical techniques, still less by being nice to children, but that they necessitate changes in personal value-positions and social policies and a blurring of traditionally sharp boundaries between school, family and community. For example, if the underachievement of the south is to be seriously tackled, parental support will be crucial, and teachers will have to encourage children and their families to question their position in ways that may be threatening to established authority. The emerging awareness that families are important for all concerned with equality of opportunity in education, and are not just an obsession of reactionary Catholics, can also be traced in the influential journal *Scuola e Città* and in rather different tones, in the PCI's journal of educational theory and discussion, *Riforma della Scuola*.

An important later contribution to, and result of this maturing of left-wing opinion was Tullio Aymone's study of the interaction of families and schools in Sesto San Giovanni, a working-class housing area with many southern immigrants in the hinterland of Milan. Aymone criticizes the Italian Left for failing to relate its generalized egalitarian-ism to 'the family, the school, the institutions of everyday living which mediate life to individuals by bringing them into touch with the organized network of civil society.'[17]

It was not until the late sixties and early seventies that these various currents of opinion — which at the time often seemed confused and ineffectual to those most concerned[18] — began to bear fruit in observ-able institutional change. The fact that that change was triggered off, as in France, by the student unrest of 1968, must not be allowed to disguise the fact that much of the initial question-raising and thinking had been done by creative minorities before 1968. Plans and attitudes had not been as thoroughly worked out as in France, and in particular grass-roots parent activity remained much more fragmentary, infre-quent and ineffectual than in France. Yet in spite of that it was possible in March 1968 for a Jesuit priest and a prominent communist spokesman to publish almost simultaneously articles on school government which called independently for local autonomy for schools as a way out of the dead-end of bureaucratic sclerosis and rigidly opposed ideologies.[19] In presenting their solutions, both were already able to argue from a certain style of thinking, even a rather tentative tradition, of which the parent journals had become the vehicles. As in France, the participatory machinery which emerged from the emotional break-through of '1968' was not a sudden magical flash of inspiration, even if it seemed so to many participants.

3.3   The Emergence of a Legal Framework 1968–74

The events of 1968 manifested themselves rather differently in Italy from in France, even if their spirit and content were similar. They were less dramatically confined to a brief revolutionary period. The first faculty was occupied by students as early as January 1966 (Trento), and the high point of student unrest was from late 1967 through the spring of 1968. The school of Barbiana's *Letter to a Teacher*, which to many Italians seemed to summarize the spirit of 1968 as it affected schools, in fact came out in 1967.[20] The students were also less successful than in France in placing their demands in the general political arena, so that the national elections of May 1968 were conducted with surprisingly little reference to the student occupations. Yet in spite of this the psychological impact was undoubtedly profound. For the first time in living memory — or so it seemed to many people — it looked as though what ordinary people thought and said might have some impact on 'the state'. People began to feel that they could, and should, 'stand up and be counted', and the impact of this feeling can be traced in various areas of Italian life over the following decade, ranging from trade union attitudes to the position of laypeople in the church, from local planning and welfare to the women's movement. Indeed, the success of the national referendum to legalize divorce in 1974 is a very good example of 'the spirit of '68' carrying through real change in the face of powerful opposition from the ruling party, the church and a large part of the media.

In the sphere of education, the governing Christian Democrats found themselves in a situation similar to that facing the French Right, though less urgently dramatic. Educational issues had after years of neglect suddenly shot to the top of the agenda. It was important for government to be seen to be doing something. As in France, there was an immediate need for something to be done about the universities, and in due course (law 910, 11 December 1969) all faculties were thrown open to all possessors of a school-leaving certificate — a supposedly interim measure passed in expectation of a more substantial reform which has not so far materialized.[21]

Schools too were in turmoil. Parental disquiet was for the moment met by a vague circular (circular 476, 26 November 1968) acknowledging parents' 'aspirations to participate actively in school life' in new ways and urging schools to listen to parents' views and 'stimulate and guide initiatives which are becoming more and more widespread.' However, this was no more than a token gesture, and it became increasingly clear that, rather against its better judgment, the government would need to evolve a plan for parent and pupil participation in the running of schools. In deciding what that plan should be, the government had to consider a wide range of factors. It had first to come to terms with developments in the schools and the community. Over many of these developments it had no control, and there can be little doubt that one of the motivations behind eventual legislation was a desire to direct popular pressures into safe channels.

The activity of parent and community groups in the years immediately following 1968 was extremely diverse and unpredictable. Parents and teachers, and sometimes pupils, would come together, often at school, sometimes at neighbourhood level. What brought them together was often some obvious injustice or official absurdity. Sometimes an alliance between teachers, pupils and parents of a progressive cast of mind would trigger off a traditionalist parents' association to fight innovations which were seen as anarchic or threatening. In many schools, the debate came to centre on the *voto* — the traditional formal mark given by teachers. Progressive teachers disliked the authoritarian implications of this system of periodic formal number grades, often allocated in public as a result of testing recall of learning homework, and its openness to abuse as an instrument of discipline or control; they also disliked the *bocciatura* system (the requirement that students who did not 'make the grade' should repeat a year), of which the *voto* was an important element. For many parents, however, the *voto* was both their main channel of communication with teachers and a guarantee of traditional standards.

The *Liceo Scientifico A. Serpieri* at Rimini provides a good example of the sort of local struggles going on in many places after 1968. Teachers refused to give the *voto*. A parents' association was formed which demanded that teachers should follow the regulations. A second, progressive parents' association was formed to defend the teachers who were refusing the *voto*. An extensive local debate ensued. Mass meetings produced emotional confrontations. The unfortunate head teacher at one time became a scapegoat for both sides, but eventually found himself supported by the progressives against the inspector who was sent in to restore order. A relatively insignificant teacher (not one who was at the centre of the 'progressive' party) was transferred to another school. After recounting these events in detail, *Cooperazione Educativa*'s informant commented:

The conclusion may be drawn that one of the teacher's tasks consists in presenting the contradictions peculiar to the school as a specific reflection of social contradictions, and at the same time providing adequate means for understanding their full historical significance.[22]

That is, such educational debates, however confused, should be seen as part of a more general process of raising public consciousness about the social, economic and political system of which schools were only a part.

A local incident of this sort casts some light on the grass-roots changes which eventually contributed to the 1973 legislation. In effect, three linked but distinct shifts were going on: in the teaching profession, in local communities and among parents.

Historically, Italian teachers have been a highly conservative profession. The combination of low pay and half-day school have made it, more than elsewhere in Europe, a predominantly female preserve, grouped in unions with Catholic affiliations. From the mid-sixties, however, this traditional image began to change. The emergence in 1967 of a relatively dynamic left-oriented union grouping (CGIL-Scuola) provided a rallying-point for the large numbers of young teachers recruited after 1968 — some of them former student leaders. Even the formerly Catholic unions distanced themselves somewhat from the church. Sections of the profession showed themselves increasingly ready to think and act politically, and in pedagogical terms to be more open to progressive ideas of the sort which had for many years been promoted by journals like *Cooperazione Educativa*, *Scuola e Città* and *Riforma della Scuola*. The early seventies saw a growing tendency for teachers of this sort to band together in local pressure-groups, with or without formal union backing. The trend for local authorities to hire supplementary teachers for assorted extra-curricular or remedial activities also tended to concentrate teachers of an idealistic and often left-wing orientation on particular schools — often in more or less deprived working-class areas. It was on such schools that much of the spontaneous post-1968 participation centred.

Local debates and campaigns on educational issues increased very markedly after 1968. No doubt part of the explanation was psychological — the feeling of release and openness engendered by 1968 — but much of it was because, for the first time, the rigid sameness of centralized provision began here and there to crumble away. Some of the crumbling, as in the Rimini incident, took place because teachers took the law into their own hands; some because local (especially communist) authorities began to spend money on facilities and buildings and on additional teachers over and above those paid for by the central state. Local authorities could found and run certain types of school (e.g., upper secondary technical schools and nursery schools); they were also empowered to hire teachers in assorted more or less peripheral roles (e.g., for play-schemes or for special activities which took place on school premises in the afternoons). The possiblility of such initiatives naturally led to an unstable but vociferous fermentation of local associations and pressure-groups, especially in urban areas and the north, often with a tendency to split along broad ideological lines. In some places local committees and consultative bodies appeared which prefigured the later national system and were often superior to it in flexibility and strength of local commitment.[23]

Not all of this activity was in the narrow sense *parent* activity, though obviously parents were heavily involved. However, as we saw in the Rimini example, change tended to generate parents' associations. As these were usually formed either to legitimate or to combat change, they tended to take on a certain ideological colouring. The next stage was inevitable: that school or local parents' associations should begin to come together in larger national groupings, initially for mutual support, comfort and information, but also for bringing pressure to bear on public opinion and legislators and adminstrators at national level. By 1971 there were, predictably, two such groupings, corresponding roughly to the bodies of parent opinion fed by *Genitori* on the Right and the *Giornale dei Genitori* on the Left. The AGe (*Associazione Italiana Genitori*) was founded as early as February 1968. Article 4 of its constitution states that it is 'independent of any political or confessional movement, but respects the values sanctioned by the Italian constitution and the Christian ethic.' Its left-wing counterpart, COGIDAS (*Centro Operativo tra Genitori per l'Iniziativa Democratica e Antifascista nella Scuola* — parents' working centre for the democratic and antifascist initiative in the school), emerged in 1971. In its early years it was closely connected with a group of progressive teachers, CIDI (*Centro Iniziativa Democratica Insegnanti*), working for new ideas in education outside the existing political and union structures of the Left.

In time, both AGe and COGIDAS became more obviously 'right' and 'left'. In the early years, however, they remained relatively loose organizations attempting with varying success to coordinate local groups which were often resistant to coordination from a 'centre' which had few resources and no traditional authority.

All this activity constituted one major input into the 'black box' of the decision-makers in Rome. But other narrower party-political considerations were also important for the Christian Democratic establishment. As the dominant party in a series of short-lived coalitions, the Christian Democrats had to take into account the views of actual and potential coalition partners, some of whom held strong views on the need to 'debureaucratize' and 'democratize' education.[24] Nor could the views of the Communist Party itself be ignored, for even before the open 'historic compromise' of 1974 successive Christian Democratic administrations relied on the tacit compliance of the PCI. When one considers in addition the internal divisions of Christian Democracy itself, and the dramatic changes in Catholic attitudes associated with Pope John XXIII and the Vatican Council, the pressures for an initiative which would as far as practicable be 'all things to all men' are evident.

Of course, even in the field of educational policy, lay participation in decision-making was by no means the only issue which preoccupied the establishment. There were other even more contentious and urgent questions, such as the long-expected reform of upper secondary and higher education. Participation differed from these issues in two important ways. It was relatively cheap; and it could be packaged in a more or less consensual way as a progressive and democratic innovation likely to appeal to all shades of opinion. To reform upper secondary education would require tough and clear-cut decisions about the nature of the curriculum, how comprehensive it should be, how it should relate to employment, etc., as well as painful financial decisions. Participation, on the other hand, could to some extent be fudged and required no decisions on financial priorities. It is presumably for these underlying reasons that Italian political circles overcame the natural inertia inherent in their political system and came to place the introduction of democratic participation on the parliamentary agenda. In some ways action on school democracy was a cover for inertia in more difficult areas of educational policy.

This is not, of course, to say that lay participation in education was uncontroversial. There were, in principle, at least three possible decisions open to the authorities, any one of which in its pure form would have raised important opposition because each would have involved substantial shifts of power. One radical solution would have been to reallocate substantial authority to local communes — a policy much more practicable in Italy than in France because of the greater activity and prestige of the historic communes. This was unlikely to appeal to the Right which feared total PCI dominance over schools, and therefore over the hearts and minds of children, especially in the big cities. Another theoretical possibility was to build on the spontaneous citizen activity of the post-1968 period and devolve responsibility in some way to *assemblee* — mass meetings of participants and consumers.

'Soviets' of this sort were not only a reality in some schools and localities, they also had a strong romantic appeal to the young and to left-wing intellectuals and to all who hankered for the supposed ideals of the Resistance to be related somehow to everyday decision-making. However, the potential anarchy of this solution was likely to appeal neither to the forces of the Right nor to a PCI whose own power structures are highly centralized and which was in any case very anxious to gain power through the ballot-box and not frighten off potential middle-class support. A third, less radical compromise would have involved hiving off bits of the education system for local or grass-roots control — perhaps, as in France, parts of the timetable, or certain aspects of expenditure. Unless it was to be merely cosmetic, this third solution ran the risk of provoking massive teacher opposition, of cutting across left-wing commitments to equality of provision, and of offending the educational bureaucracy with a solution that was bound to be messy, unstable and politically explosive.

In some ways all these issues revolve round the parental role. If control of education is placed firmly in the hands of democratically elected local authorities, parent participation must remain secondary and peripheral. If power is to be allocated to mass meetings, then it becomes crucial to decide what power and at what levels, as well as to determine who has the right to attend the meetings; to take an extreme example, a school mass meeting deciding on school policy could be dominated by parents simply because they are numerically a majority. The hiving-off compromise raises similar questions.

The neat and orderly way of coping with these issues is obviously some form of representative democracy. This was the solution eventually adopted in Italy, but elements of the three other possibilities are present in the 1973–4 scheme, and it is those elements which underlie the arguments which led to the final compromise. This should be borne in mind as a clue to the way Italians discuss and evaluate the participatory system. They are often hankering after two possibilities: crudely, 'all power to the soviets' or 'all power to the communes'. Sometimes they try to mix the two, with unhappy consequences for logic and consistency. It is partly through these lenses that the parental role in school decision-making is seen. Are schools a function of the state (the socialist and communist line) or of the family (the Catholic line)? Are parents to be involved with schools so that they can exercise some control over the powers they have delegated to teachers, or are they as parents present simply to receive and transmit information, with actual power and control reserved to democratically elected citizens who may also happen to be parents? Tristano Codignola, the education spokesman of the PSI, puts a characteristic point of view in his reactions to the new arrangements. After admitting that parents need to be involved at class level so that teachers can base their work on real knowledge of the 'socio-educational environment of the pupil', he goes on to say: '*But beyond this point, the parent should give way to the citizen.* There is no good reason why I should be more interested in a technical school simply because my son is studying there than any other citizen living locally. This is a typical projection of the personalistic and individualistic Catholic mentality, as opposed to the communitarian and social attitude of Marxism.'[25]

The decisions of government and the tortuous journey through parliament of the new legislation displayed in full measure the confusion of underlying ideas and the complexity of the negotiations and debates which eventually produced the compromise of the 1973 Act (Law 477, 30 July 1973) and the *Decreti Delegati* of 1974. A blow-by-blow account of the protracted process is unnecessary here.[26] No less than three bills incorporating forms of 'social management' (*gestione sociale*) were passed by varying majorities in the Chamber of Deputies between 1971 and 1973, and two of them were rejected or emasculated by the Senate. The third (Law 477) was passed only under threat of a general strike. What happened was that the triennial negotiation on wages and conditions of service, which in Italy is a massive national process, broke down in the spring of 1973. Certain educational measures (notably time off by right for workers to follow adult education courses, and *gestione sociale*) had then become part of the political bargaining and were included in the package of measures eventually agreed between unions and government. In other words, in the five years after 1968 lay participation in the running of schools had become generally accepted as an understood objective of the Left and featured naturally in a compromise package between Left and Right. As well as the provisions for participation, the Act contained others to encourage in-service training, experimentation and the study of education.

Law 477 had been preceded by circulars 375 and 376 of 23 November 1970, and circular 001/STC of 20 September 1971. Again, the details are unimportant, but these circulars permitted the 'experimental' establishment of parents' and students' councils and especially of a 'school-family committee', consisting of parent and teacher delegates, and students in upper secondary schools, who were to meet with the head teacher, etc. This committee was to be consulted on 'questions relative to school welfare and health and extra-curricular activities'. These 'Misasi committees', as they were called after the then Minister, seem to owe their origin to the desire of a new Minister to present an energetic and reforming image. From the 1977 report of the *Centro Didattico Nazionale* it seems that about a quarter of upper secondary schools and a third of middle schools produced committees, and that real success was relatively infrequent.

> The majority [writes Dina Lombardi of the upper secondary school] had in fact been set up purely as a formal gesture, in outward conformity to the minister's request and had remained entirely passive: the parents had often been chosen by the head teacher for their docility and their readiness to accept any decision the school might make.[27]

In some cases head teachers had used the existence of these committees to head off requests for parent associations or *assemblee*, which were less likely to be docile.[28] Elementary schools were excluded from this 'experiment' — an exclusion described by one observer as 'inexplicable' in view of the fact that the most effective participation was taking place in that sector.[29] In fact the 'Misasi committees' bear all the marks of hasty interim arrangements rather than a considered preparation for the national system which got off the ground in 1975. They constituted another element in the general post-1968 ferment and can hardly be considered a substantial government initiative.

The participatory framework eventually set up in the 1973 Act and the consequential decrees (*Decreti Delegati*) which established most of the concrete details bore the marks of the tortuous negotiations carried on over more than half a decade. In general, it was a conservative (or individualist) interpretation of participation which carried the day.[30] The network of elected committees was based on the representative principle. Delegates were to be elected even for class councils, and although mass meetings (*assemblea*) were permitted, at no level did they carry any formal authority. The local authorities were excluded from representation at school level. Although the Act declared its intention to establish the school 'as a community which interacts with the broader social and civic community',[31] that 'broader community' was represented only by parents, who were in any case always in a minority on all committees. The local authorities had their main role on new district councils. Throughout, functions were left somewhat vague and no real attempt was made at school level to define the sort of decisions to be made or to alter the balance of power. Behind the rhetoric, it was a case of the basic structure continuing as before with committees as *appendices* at class and school level. How the new system would function in practice would inevitably depend on the spirit in which the new regulations were applied.

3.4 Participation in Schools

The *Decreti Delegati* presenting the detailed regulations for putting the 1973 Act into effect were published in November 1974,[32] and the ensuing school elections took place in February 1975. There was then a gap of almost three years before the district, provincial and national elections of December 1977. Thus for a substantial period the pyramid of councils remained incomplete, and this must be borne in mind in reading this section, which necessarily concentrates on participation at *school* level.

In schools there were to be two basic sorts of committee, at class and school level. The exact provisions varied somewhat according to the level of school. For example, the normal 'class council' in the elementary school was normally a *consiglio d'interclasse*, combining two or more classes within a year or grade working in one school building (*plesso*). Italian elementary schools often consist of two or more *plessi* grouped into a *circolo*, or multi-site institution under a single head. Hence the elementary school council is known as a *consiglio di circolo*. Its equivalent in the middle and upper secondary schools is the *consiglio di istituto*. Parents and teachers are represented at class and school levels in all types of school. In addition, students are represented in the upper secondary school, with a corresponding reduction in parent representation. Non-teaching personnel are represented on school councils. Different numbers of representatives sit on the school councils according to the size of the school (whether above or below 500 pupils). To list all the details at different levels would be tedious, but the middle school arrangements give a good general idea of the arrangements. The class council consists of all teachers who teach that class and four annually elected parent representatives. It is chaired by the head or by a teacher delegated by the head. There is no required frequency of meeting. The decree 'defines' the duties of the class council as: 'to present to the teaching staff of the school proposals for educative and didactic action and for new experiments, and to facilitate and extend good relations between teachers, parents and pupils' (Article 3).

The school council of a small middle school (less than 500) has fourteen members: the head, six elected teachers, one member of the non-teaching staff, and six elected parents. Elections are by proportional representation for a three-year period, and representatives who resign or leave are replaced by the next highest on the voting list. The main function of this body, according to Article 2 of the decrees, is to control funds allotted by the state for the running expenses of the school. Between meetings, a six-member executive committee (*giunta esecutiva*) elected by the council is responsible for the conduct of affairs. Middle schools *must* also have a formal 'discipline council' to deal with serious breaches of discipline. They *may* also have general parents' meetings (*assemblee*) at class or school level, and a school parents' committee.

The reception accorded to the new arrangements was predictably varied. Much of the rhetoric emanating from the Right and Centre of the political spectrum saw the new councils as a major change of direction for Italian education — away from the well-known, sclerotic *sistema napoleonico* towards an unknown and somewhat mythical *sistema anglosassone* in which public-spirited individuals and groups would somehow take instant responsibility for the democratic transformation of the traditional school into a free and open community institution. The far Left, on the other hand, saw the whole exercise as one of mystification, a re-valuation of reactionary ideals of the family:

> The divorce referendum failed to reconstruct a Christian Democrat ideological hegemony by raising the cry of tradition, of maintaining the old order within the family, which was to have been the first stage towards the building of a front for law and order. That objective is now raised in another form by calling students, teachers and parents (especially the latter) to the repressive joint management of the institution, and deploying for that purpose the values of a school which must be serious, rigorous, selective, efficient, laying stress on merit and ability . . . .[33]

Somewhere between these extremes of idealism and scepticism lay the majority of informed and interested observers, their views and judgments often bearing the stamp of the idealistic participatory centre or the sceptical Marxist Left, but seeing also that new structures offered some hope of change, however limited and unpredictable. 'Who knows?' was the feeling. The new participatory system might produce the motive power for real grass-roots change: '. . . to call millions to vote for the governing bodies of schools, and hundreds of thousands to become members of them, must mean that we achieve an effective stimulus and contribution to the search for solutions to the problems of the school. . . .'[34]

If this were to happen, the complex mechanics of the new structures were likely to be a stumbling-block. Much disquiet was focused on class councils, as many felt that it would have been both simpler and more democratic to involve *all* parents in meetings with teachers, not just elected representatives. 'The first and truest function of schools is to educate,' wrote one Catholic commentator, 'and *in education there can be no authority.*'[35] Other criticism, more usually but not always from the left of centre, deplored the failure to involve local authorities and bodies such as trades unions. The general feeling was, however, that while the new structures were far from ideal, nonetheless the spaces, the nooks and crannies in the new machinery offered the possibility to citizens of goodwill of making concrete progress, of a slow maturing of public consciousness of, and responsibility for the schools of Italy. 'Spaces' (*spazi*) thus became a central term in discussion. A pragmatic and moderately hopeful willingness to 'fill the spaces' characterized a wide spectrum of informed opinion ranging, with differences in vocabulary, tone and emphasis, from PCI to DC.

Yet in the event *informed* opinion in the run-up to the first school elections in February 1975 was much less important than *uninformed* opinion, in the sense that the most striking (and, to many, unexpected) feature of the 1975 elections was the great surge of public enthusiasm for the possibilities of the new structures. What had hitherto been for many a rather recondite discussion among enthusiasts, experts and legislators suddenly caught light. The electoral campaign gathered increasing momentum during the months before February 1975. The turn-outs of the separate electorates were, even by Italian standards, gratifyingly high: 90 per cent for teachers, 70 per cent for parents, 67 per cent for upper secondary students: an overall average of over 70 per cent. Over four million parents (26 per cent of the parent electorate) spoke in electoral meetings; 60 per cent went to one meeting, 32 per cent to more than one.[36] This massive participation was in some ways a defeat both for the extra-parliamentary Left and for any on the Right who had assumed that Catholic parents would automatically control the new bodies, as well as a reminder to many doubting Thomases in government and elsewhere of the popularity of involving people in the running of schools. What was particularly impressive was not only the casting of votes (turn-out in all Italian elections since the war has been consistently high) but the level of public discussion which preceded the debate, the extent to which a high proportion of the parent electorate took the trouble to go to local meetings and make real efforts to inform themselves and discuss what the election meant. This ferment of lay activity was clearly reflected in the contemporary press and contrasted markedly with most similar electoral processes in other European democracies.

Yet a single campaign, however lively, will not solve the problems of Italian schools. Two initial doubts arise from the electoral process itself. Firstly, the incidence of participation was by no means as even as contemporary euphoria suggested. The north and centre participated more wholeheartedly than the south, urban areas more than rural and elementary and middle-school parents more than secondary-school parents — a trend which appears to be international and presumably reflects the greater closeness (both attitudinal and physical) to the family of the primary school. The middle classes and men tended to be disproportionately represented among the elected delegates, especially at levels above the class council.

This patchiness was predictable to anyone with a modicum of sociological awareness or historical commonsense. A much more problematic question was: *what did all this activity mean?*

Contemporary press accounts of the February elections did not find this a difficult question. They presented the campaign in traditional terms as a *political* struggle between Left and Right. There was a good deal of sense in this analysis: from one point of view the enthusiasm of the February elections reflected the progressivist euphoria of the successful divorce referendum of 1974 and was also reflected in marked communist and socialist gains in the June 1975 local elections. Yet while this may capture one aspect of the situation, as an account of all that was going on it distorts and oversimplifies.

Loredana Sciolla's detailed account of the elections in Turin reveals a much more complex picture.[37] The elections were, like all Italian elections, by proportional representation, which necessitates groups of candidates coming together to form common programmes or 'lists'. Most parents in Turin were required to choose between three or four lists: something like 90,000 different lists were registered throughout Italy. To label these lists neatly as 'Left' or 'Right' is often highly misleading. In Sciolla's view, the media tended to assume that all groups not clearly on the left-wing ticket (*liste unitarie, confederali*) were on the Right, thus overestimating the support for the *status quo*. It was easier for this to happen because the PCI (very powerful in Turin and strongly rooted in an active trade union movement) tended to distance itself from the elections and distrust 'family politics' as a Catholic preoccupation. The result was partly that Catholics made a better showing in Turin than they really deserved — partly that the Right was able to claim various types of 'independent' list for its camp when in fact many of these programmes were strongly critical of the schools as they were. On concrete issues such as the introduction of whole-day school or the provision of remedial assistance or class libraries, parent opinion was strongly in favour of change.

Whatever the realities of 1974–5, media presentation of the participatory debate as a relatively simple Right-Left division obviously affects the way people think about what they are doing. Certainly one of the trends after 1975 was for the initial more or less spontaneous popular impulses of the first elections to become increasingly polarized and stereotyped. The growing role of the national parent associations (AGe and COGIDAS, later CGD) and the extension of a specialized 'parent press' after 1975 are both signs of this process, which by the late 1970s had led some to see the annual school elections at class level almost as a straightforward AGe/CGD conflict.

As new and relatively loose organizations, AGe and CGD are more difficult to characterize than their French counterparts. In terms of membership and resources, they are much less impressive than the French parents' federations: both give the impression of dedicated minorities struggling to keep the ship afloat. Yet their influence on the politics of participation is greater than their membership suggests. It lies above all in defining issues and highlighting problems for public and parental attention. Of the two associations, AGe emerged earlier, and seems to have found it easier to define a consistent line which on the whole corresponds to a traditional interpretation of Catholic doctrine, and is certainly not assented to by all contemporary Italian Catholics. AGe's leadership, and hence its publications, tend to present rational arguments for the orderly conduct of schools, for strong parental control of sex education, against 'political' influence on the school curriculum, against the legalization of abortion, etc. The grass-roots appeal of the AGe line is less rational, and many of its more vocal supporters are members of a worried middle class seeking the security of older verities.

The CGD (*Coordinamento Genitori Democratici* — Grouping of Democratic Parents), which emerged from its predecessor COGIDAS in 1976,[38] is as yet less settled and sure of its own opinions than the older AGe. As its name suggests, it tries to coordinate or group a wide range of local parent groupings of a roughly 'democratic' or 'antifascist' character — the term 'democratic' being used on the Left, to the irritation of democrats on the Right, as shorthand for 'left-inclined'. By 1980, when the author visited a number of local groups, CGD had all the marks of a new and lively grass-roots movement. Its exact character differed a good deal from place to place, depending on its local leadership and on the local political background.

In some places — e.g., the 'red city of Bologna' — it was heavily dominated by the PCI establishment and on many issues fell readily into the role of another broad-based party organization. In other places — e.g., Arezzo, a small market town on the southern borders of Tuscany — it seemed to be broadly based, with substantial socialist and even left-wing Catholic contributions. Other differences related more to the predominance of one social class or another in an area. Thus in municipal housing estates on the periphery of Florence and Turin the impression was of groups run by lively and vociferous housewives, for whom CGD provided an opportunity to explore their own social and personal roles and to increase their social and political awareness. Other groups seemed to be more dominated by intellectuals, especially teachers who were also parents. In many areas — e.g., large parts of the south, small country towns, etc. — CGD did not exist or maintained only a struggling token presence, perhaps supported by local left-wing trade unions. Trade union premises were often used for meetings. The nature of much of the grass-roots activity, as with AGe, was not overtly political — public lectures on the drugs problem among teenagers, regular advice sessions for parents to discuss educational problems. Nonetheless, the ideological input was greater than it would have been in some European countries, partly because much of the impetus for CGD was the need to organize parent lists for the annual school elections. This gave a certain direction and a certain regular annual pattern of activity to both CGD and AGe, and would obviously tend in the long run to produce a more unitary and centralized style of confrontation. Yet in 1980 CGD remained relatively diverse and unpredictable, with some criticism from the more hardline local groups of a central leadership which some felt to be too dominated by intellectuals in Rome.[39]

The emergence in the middle and late seventies of a strong communications network aimed at parents is another aspect of the consolidation and polarization of parents as a recognizable electorate and body of opinion. *Genitori* (Catholic) and *Giornale dei Genitori* (left-oriented) had existed since the 1950s and now came to play a role in the new associationism. AGe used *Genitori*, which retained its independence, for the insertion of a special AGe inset. The CGD was launched from the *Giornale dei Genitori*, and one of CGD's local activities is sale of that magazine. 1975 also saw the launch of two new monthlies: *Genitori e Scuola* in October, *Tuttoscuola* in November. The former is overtly Catholic, and published by the Catholic publishing house of La Scuola, Brescia. It is a sort of up market version of *Genitori*, which still retains something of the air of a 1950s parish magazine. *Genitori e Scuola* is larger, glossier, rather more intellectual in tone and contains advertizing. *Tuttoscuola* is different again. Clearly modelled on mass-circulation magazines, with innovative use of photographs, eye-catching headlines, etc. and a great deal of advertizing, it is aimed at commercial success. It provides 'what the modern parent needs to know', and claims to be independent of any party influence. It publishes news of AGe — indeed an actual insert since 1977 — but also occasional contributions from or about COGIDAS and CGD. However, its proclaimed independence and objectivity and its penchant for presenting snippets of opposed opinion do not prevent it from taking a strongly anticommunist line on many issues. For example, the January 1977 issue carried on the cover a photograph of a pathetic little girl wearing the red scarf of the Soviet Young Pioneers with 'PCI' embroidered on it in addition to the hammer and sickle. This introduced the theme of 'the red nursery school' — the way in which pre-school institutions in communist municipalities were supposedly being used to indoctrinate children. *Tuttoscuola*'s main foreign correspondent, W. Kenneth Richmond, regularly reports on the alleged disasters of comprehensive education in Britain and elsewhere. In a word, *Tuttoscuola* aims at a mass audience of the aspiring lower-middle classes, many of whom are only a generation away from the peasantry and need information and reassurance about many aspects of their new life-styles, including their own children's schooling.

The existence, in a country which rightly bewails the fact that so few of its citizens read, of four specialist parent monthlies is one measure of the success of the *Decreti Delegati* in launching parent opinion as a social reality. Let us now turn to the working of the *organi collegiali* in schools: the reality which the journals reflect and which in turn provokes parents to want to read the journals.

The elected committees at class and school level began work in the spring of 1975 with the great advantage of the substantial public support and interest evinced in the election campaign. In some ways, however, that rousing send-off turned out to be more of a liability than an asset, in the sense that public expectations of what could be achieved were unrealistic. The practical problems which beset the newly elected parent councillors were similar to those of their French counterparts. Teachers were often unhelpful or directly hostile. As parents were not compensated for absence from work, they often could not attend daytime meetings. When they did attend they were often unfamiliar with the procedures of formal meetings and intimidated by the professionals operating on home territory. *Genitori e Scuola* printed a wry vignette of a school council in Rome:

> the lady teachers regularly arrived for Councils in mink coats, as though to intimidate us. . . . They were almost all the wives of lawyers, doctors and generals, and anxious to remind us of the fact: one went so far as to declare that 'the Magistrature and the Army will save the school!'[40]

The crucial problem, however, was that there were few, if any, decisions to influence or control, for Italy had chosen the same path as France — to set up elected committees as appendices without altering the power structure of schools by devolving decision-making from the centre. As ever in such matters, councils found that finance was the crucial touchstone. The sums provided by the Ministry were small:

> There are schools of more than 500 or 600 pupils . . . which have had about a million lire to spend: when one thinks that more than half a million is needed for the annual elections, that leaves for these middle schools 300,000 or something of that sort, hardly enough for a few balls or something, and still requiring the assent of higher authority. . . .[41]

The expense of the electoral process, the running expenses of the new committees and their bare offices — 'cleaning materials, toilet paper, detergents, taxes to be paid to the Commune for refuse disposal, telephone, etc.'[42] — consumed almost everything. Thus school councils usually found themselves simply acquiescing in trivial decisions on the spending of minute sums of money, or interesting themselves in peripheral matters such as how the school should celebrate the anniversary of the Liberation. They became effective only in a minority of cases. Sometimes a school council could act as a pressure-group and rally local opinion to right some obvious inadequacy or injustice. Even when this occurred, there was no guarantee of success, as the purse-strings to provide repairs, new buildings, sports facilities or teachers were held by other hands. Other councils, often starting from a local campaign, became effective parts of 'the wider community', serving as channels of information and action for teachers, parents and local politicians. This sort of development depended on teachers' attitudes being sympathetic, and tended to happen largely in schools where left-wing staff were concentrated and could collaborate with like-minded, usually working-class parents.

Similar problems beset the class councils, and were compounded by the need for annual elections of parent representatives. As these took place in the latter part of the autumn term (and in 1975 half-way through the spring term), there was no opportunity to involve parents in discussions of class policy at the point when teachers were planning the year's work. It was also difficult for parent representatives to refer back to their electorate: not only was the school year almost over by the time they had got themselves established, but also the pedestrian problems of finding a room and a caretaker prepared to open it and lock it up could loom large unless positive assistance was forthcoming from the school authorities to make a reality of the optional general parent meetings set up in theory by the 1974 decrees. In any case, as much of the business of a class council centred on children's progress, as reflected in the formal grade or *voto*, any teacher who chose to take a restrictive stand on confidentiality could make a nonsense of the whole proceedings.

The issue of confidentiality was an important one in the first year of operation of the new committees. A circular of 20 March 1975 required that the proceedings of school councils should be closed to the public, thus rendering extremely difficult any real interaction between schools and the parent body as a whole, or any feedback from parent representatives to those who had elected them. A number of school councils ignored the decree, or devised ingenious subterfuges to observe its letter but not its spirit, and the circular was eventually withdrawn after loud protest from all quarters of the political spectrum. However, the incident underlined two facts about the new structures: the continuing opposition in parts of the ruling party and the bureaucracy to the idea that the new committees might function really effectively, and the degree to which these committees were dependent on the goodwill of the powers that be for their effective functioning.

At local level they needed a combination of sympathetic principals and teaching staff with lively and enterprising parents — and preferably also a left-wing local council — if campaigns for the spending of money on extra teachers, resources or materials, or an extension of school hours were to come to anything. Such combinations were necessarily the exception rather than the rule. Much more usual was a growing disillusion. This tended to go hand in hand with a trend towards ideological polarization. The imperatives of annual re-election of class delegates, the interests of parties and the media in treating those elections as dummy runs for the real thing, the increasing importance of AGe and CGD and the growth of centralized information networks — all these factors made the often euphoric spontaneity of 1974–5 look increasingly dated and unrepeatable.

Disillusion with the *organi collegiali* came to a head at the end of the decade, but the tide was already setting strongly in that direction in 1977, when after two years' experience at school level, the new district, provincial and national councils began to function. It is to these higher levels of representation, and particularly to the district, that we must now turn.

3.5 Participation through District, Provincial and National Councils

The district (*distretto*) was in theory created to provide the middle ranges of participation in a pyramid based on class councils and moving up through school and district councils to provincial and national levels. In practice, however, the upper reaches of the participatory system (provincial and national) provoked much less public interest and discussion than the district. To consider why this was so helps to explain the pivotal position of the district in the Italian participatory apparatus sketched in the 1973 Act.

At national level, there had long existed a 'National Council of Public Instruction'. Originally modelled on its French counterpart, this had been a purely consultative organ entirely dominated by the ministerial bureaucracy: its main function was the formal ratification of ministerial decisions. Although the 1974 decrees made certain changes in membership and function, these were largely cosmetic. Neither parents nor students were involved at all, and of seventy-one members only five were to be nominated to represent 'the world of the economy and labour'; the council was thus overwhelmingly composed of persons dependent upon the bureaucracy — teachers, school principals, inspectors and administrators. One of the main new functions of the council was to draft and approve an annual report on the Italian education system; it failed to do so because the civil service refused to reveal the requisite information.[43] For the first year of its operation the national council had neither office staff of its own nor even an office.

At first glance, the provincial councils set up by the 1974 decrees looked a little more promising. Yet their main problem was that they did not correspond to the realities of power. Historically, provinces have been 'more significant as geographical or field areas for the central administration than as a form of local government.'[44] In the administration of education, the province has traditionally been important as the main local focus of central government control. In each province, a local executive officer, the *Provveditore*, is assisted by inspectors in transmitting information to and from Rome, and in ensuring that central rules and regulations are carried out locally. He may interpret his task in a highly restrictive way, and is assisted in that by the frequent vagueness of ministerial instructions. When the *Provveditore* of Savona, for example, transmitted to schools a 1972 circular urging collaboration between school and family, he included his own covering note of interpretation. At a time when many schools were experimenting with the study of newspapers (which had not traditionally been allowed into schools as being partisan and controversial), he instructed that such reading was to be limited 'as far as possible'; as for sex education, 'until receipt of more precise instructions from the Minister, I also forbid in all schools of this province any form of sex education.'[45] High-handed attitudes of this sort are made easier by two facts. Firstly, *Provveditori* are responsible directly to the Ministry of Public Instruction, and are not subject to the local Prefect, who is responsible only for affairs falling into the ambit of the Ministry of the Interior. Secondly, although elected provincial councils exist, their powers are 'extremely limited', and their financial position even more parlous than that of the communes.[46]

Thus, while in theory a provincial school council as established by the 1974 decrees had considerable scope for making its views felt, in practice it was bound to be otherwise. The real political weight, and the real possibilities of educational change were not located in the province. The increasing readiness of local authorities to take educational initiatives occurred throughout the seventies at levels either *above* the province (the region) or below it (the commune). Thus the *Provveditore* was left in the middle exercising his traditional functions of control over the compulsory core of the system, while regions and communes, at least in some areas, busied themselves with those relatively peripheral matters where central government permitted their intervention – e.g., the provision of regional funds for scholarships or travel to school or the erection with communal funds of nursery schools or technical schools. This trend meant that provincial councils were inevitably removed from those levels of decision-making which carried some political clout, and this is shown by the vagueness of the councils' functions as defined in Article 15 of Decree 416 of 31 May 1974, where almost the only concrete task seems to be responsibility for the planning and use of school buildings.

Behind the difficulties of the provincial councils lies a prior decision not to involve either regions or communes in any substantial way in the hierarchy of formal participation. That decision was an essentially conservative one, designed to disturb the *status quo* as little as possible. This, rather than their complex statute or the low proportion of elected parents (25 per cent) or their politicization, was the real reason for their ineffectiveness. The realities of their functioning showed that the *Provveditorato* retained almost total control. If a local *Provveditore* was unsympathetic, it was easy for him to withold information and blackmail councils into acquiescence; if they refused to sanction his plans, the result was either administrative paralysis or an actual strengthening of the executive which was obliged to act to keep the machinery turning.

However, most provincial councils seemed simply to muddle along with their more or less trivial and meaningless tasks rather than seeking grand confrontations, and absenteeism was widespread.[47]

As both national and provincial councils were unlikely vehicles for genuine change, and as public disappointment with class and school councils grew, it is not surprising that by 1977 hopes of change were pinned almost entirely to the district.

For a foreign observer to undertand the emotion invested in the school district is quite difficult. It is after all only a middle-level administrative unit, notionally catering for a population of 100,000 (or in urban areas up to 200,000) and including all forms of education up to 18. Yet for a brief period the idea of the district managed to focus frustration with the rigid bureaucracy and centralization of the past, local patriotism, and hope for a new progressive future liberated from the sterile ideological confrontations of tradition. It was able to focus these feelings because it was a new and untried institution, quite separate from any existing unit. In its newness and unattachedness lay both its attractiveness and its weakness.

Different forms of decentralization and devolution had had a long history in Italy. The post-war Republic was intended to mark a new departure with the institution of regions. Although regionalism was written into the constitution, it is an indication of the difficulty and controversiality of devolution that most of the regions did not exist till 1970. If historically centralization had been seen as a guarantee against local church dominance, so that decentralization came to have a Catholic tinge, the emergence of the PCI as a real power in the 1950s turned that argument on its head, and many feared permanent communist control of the regions, especially in central Italy. From one perspective, the district was an attempt to break out of that strait-jacket by setting up a relatively small-scale local unit whose main tasks would be essentially concrete and pragmatic, the coordination and planning of the educational enterprise in a given area. Since the end of the war, some educationalists had been strongly attracted by what they called 'the Anglo-Saxon model' of administration, an often dimly conceived and idealized amalgam of the English local education authority and the American school board. The parallel with the LEA continued to be drawn even after the institution of the district, though as will be seen there was little similarity between the two institutions.

First adumbrated in a 1963 commission of enquiry as a possible solution to the grave inequalities of provision (town and country, north and south, etc.), the district had emerged more definitely into discussion in 1970, dropped from view again in 1972, then re-emerged in the negotiations with the unions which resulted in the 1973 Act.[48] Its attraction at that point lay in its connotations of untainted progressiveness and in the fact that it could be realized without encroachment upon existing jurisdictions. As fleshed out in the 1974 decrees, the district retained this air of being all things to all men. 'The school district actualizes the democratic participation of local communities and of the social forces in the life and management of the school' (Decree 416, Article 9). Regions were empowered to work out the boundaries of the new districts. The sole institutional expression of the district was its council, consisting of twenty-six elected members (ten teachers and heads, and seven parents, two non-teaching staff, seven students) and eighteen nominated members representing the 'social forces' — eight representing unions, workers, chambers of commerce, cultural associations, and ten from communal and provincial councils. The inclusion of 'social forces' was intended to meet left-wing objections to their exclusion from the school councils. A novelty was the inclusion of representatives from private schools, regarded by some on the Left (especially socialists) as the thin end of the ecclesiastical wedge.

The functions of the district council related principally to local planning. By July of every year it was required to draw up a district plan for the following year. Article 12 defined what should be included in the plan, and these defined matters, although some of them were potentially very significant, dealt essentially with the periphery of the educational process: 'extracurricular and out-of-school activities, and those which involve more than one school', guidance, counselling and welfare, medical and psychological services, adult education, experimentation, etc. In addition the council had more generalized responsibilities for making proposals on

> everything relating to the institution, establishment and effective running of schools, as well as the organization and development of services and ancillary structures, with the purpose of constituting scholastic units which are territorially and socially integrated, and to assure as a norm the presence within the district of state schools of every order and level. . . .' (Article 12)

This council was to constitute, in the words of the PSI's education spokesman, 'a *political* body of great potential, a centre where requests, pressures and proposals can be harmonized and which could become a force for internal cohesion within a strongly centrifugal reality.'[49] Another writer brought out another of the attractive aspects of the district as seen by many Italians: its potential for breaking out of the magic circle of the teaching profession and bringing the school into contact with a wider world: 'The really innovative body, i.e. the district, in which the social forces beyond the teaching profession carry greater weight, certainly has an obvious political clout; but,' he added significantly, 'no corresponding administrative power.'[50] For it was at this point that the very attractiveness of the district contained the seeds of its own downfall. The district was attractive because it was outside the established structures, because it offered escape from sterile confrontation, because it stressed apparently consensual and pragmatic functions — planning , coordination, etc. Some maintained quite sincerely that 'the district council is not, and must not be an executive body, because in so far as it is executive it is a state organization and as such subject to the power of the central bureaucracy....'[51] Yet, like the rest of the participatory machinery, it too was an appendix rather than an integral part of decision-making. 'The new structure tended not to *replace* the old, but to be *added* to it.'[52] Above all, the absence of concrete powers, the reliance on consultation, the failure to allocate funds meant that once again real changes had been evaded. The district council was doomed to remain a talking-shop which in reality was almost entirely parasitic upon the holders of purse-strings — i.e., communal and, above all, central government.

Thus to talk to district councillors in the spring of 1980, towards the end of their first three years of office, was in many ways a disheartening experience. The district had been visible on the horizon since 1973. Its birth had been unduly protracted, partly because of the time taken by many regions to work out the boundaries of the new districts. By the time the first district elections took place in December 1977, the climate of public opinion towards participation had changed markedly since February 1975. Disillusion with the school councils and weariness with the annual class elections contributed to a slump in electoral turn-out, and only 45 per cent of eligible parents voted; the figure was a great deal lower in some areas, and this was widely interpreted by the press as betokening a crisis for participation. In addition, shifts in the broader political scene meant that the Right did relatively well in the 1977 district elections.[53] By then, AGe in particular had built up a substantial organization at local level, and this meant that as the new district councils began to flex their muscles and define their rather elusive functions they contained many people who preferred to define those functions in a fairly restricted way. Much more important, however, was the basic impossibility of the tasks set to councillors.

The work of the district is not easy [wrote one participant[54]].
Planning means the assembling of experiences and demands,

the evaluation of available resources, the refusal to write out lists of unrealistic and demagogic requests, establishing priorities. And even when the plan has been worked out, one must know how to use it politically by exerting appropriate pressures on the authorities to whom the plan is addressed and who are the actual decision-makers.

This complex task was made no easier by frequent failure to provide adequate premises and support for the new councils. Often a district was run from a school office, and shared the services of a school secretary who was not present in the afternoons — which was the only time when parent councillors or parents wishing to make enquiries could attend or telephone.[55] District councillors themselves were often active in many different spheres and had little time or energy to spare for the infuriatingly insubstantial work of planning a system in which it seemed that all the significant decisions were still reserved to Rome. Unsurprisingly, the district councillors with whom I spoke in the spring of 1980 recorded almost universally feelings of frustration and disappointment in spite of their initial idealism and enthusiasm. This disillusion was reflected in absenteeism, and many councillors were removed from office for having failed to attend three consecutive meetings.[56]

3.6 Balance-Sheet

Thus by the end of the 1970s disillusion with the participatory system was universal. It was crystallized in the winter of 1979–80 by the refusal of the student element to participate in the electoral process of November 1979. Parliament eventually required the Minister (Professor Valitutti) to postpone the election of student representatives till February 1980. This he did, against his own better judgment.[57] At the same time he called national conferences to discuss the future of the participatory system and the media were full of gloomy discussions of what all held to be 'yet another Italian failure'.[58] The gloom was even deeper than in France, and for that there were two basic reasons: the unrealistic expectations of only five years before, and the absence of any prospect of real political change at the centre.

The differences in style and tone of voice between the parent movements of France and Italy are ultimately reflections of different historical backgrounds. The French parent federations are offshoots of a longstanding centralizing habit of mind. They react to and attempt to modify a bureaucratic machine whose functioning is consistent and in some ways effective. Their Italian counterparts on the other hand can still draw upon a substantial residue of local pride and grass-roots initiative, for which the relative ineffectiveness of Roman control gives considerable scope. Even if AGe and CGD were less recently founded and better funded and coordinated, one suspects that they would still be more variable and unpredictable than their French counterparts, simply because the system within which they operate is less monolithic.

Yet the differences are more of style than of substance. Most of the general judgments made on the French participatory system in section 2.7 apply also to Italy. In particular, the circumstances in which Law 477 and the *Decreti Delegati* were formulated show as clearly as in France that the new structures emerged as 'attempts by the ruling elite to achieve greater levels of legitimation' (Table 3). The Act was passed to get the government off the hook of a difficult wage negotiation; in a longer time scale, it was passed because of uncertainties about the legitimacy of the whole political and social system which were symbolized in the shorthand of '1968'. The various educational items included in Law 477 (funds for adult education and educational research as well as the participatory framework) had the merits of apparent progressivism and relative cheapness. They were also nicely calculated to contribute to the extension of the 'historic compromise' between Christian Democracy and PCI, by providing arenas in which appropriate left-wing activity could be permitted. They could thus be expected to contribute ultimately to the stabilization of the Italian state. In this, the *Decreti Delegati* resembled the 1970 legislation on the regions which from one perspective marked an acceptance by the DC of the legitimacy of PCI contributions at levels below central government.[59] It is this relative openness of the right-wing elites to their leftist counterparts which explains the main structural difference between the French and Italian systems of participation: the achievement of the district in Italy, and its failure to appear in France. It also helps to explain the relative absence in government justifications of the new structures of the French emphasis on 'responsiveness', on the desire to depoliticize education and present the parental influence as purely individualistic and as a necessary counterweight to the Marxist onslaught. In an odd way, the Italian structures were more the products of consensus than their French counterparts.

This did not mean that the Italian machinery was more realistic. As in France, the new councils were grafted on to an existing system which remained in its basic power structures virtually unaltered. This was true even of its most potentially innovatory element, the district, and reflected the overriding concern in the creation of the new structures with 'legitimacy'.

Six areas of possible parental influence were specified in section 1.5. In terms of the formal arrangements set up by the *Decreti Delegati*, (ii) (curriculum and internal organization), (iii) (appointment and control of personnel) and (iv) (resourcing) were hardly considered as proper areas for outside influence. Areas (i) (progress of individual pupils), (v) (planning of school provision) and (vi) (improvement of school-community relations) were formally allocated to class, district and school councils respectively. Yet (i) and (v) turned out to be highly frustrating, and even (vi) was effective only when backed by progressive teachers. Area (iv) was a constant problem round which the other problems revolved. The other areas will be discussed a little later in this section in relation to the possibilities for innovation in 'experimental' schools, but neither the *Decreti* nor the early stages of the new councils showed much evidence of any real attempt to engage with aims beyond the area of 'legitimacy'.

When compared with France the Italian case appears at first glance to confirm the second clause of the 'general crisis theory', that legally attested forms of parent participation are 'established earlier and more easily in polities where the threat to the ruling elite is most urgent' (Table 3). It is true that the immediate threat to Italian political stability was more diffuse than the May events in France and that it took five or six years longer to establish school councils in Italy than in France. Yet the difference is less clear-cut than it seems. One might argue that school councils in *all* French schools were required only from 1977, while Italy had reached that stage in 1975. The fact is that both systems emerged from the general shift in attitudes focused on '1968', and that for both France and Italy the first half of the seventies was a period when hastily erected participatory machinery was evolving. The similarities were too great, and the time-difference too short, to permit any very general conclusions to be drawn on this aspect of the theory: for that, West Germany is a more instructive example.

Differences between France and Italy emerge a little more clearly when the evolution of the two systems is considered in relation to the four aims (Table 4). As conceived by government and bureaucracy, the Italian participatory system clearly resembled its French counterpart in placing the main stress on 'legitimacy'. By 1980, the end of the first three-year period of office of district councillors, there was much discussion of changes in the rules,[60] but little evidence of will to change the system. To allocate any real power to the districts or to alter the basic arrangements of educational finance would by 1980 have disrupted the delicate web of compromise spun between Right and Left since 1975, allowing some 'progressive' advances within a generally 'conservative' framework. In that sense, legitimacy remained a dominant concern both of the Christian Democrat 'ruling elite', which remained in power in Rome and in many regions and communes, and of the communist and socialist local governments, which had achieved local power in other regions and communes. Because of the more even spread of power between Right and Left in Italy, the participatory structures could be used by *both* sides to launch change or resist it. Thus the new councils were rather less obviously than in France a government-run confidence trick, if only because 'ruling elite' in Italy is a more elusive and flexible notion, less obviously tied to a central ruling coalition than in Giscard's France: the communist rulers of Bologna or Siena are really as much of an 'elite' as are the nabobs of the DC in Rome or Venice.

This is partly what makes it more difficult than in France to trace lines of development since 1975. Italian politics and society are more diverse and multi-faceted. Once the participatory system had been erected, the initiative lay much more than in France with the grass-roots — with communities and parent groups. If one may generalize from talking to class, school and district councillors, and from sampling the large amounts of literature produced about participation since the late sixties, there would seem to be less stress in the Italian discussion than in the French on 'responsiveness' and 'personal development', and more on 'overcoming alienation'. In other words, parents are less commonly distinguished from the community of which they are a part. One thinks, for example, of the parents in the Florentine *quartiere* of Le Cure who worked out their highly creative relationship with their local schools in a series of public meetings, exhibitions and open committees designed to inform and involve the entire local community.[61] While no doubt their experience was exceptional, conversations in 1980 with CGD groups regularly threw up at least the strongly felt desire to relate to the community base. The *assemblea* or mass meeting (an optional extra in the official structures) was the characteristic institutional expression of this mood. On the Left at least, parents were seen less as a tightly defined group with a separate quasi-legal existence, and more as persons whose natural interest in their own children might lead them to be active in schools *and* in the local community.

This emphasis may reflect several factors particular to Italy. One is the ineffectiveness of the government and bureaucratic machine. Quite simply, parents, teachers and local authorities (communes and regions) can 'get away' with initiatives which in France would either not have been thought of or would have been rapidly squashed — e.g., by the inspectorate. Another factor may be the lack of 'concreteness' typical of much Italian educational discussion, and which may flow from a long history of authoritarian rule — an unawareness of or disinterest in all those pragmatic 'theory-into-practice' activities placed in Table 4 under the 'responsiveness' heading. A third factor may be the greater openness of traditional Italian social life, with its conversations in bar and barber's shop, its twice-daily *passeggiata* or public promenade, etc. Finally one must consider the success of the Italian Left in building up over a long period a general consciousness of alternative interpretations of history and society. Maybe the rhetoric so often heard on the Left about the people taking command of its own destiny — as in the Resistance — is less empty than it sometimes sounds.

Whatever the explanations or interpretations, this stress on 'overcoming alienation' is revealed not in institutional changes or demands for new voting systems, but in a remarkable enthusiasm for participation in the face of much discouragement. The widespread public interest in the 1975 elections of school and class councillors and in the 1977 inauguration of the district have already been described (in sections 3.4, 3.5). Although this level of enthusiasm for participation among ordinary parents is unevenly spread through society and is often ill-informed or naive, it seems to have staying-power. The evidence for that is the continuing growth and activity of associations like AGe and CGD, and the viability of the network of parent journals at different levels of sophistication and aimed at parents of different classes and ideological positions. That this interest and activity are maintained by so many in spite of the judgment of educational experts and parent militants that the participatory structure is at best defective and at worst an elaborate deceit is puzzling. It may mean that the Italians are peculiarly gullible. It is more likely to mean that the problems of Italian education are so manifest that any structures which seem to offer a chance of improvement will command public support. It may also mean that the task of 'consciousness-raising' undertaken by the Left since the 1950s has really had some impact, particularly in the urban areas of the centre and north where the parent movement has been most lively.

An emphasis on 'overcoming alienation' may be at odds with the more humdrum aims associated with 'responsiveness'. Nonetheless, the rhetoric about community involvement seems to run in parallel with a growing network of pragmatic lay improvement in school affairs. As this does not loom very large in the rhetoric, it tends not to register as commitment to some explicit aim of 'responsiveness'. Indeed, Italian informants point frequently to their own failure to achieve 'concreteness' (to back up words with deeds) and compare their own efforts unfavourably with a supposed 'Anglo-Saxon pragmatism'. Nonetheless, there is surely an observable trend since 1975 towards using the 'spaces' afforded by the new system, and to developing the individual identity available to a school through possessing its own council. In circumstances where teachers, parents and communal authorities are of like mind, it is possible to proceed to radical school-based reforms of a kind almost unthinkable a decade before. It is now relatively easy for a school council to request experimental status; the fact that such a request comes from a mainly elected body with parental representation gives it some legitimacy in coping with the bureaucracy. Experimental status then legitimizes a wide range of deviations from the centralized norm. Perhaps the best publicized and most hopeful are those associated with *tempo pieno* — the move away from the morning-only timetable into whole-day school,[62] usually achieved with financial and staffing support from the local commune — usually a communist or socialist commune. Particularly in urban areas, which is where most such changes have happened, these developments are gradually producing a much more variegated and unpredictable pattern of schooling. Teachers of an idealistic, often left-oriented frame of mind are attracted to whole-day schools, so that a further polarization of school provision occurs. However one rates these changes, they are certainly a concrete reminder to parents that the system can be made more 'responsive' than it outwardly appears to be. Such developments motivate parents with strong views to be active in class and school councils and in parent associations in order to promote or resist such changes. Thus in a sense the pragmatic aims associated with 'responsiveness' grow from the less promising soil provided by 'legitimacy'.

Another illustration of this process is provided in school choice of textbooks.[63] A certain polarization of schools since the late 1960s has been accompanied by a drive on the part of left-wing publishers and authors to provide school texts alternative to Christian Democrat orthodoxy. Thus what had, prior to 1975, been the largely formal task of deciding texts for the coming school year and informing parents what they were so that they could buy them, rather unexpectedly became a focus of real parental concern and activity, supported by the emerging parent associations. Thus in this important detail of the annual routine of schools, we again see the pattern of structures set up to promote 'legitimacy' being used in fact to extend 'responsiveness' and resulting in a more overtly pluralist school system — at least in urban areas where schools are to some degree in competition.

To summarize, we can now see that in terms of the four broad aims outlined in section 1.2 and in Table 4, the Italian case may be differentiated somewhat from the French.

> Pre-1968: The idea of parent participation evolves in two streams, not very closely connected: (i) stresses 'responsiveness' (see publications of Rome Centre for Study of School-Family Relations); (ii) stresses 'overcoming alienation' and emerges from currents of opinion on the Left (PCI, PSI) which are increasingly attracted to regionalization, workplace democracy, etc.
> 1968–73: A period of some turmoil in which a variety of well-publicized local experiments stress 'overcoming alienation'.
> 1973–5: Government proposals highlight 'legitimacy' (as in France). The 'responsiveness' element remains largely rhetorical.
> 1975– : Structures whose main goal is 'legitimacy' naturally produce tensions when operated by persons preoccupied with 'overcoming alienation'. Major confrontations or sweeping changes are, however, avoided because central government takes a low profile and has in any case less control over the system than is the case in France. Hence 'responsiveness' begins to emerge from the activities of some school councils in a relatively pragmatic way as individual schools try to work out improvements. The 'legitimacy' system is thus side-stepped by devices like 'experimental status' rather than rethought to accommodate new aims.

Chapter 2 concluded with an attempt to restate in the light of French experience some of the theoretical models enunciated in Chapter 1. As might be expected from the broad similarity in terms of centralization, Left-Right polarization and the need for crisis management posed by '1968', the Italian case appears to confirm that general statement. The greater completeness of the Italian participatory structures, notably at district level, probably reflects a greater willingness on the part of Italian Christian Democracy to admit a communist-socialist presence in society. Events in Italy seem to confirm that legally required participatory structures involving parents originate in government desire for 'legitimacy'. The mix of the other three aims, different from that in France where 'responsiveness' is more prominent as a declared aim, does not suggest any invariant order of appearance. Rather the mix of 'responsiveness', 'overcoming alienation' and 'personal development' seems to depend partly on national styles of rhetoric or analysis (in Italy affected by Marxist traditions), partly on general political and administrative circumstances (for example, the greater independence of Italian local authorities relative to those in France). In neither country does 'personal development' seem to feature at all prominently in public discussion: this raises the question of whether it is a useful category in this discussion.

The growing importance of 'responsiveness', at least in urban areas and the north, suggests that in Italy participation is not simply another area for ancient political confrontation (though it is that) but may have its own pragmatic dynamic. That is one answer (which must for the moment remain tentative)to the question posed at the end of section 3.1.

Notes

1 These figures are from DE FORT, ESTER (1979) *Storia della Scuola Elementare in Italia, Vol. 1, Dall' Unità all' età Giolittiana*, Milan, Feltrinelli, pp. 15, 48, 49.

2 AYMONE, TULLIO (1972) *Scuola dell' Obbligo: Città Operaia*. Bari, Laterza, p. 249.

3 FILIPPETTI, ANTONIO (Ed.) (1977) *Informazione, Fabbrica, Scuola, Società*, Naples, Istituto di Studi e Ricerche per lo Sviluppo dell' Informazione Regionale.

4 ACQUAVIVA, S.S. and SANTUCCIO, M. (1976) *Social Structure in Italy: Crisis of a System*, Boulder, Color., Westview Press, p. 110.

5 DE FORT, *op. cit.*, pp. 124–8.

6 LOMBARDI, DINA (1973) *Il Rapporto Scuola-Famiglia nella Comunità Educante*, Rome, Ministero Pubblica Istruzione, Centro Didattico per i Rapporti Scuola-Famiglia e per l'Orientamento Scolastico, pp. 30–1.

7 LOMBARDI, *op. cit.*, pp. 32–3.

8 *Centro Didattico Nazionale per i Rapporti Scuola-Famiglia* — to which was added in 1963 the phrase *e per l'orientamento scolastico* ('and for educational guidance'.) The history of the Centre is set out at length in CENTRO DIDATTICO NAZIONALE PER I RAPPORTI SCUOLA-FAMIGLIA E ORIENTAMENTO (1974) *Venti Anni di Attività 1953–1973*, Rome, MINISTERO P.I., Centro Nazionale. . . . Much of what follows is based on this, and on conversations with Professor Franco Bonacina, Director of the Centre.

9 For example, as early as 1953 Lamberto Borghi, a prominent socialist educationalist, was proposing to strengthen family and school by linking both so that parents would 'consider the school as the living centre of the community, as a home from home (come la loro stessa casa)' (BORGHI, LAMBERTO (1953) *L'Educazione e i Suoi Problemi*, Florence, La Nuova Italia, p. 43). For broader historical treatment of this period, see TOMASI, TINA (1977) *Scuola e Pedagogia in Italia, 1948–1960*, Rome, Editori Riuniti.

10 Especially the regular journal *Servizio Informazioni Scuola e Famiglia*,

many of whose numbers are in fact independent monographs on aspects of parent-school relations.

11 ANON. (1974) 'Genitori' ha venti anni', *Genitori*, 200, February, p. 1.

12 CHIOSSO, GIORGIO (1977) *Scuola e Partiti tra Contestazione e Decreti Delegati*, Brescia, Editrice La Scuola, p. 71; TOMASI, *op. cit.*, p. 20. For an interesting review article of the PCI's cultural offensive, see LOVETT, CLARA M. (1980) 'Marxism and culture in Italy', *Problems of Communism*, 29/6, pp. 77–80.

13 *Giornale dei Genitori*, No. 27 new series (Vol. 18, December), 1977 contains a review of the years 1959–78. On Gobetti herself, see ANON. (1970) 'Ricordo di Ada Gobetti', *Riforma della Scuola*, 17/2, pp. 28–9. For the link with *Riforma della Scuola*, see RADICE, LUCIO LOMBARDO (1974) 'Venti anni', *Riforma della Scuola* 20/1, p. 7.

14 CENTRO NAZIONALE DIDATTICO PER I RAPPORTI SCUOLA-FAMIGLIA, *op. cit.*, p. 41.

15 CORRADINI, LUCIANO (1975) *La Difficile Convivenza: Dalla Scuola di Stato alla Scuola della Comunità*, Brescia, Ed. La Scuola, p. 88.

16 TOMASI, TINA (1977) *Scuola e Pedagogia in Italia 1948–1960*, Rome, Editori Riuniti, pp. 108–15.

17 AYMONE, TULLIO (1972) *Scuola dell' Obbligo: Città Operaia*, Bari, Laterza.

18 See, for example, the self-criticism published in various numbers of *Cooperazione Educativa* in 1968, especially issues 5 (May) and 8–9 (August-September).

19 REGUZZONI, MARIO (1968) 'La partecipazione delle comunità naturali alla gestione della scuola' *Aggiornamenti Sociali*, March pp. 173–86; April, pp. 277–286; and BINI, GIORGIO (1968) 'Parità e scuola comune', *Riforma della Scuola*, 15/3, pp. 29–31.

20 SCUOLA DI BARBIANA (1967) *Lettera a una professoressa*, Florence, Libreria Editrice Fiorentina. .

21 DE FRANCESCO, CORRADO (1978) 'The growth and crisis of Italian higher education during the 1960s and 1970s', *Higher Education*, 7, pp. 193–212.

22 ANON. (1970) 'Repressione a Rimini', *Cooperazione Educativa*, 19/6, pp. 1–4; here, p. 4. For similar incidents, see ANON. (1971) 'Repressione ad Ostia', *Cooperazione Educativa*, 20/8, pp. 19–28.

23 See, for example, the 1973 constitution from Sesto Fiorentino reprinted in ANON. (1974) *I Rapporti Scuola-Famiglia nella Scuola Materna*, Rome, Centro Didattico Nazionale per i Rapporti Scuola e Famiglia, pp. 121–3; or the multifarious pre-1975 activity in Florence described in COMITATO SCUOLA LE CURE (1978) *Un Quartiere Sperimenta*, Rimini and Florence, Guaraldi, or RONCHETTI, LUCIANO (1972) 'Gestione sociale al Fermi di Modena', *Riforma della Scuola* 18/4, pp. 14–16; or VARIOUS (1972) 'Gestione sociale per il rinnovamento didattico', *Riforma della Scuola*, 18/6, pp. 27–31.

24 For a detailed description of the Christian Democrats' position see CHIOSSO, *op. cit.*, pp. 27–70.

25 CODIGNOLA, TRISTANO (1974) 'Strumento per una battaglia', *Scuola e Politica*, 4/5, pp. 1–3; here, p. 3.
26 For a brief chronological account bringing together many references, see PELOSI, GABRIELE (1975) 'La gestione della scuola — problemi e riferimenti bibliografici', in VARIOUS (AGAZZI, ALDO, *et al.*), *La Nuova Scuola della Partecipazione. Prospettivi Organizzative e Pedagogiche*, Milan, Vita e Pensiero, pp. 96–106.
27 CORTELLESE, M. and LOMBARDI, D. (1977) *Il Rapporto Scuola-Famiglia: Esperienze, Problemi, Prospettive*, Rome, Centro Didattico Nazionale per i Rapporti Scuola e Famiglia; here, p. 155.
28 MONASTA, ATTILIO (1971) 'L'istituzione affermata', *Cooperazione Educativa*, 20/4, pp. 26–7.
29 CHIOSSO, *op. cit.*, p. 38.
30 For a full account from the PCI angle see ZAPPA, FRANCESCO (1974) 'Il consiglio di istituto, un punto di partenza', *Riforma della Scuola*, 20/8–9, pp. 4–8. For the PSI analysis, see CODIGNOLA, *op. cit.*
31 Law 477, 30 July 1973, Section II, Article 5.
32 Circulars 283, 14 November 1974, and 301, 30 November 1974.
33 GATTULLO, MARIO (1974) 'La gestione della scuola', *Scuola Documenti*, 5, pp. 1–38; here, p. 34. *Scuola Documenti* is published by a 'Centre of basic documentation and counter information' in Pistoia.
34 NAPOLITANO, GIORGIO (1974) 'Democrazia per la riforma', *Riforma della Scuola*, 20/8–9, pp. 2–3.
35 PERUCCI, CARLO (1975) 'L'azione educativa collegiale: il consiglio di classe' in VARIOUS (AGAZZI, ALDO, *et al.*), *op. cit.*, pp. 57–78; here, p. 68: his italics.
36 ANON. (1977) 'Un primo bilancio dei nuovi strumenti di governo della scuola', *Quindicinale di Note e Commenti CENSIS*, 261/262, Vol. 13, 1 January, pp. 20–30. This statistical account by the research association CENSIS is the source for most of the considered commentary of the late seventies.
37 SCIOLLA, LOREDANA (1977) *La Partecipazione Assente. Gli Organi Collegiali della Scuola dall' Utopia alla Crisi*, Rimini and Florence, Guaraldi Editore.
38 It was formally launched at a conference in Rome organized by the *Giornale dei Genitori* on 18 and 19 December 1976 and attended by many parties and groups — e.g., PCI, PSI, PSDI, MCE, COGIDAS. (See *Giornale dei Genitori*, 18/15–16 Dec. 1976/Jan 1977.)
39 These remarks are based largely on meetings with CGD militants in February–March 1980.
40 PERONI, ANGELO (1977) 'Testimonianze sulla partecipazione', *Genitori e Scuola*, 2/7 pp. 23–30; here, p. 23.
41 RUGIU, ANTONIO SANTONI (1977) 'Scuola e politica ieri e oggi' in QUAZZA, GUIDO (Ed.) *Scuola e Politica dall' Unità and oggi*, Turin, Stampatori, pp. 9–29; here, p. 21.
42 ZUCCHINI, GIAN LUIGI (1979) 'A proposito di elezioni scolastiche', *Genitori e*

Scuola, 4/5, pp. 9–11.

43 ROMAN, OSVALDO (1979) 'Anche il consiglio nazionale è in crisi', *Riforma della Scuola*, 26/11, pp. 13–16.

44 ALLUM, P.A. (1973) *Italy: Republic without Government?* London, Weidenfeld and Nicolson, p. 216.

45 URBANI, GIOVANNI (1973) 'Una proposta per la democrazia organizzata', *Riforma della Scuola*, 19/1, pp. 7–14; here, p. 11.

46 ALLUM, *op. cit.*, p. 220.

47 For accounts of the functioning of provincial councils, see LICHTNER, MAURIZIO (1979) 'Che cosa fa il Consiglio scolastico provinciale di Roma?' *Riforma della Scuola*, 26/10, pp. 32–3; and FIORAVANTI, GIOVANNI, 'Un documento del Consiglio scolastico provinciale di Ferrara', *ibid.*, pp. 33–4.

48 For a more detailed account, see CORRADINI, *op.cit.*, Ch. 4. The relevant quotations from government reports and other documents are conveniently gathered together by TELMON, VITTORIO (1974) 'Cronache di una laboriosa gestazione', in VISALBERGHI, ALDO (Ed.), *Il Distretto Scolastico*, Florence La Nuova Italia, pp. 11 ff.

49 T.C. (TRISTANO CODIGNOLA) (1974) 'La costituzione entra nella scuola', *Scuola e Città*, 25/9, pp. 363–5, 378; here, p. 365.

50 BERTIN, GIOVANNI MARIA (1975) 'Partecipazione al governo della scuola', *Scuola e Città*, 26/1, pp. 11–19; here, p. 17.

51 RIZZI, RINALDO (1977) 'Distretto scolastico: compiti, funzioni, prospettive, impegno', *Cooperazione educativa*, 26/7–8, pp. 253–259; here, p. 258.

52 CHIOSSO, GIORGIO (1979) 'Intervista all' on. T. Codignola', *Genitori e Scuola*, 4/7, pp. 6–8; here, p. 6.

53 *Genitori e Scuola*, 3/5, 1978 contains several interesting analyses of this interaction of national and school district politics.

54 CASCIOLI, P. (1978) 'I distretti entrano in fase operativa', *Genitori e Scuola*, 4/1, pp. 15–16; here, p. 16.

55 CASCIOLI, *op. cit.*, For a plea for more generous funding of districts, see ROMAN, OSVALDO (1978) 'Il borsellino del distretto', *Giornale dei Genitori*, 20/31, pp. 12–13.

56 CHIOSSO, GIORGIO (1978) 'L'esperienza di Torino', *Genitori e Scuola*, 4/2, pp. 32–3.

57 Speech of 6 February 1980, cyclostyled (Biblioteca Nazionale Centrale, Rome).

58 For a typical analysis in the general press, see GRANDORI, LUCA and PINNA, ANTONANGELO (1979) 'Il riflusso', *Panorama*, 2 January, pp. 40–6.

59 See PRIDHAM, GEOFFREY (1981) *The Nature of the Italian Party System: A Regional Case Study*, London, Croom Helm.

60 For a useful summary, see BRUNI, NICOLA (1980) 'Organi collegiali: è il caos se non arriva la riforma', *Tuttoscuola*, VI, 104, pp. 9–12. See also PASOTTI, PIETRO (1978) 'Semplificare le elezioni: una proposta', *Genitori e Scuola*, 3/5, pp. 27–8, (Catholic); RODANO, MARSIA (1979) 'La crisi della partecipazione', *Riforma della Scuola*, 25/1, pp. 3–8 (communist).

61 COMITATO SCUOLA LE CURE (1978) *Un Quartiere Sperimenta: Il Movimento per il Tempo Pieno a Firenze*, Rimini and Florence, Guaraldi.

62 For an excellent concrete description of these changes in Florence, see COMITATO SCUOLA LE CURE, *op. cit.* A more theoretical account is DE BARTOLOMEIS, FRANCESCO (1972) *Scuola a Tempo Pieno*, Feltrinelli.

63 For some of the complexity behind this question, see BEATTIE, NICHOLAS (1981) 'Sacred monster: Textbooks in the Italian educational system', *British Journal of Educational Studies*, 29/3, pp. 218–35.

4 German Federal Republic

4.1 General Approach

West Germany differs from France and Italy in having a federal system of government in which education is essentially a responsibility of the constituent states or *Länder*. The existence of eleven distinct systems[1] greatly complicates the task of describing and analyzing the participation of parents in school government. Substantial differences between the *Länder* have to be balanced against the fact that educational discussion and controversy are often directed at a *West German* public, even though decisions are reserved to the local level. An additional complication is that legally required structures of parent participation in school management have a much longer history than in France or Italy, going back in some cases to before the First World War, but interrupted during the Nazi period. To do justice to this complex and variegated scene without losing one's way in a mass of detail is difficult. In presenting the west German case, two basic decisions have therefore been taken:

(i) to concentrate on four *Länder* out of the eleven;
(ii) to present these local cases in three stages:
  (a) the origins and emergence of legally required structures of parent participation;
  (b) their subsequent development by *Land* governments as formal structures;
  (c) the related evolution of parent groups as a more or less independent force.

Stages a) and b) are similar to those used to organize Chapters 2 and 3, and relate to the basic model expounded in section 1.3. The interest of stage c) is that it represents a phase of development which is still hardly visible in France and Italy because of the recency of the participatory system in those countries. We shall therefore need to ask whether recent developments in West Germany reflect forces peculiar to that country, or are generalizable to others.

Stages a) and b) will be illustrated through events in Hamburg and Bavaria, stage c) through Hessen and North Rhine-Westphalia. These four *Länder* provide a good variety of political and participatory tradition, as well as a useful geographical spread from north to south and from a city-state (Hamburg) to larger areas. It will be argued that 1945 represents a natural chronological starting point, but Hamburg will also provide a good example of the ways in which older traditions were influential; this will necessitate a sort of flashback technique.

The complexity of the federal system makes a straightforward chronological narrative in the style of Chapters 2 and 3 difficult to sustain. Chapter 4 will therefore be more fragmented into sections and somewhat longer. However, the ordering is still roughly chronological, with section 4.2 relating mainly to the immediate post-war period (1945–9), and 4.3 carrying the story through to the early seventies. Sections 4.4 and 4.5 return to the 1950s and 1960s to present a counter-case. After a brief overview in 4.6 of the stage of development reached by about 1970, sections 4.7 and 4.8 present two illustrative educational controversies involving parents, one from 1972–3 and one from 1977–8.

4.2 The Establishment of Parent Participation: Hamburg and Bavaria.

Hamburg in 1945 was an unlikely setting for experiments in the participatory management of schools. The mere maintenance of some semblance of civilization was a sufficiently daunting prospect. The numbers killed in the apocalyptic fire-storms of July 1943 were literally incalculable.[2] The misery of the remaining inhabitants was increased by the influx of refugees from the east. Out of 483 schools, a hundred had been destroyed, and two hundred badly damaged.[3] There were virtually no teachers under the age of thirty as all younger teachers had either been called into the armed forces or were suspect as having been trained since 1933: the average teacher was over fifty.

In these circumstances, people's minds turned naturally to the past. The first Burgomaster of occupied Hamburg, nominated by the British forces shortly after their takeover, declared in his first speech amid the ruins (15 May 1945) that the only thing that gave him the courage to take up the job was: 'trust in the blessing of God and of His Son Jesus Christ . . . whose name, on account of His race, has not been uttered by government in Germany for these last twelve years.'[4]

Over the next few years this renewal of Christian commitment was to affect the evolution of education in Hamburg in several ways. It was to place on the local agenda the issue of whether denominational schools should be introduced.[5] It was to contribute to the emergence of the Christian Democrats (CDU) as the main opposition to the Social Democrats (SPD). It was to inform the statement of parent rights enshrined in the federal Basic Law which would be incorporated word for word into Hamburg legislation.

But there was another aspect of the Hamburg tradition which was even more frequently invoked: that of *Reformpädagogik* and the 1920 Education Act.[6] Thus in April 1947 it seemed natural to open a rally of SPD parents by describing the 1920 Act, by comparison with which existing arrangements for school government were shown to be inadequate and unprogressive.[7] In the same spirit, the first issue of the *Hamburger Lehrerzeitung* (April 1948) stated in its editorial:

> A greater obligation than ever before is laid upon a teachers' journal to involve younger members of our profession in the ethos and tradition of the fertile period before 1933, when Hamburg's educational life had an impact beyond the boundaries of the city and throughout the *Reich* itself. . . .[8]

In November the *Lehrerzeitung* commissioned an article from the 83-year-old Ernst Lübkert in which he outlined educational developments in Hamburg from the first Schools Act of 1870.[9] In May 1949, when a new Hamburg Education Bill was under discussion, a Hamburg speaker attended a trizonal discussion on school government and administration. Again the excellence of the 1920 Act was stressed. A particular responsibility lay on Hamburg, he felt, to revive democratic participation in school government, for the other main pre-1933 proponent of progressive ideas in this area, the tiny *Land* of Lippe, had been swallowed up in North Rhine-Westphalia.[10]

Thus one of the first questions to ask about the new, post-1945 system for involving parents and teachers in the running of Hamburg's schools is whether it was in fact new, or whether it was a simple revival of the 1920 arrangements. The 1920 Act had set up a network of elected parent councils (nine parents and three teachers) for each school, both primary and secondary. The most controversial function of these councils was the selection of head teachers. There was also at *Land* level a *Schulbeirat*, or Schools' Consultative Council, on which both teachers and parents were represented. Teachers had similar representation at school, district and *Land* levels.[11]

This bald description of a network of elected committees gives little real idea of the spirit and significance of the 1920 innovations, which must be seen as the product and battle-ground of three forces or movements, evolving over a considerable period: parliamentary democracy, socialism and *Reformpädagogik*. The 'free Hansa-city of Hamburg' had been governed by its own parliament, or *Bürgerschaft*, since the Middle Ages. This was not democratic government in the contemporary sense, but government by an oligarchy of 'burghers' or patrician merchants. In the nineteenth century the electorate was gradually extended, but control of government remained with the upper and middle classes.[12] In the latter part of the nineteenth century as Germany, and Hamburg as its main port, became increasingly industrialized, the socialists (SPD) emerged as a working-class opposition. By the early 1900s the SPD in Hamburg was committed to a radical education policy on the *Reformpädagogik* model. The school was to be controlled by the community it served. By 1906 'the direct election of parent representatives at all levels of school administration' was part of the SPD's programme in Hamburg. The party proceeded to set up socialist 'parents' circles' in connection with individual schools, though these had no legal status.[13] These innovations were inspired by an explicit wish to break down the barriers between working-class communities and bureaucratic 'bosses' schools' — i.e., they fell broadly into the 'overcoming alienation' category. Such participatory aspirations were disliked by the conservatives who controlled the *Bürgerschaft* and by most teachers who had since 1870 had their own professional assembly, the 'teachers' synod'.

When the *Reich* collapsed in November 1918, SPD-controlled councils or soviets (*Räte*) sprang up spontaneously, and for several weeks Hamburg had two governments: the *Bürgerschaft* and the soviets. In accordance with what had been SPD policy for a dozen years, schools acquired their individual *Elternräte* (or parent soviets), which were often spontaneously formed. On 20 March 1919, the day before handing over power to the newly elected and reformed *Bürgerschaft*, the Hamburg Workers' and Soldiers' Council incorporated these parent councils into a new city-wide system of school administration, which was promulgated by decree.[14] In due course, as the *Bürgerschaft* reasserted its authority, the new Schools Act of 1920 incorporated the councils into the machinery of school government. A double system of elected parents' and teachers' councils was consolidated, culminating at *Land* level in a parents' assembly and a teachers' assembly which could meet jointly as a consultative *Schulbeirat*. Both groups were also represented in the *Schulbehörde* or executive body.

The circumstances of the *Elternrat's* birth thus gave it from the start a certain utopian inheritance, an impetus towards the aims labelled in Chapter 1 'overcoming alienation'. A speech of 7 February 1919 catches the tone:

> It is towards love that we are striving when we talk of a new social life in the school. It's no longer a case of instructing children, nor even merely of working with them, but of living with them, living in unconditional comradeship — that is our will.[15]

For some the parents' council was almost the sole official recognition that this new era of transformed human relationships had dawned, and that the alienation inherent in capitalist society could be combated by ordinary people.

A second and more lasting inheritance was politicization. Socialist parents were organized as a separate grouping in 1919 and by 1926 had their own newspaper, the *Hamburger Elternzeitung*, with the avowed aim of building up a 'mass army of fighters in educational politics'. Conservative and Lutheran groupings also emerged, and biennial elections to parent councils became variations on and preparations for *Bürgerschaft* elections. Nazi distaste for this system was predictable. A report of 1935 states:

> The parent councils, perhaps originally conceived as a link between school and parents, rapidly became a cockpit for party-political confrontations which became so serious that the nine parent representatives on a parent council quite often split openly into several opposing groups.[16]

The Nazis in Hamburg moved rapidly to eliminate this undesirable element of democracy. A new 'School Administration Act' passed through the Nazi-controlled *Bürgerschaft* on 23 June 1933. The '*Führer*-principle' meant that the crucial authority in the individual school was allocated to the head teacher. *Elternbeiräte* (parent consultative councils) were now to be appointed by the head and were simply to support the school by organizing 'lectures and film-evenings, sports festivals, school and *Volk* ceremonies, rambling expeditions, etc.'[17] This system was short-lived. When all education was brought under central *Reich* control, even these councils were replaced by *Schuljugendwalter*, or parent advisers nominated by the head.[18]

In the circumstances of 1945 there could be no simple reinstatement of the pre-1933 traditions. The pressing physical needs of the moment encouraged a different, more informal and pragmatic style of parent involvement — for example, in repairing school buildings. For a time schools served a certain welfare function (feeding, issue of coupons for shoes, etc.) which had not been part of their traditional work. Hopes of radical change were disappointed. Some SPD supporters had hoped that 1945 would see the people seizing power in the style of 1918, but the physical and moral exhaustion were too great for that to happen, nor were the British occupying authorities initially very sympathetic.[19] The *Einheitsschule* reform (comprehensive) was disinterred from the 1920s and briefly discussed in the summer of 1945 but in fact the schools reopened as a tripartite system.[20] For the next two or three years educational debate in Hamburg was dominated by the confessional and comprehensive issues, which demonstrated that democracy was still about reconciling contrary values, and that no utopian leap forward into a new harmony had taken place. In many ways the questions addressed were still those of fifty years before. Should church schools be permitted? Should religious education be permitted? Should religious education be compulsory, and in what form? Could an SPD-dominated *Bürgerschaft* impose on *Gymnasium* teachers a radical reform which they bitterly opposed? On such issues party political differences emerged rapidly and fed local fears of a reversion to the politicization of school government which had occurred in the 1920s. In conjunction with the international situation (Cold War, Berlin blockade, the emergence of 'West Germany' as the frontline of American commitment in Europe) this meant that the 1949 Schools Act was considerably less radical than many had hoped. It did not deal in detail with the question of school administration. The contentious issue of the exact rights of parents in relation to religious education was glossed over by the simple insertion of the formula from the federal Basic Law, which had been agreed only shortly before. This had itself been the product of prolonged controversy resulting from Catholic attempts to write in the primacy of parent rights in education. Article 6.2 reflected that pressure by stating: 'The care and education of children are a natural right of parents and a duty which is in the first instance laid upon them.' This was the only point at which the Basic Law used the phrase 'natural right'. However, the next sentence represented a dilution of this clear principle and reflected the intense controversy among the drafters: 'The community of the state supervises the way in which that care and education are exercised.' Article 7.1 stated firmly: 'The entire school system is under the supervision of the state.'[21] In other words, parents had rights, but so had the state: the relationship between those two sets of possibly conflicting rights remained to be worked out.

In 1949 even this compromise formula proved unacceptable to the Hamburg CDU and FDP (Free Democrats or 'Liberals') who walked out of the city parliament rather than assent to a law which they judged to be dangerously secularist and socialist.[22] However, the points at issue were more confessional and party-political (i.e., the CDU's distrust of a strongly entrenched SPD regime at the height of the Cold War) than related to school management. In fact the basic structures of participation in the operation of schools were already three years old. They had been established in an executive order (*Verwaltungsordnung*) of 1946. Separate parent and teacher councils at school level fed into similar councils at *Kreis* (district) level. All-Hamburg teacher and parent assemblies (*Lehrer-und Elternkammern*) were added in 1953; sitting jointly these were to constitute a schools consultative council (*Schulbeirat*). The entire structure was consolidated in legislation only in 1956.

By comparison with the 1920 Act, whose spirit was so frequently invoked, the 1946/56 arrangements seemed relatively timid. The participatory structures were firmly subordinated to the bureaucracy, and the functions of parents and teachers were consultative, not decision-making. The provisions for the separate teachers' and parents' councils to sit jointly remained largely a dead letter, so that Hamburg had two separate and to some extent competing systems which tended to cancel each other out. The voting arrangements in particular removed the councils from the realm of direct democracy. In contrast to the 1920s teacher representation was organized through the unions, and the base of parent representation was the class, not the school, i.e., a school parent council consisted of representatives elected by very small groups of parents, thus minimizing any possibility of politicization.

Thus, however frequently the 1920 Act might be invoked in rhetoric, the spirit of all this was very different from the 'teachers' and parents' soviets' of November 1918. The 1946 machinery was an attempt to consolidate and legitimize normal bureaucratic modes of administration which for a time in 1945 had almost vanished and which in any case suffered from a desperate need to appear democratic. By the mid-fifties SPD cadres, which were very firmly in local control in the context of Adenauer's Germany ('No experiments!'), were most unlikely to promulgate legislation to push the participatory machinery towards the spirit of 1918–20. The aims of 'legitimation' thus remained dominant in Hamburg.

These developments took place with little encouragement or discouragement from the occupying power, which in Hamburg happened to be British. A critical difference in Bavaria, our second example, was the relatively strong pressure from the occupying Americans, anxious to make a reality of the Allied Control Council directive which required all concerned 'to ensure effective participation by all citizens both in the reform and organization of education and its adminstration.'[23] Another major difference was in political and cultural traditions. Where Hamburg was urban, Protestant and socialist, Bavaria tended to be rural, Catholic and conservative. These two basic differences — in occupying power and native traditions — meant that the whole question of parent participation presented itself very differently to the Bavarians. Crudely, parent involvement was imposed rather than achieved as a natural outgrowth of local traditions.

The conservative CSU (Christian Social Union) had emerged quite early as the effective interlocutor of the American forces. For them, the central problem was how to preserve the essential traditions and values of Bavaria as they saw them from the depredations of their new overlords, who tended to equate democracy with American practice. American efforts to install a version of the American high school were met by polite but effective resistance from the Bavarian side;[24] this was after all a reform of substance which would have clashed very directly with the highly differentiated school system specified in the new Bavarian constitution.[25] PTAs, on the other hand, promoted by the Americans as a necessary part of democracy, were less objectionable. In due course, after considerable stalling on the Bavarian side, *Schulpflegschaften* (roughly, school consultative councils)[26] were restored on 27 July 1948. By 1 October 1948 the American Military Government directed the Bavarians to set up a unified *Landesschulbeirat* to coordinate activity at school level,[27] but this was done only in 1955, long after the Americans had ceased to control German internal affairs, and then only as a consultative body nominated entirely by the Minister of Education, and with a minority of parent representatives (currently six out of thirty-four).[28] However, the American pressure had at least served to precipitate a Bavarian policy on parent participation which was to remain unchanged in principle up to the present day. Basically, formal elective bodies were to be (i) limited to school level with no attempt at wider coordination in a pyramid structure corresponding to the state administration; and (ii) simply grafted on to the existing administrative system, which would not be modified to allow for any lay influence over decision-making. This showed that the underlying purpose was not to criticize or modify the system, still less to devolve power from the centre, but to improve its functioning by increasing the flow of information to and from parents.

Thus in their different styles both Hamburg and Bavaria demonstrated the overriding importance of *legitimation* in the establishment of participatory committees in the immediate post-war period. In more catastrophic circumstances, Hamburg in the mid-1940s was in a very similar position to France and Italy in the late 1960s and early 1970s: the authorities needed to justify their power in the aftermath of a major shift by opinion (and in the German case a shift in real power). If the rhetoric of 1920 ('overcoming alienation') was used by politicians in Hamburg in the same way as Edgar Faure used the rhetoric of participation in France in 1968–9, that did not necessarily imply any deliberate intention to subvert the idealism of enthusiasts for participation — simply that the options open at the time were extremely limited, and that anything that would attract support for the post-Nazi state was useful. The Bavarian situation was rather different. There seems to have been no need to use the *Schulpflegschaften* to rally Bavarian opinion behind the CSU regime. There was a considerable need to establish legitimacy *vis-à-vis* the Americans, and a token parental presence was a cheap concession to make. In both *Länder*, however, legitimation would appear to have been the predominant concern. This highlights the real break between the 1920 system in Hamburg and its 1946 successor; 1918 was quite distinct from 1945, and so were the arrangements for parent participation which flowed from those two important turning points. We can recall the pre-1933 traditions and recognize their impact on some post-1945 thinking without denying that 1945 did represent a genuinely fresh starting point.

4.3   The Development of Parent Participation: Hamburg and Bavaria

The period from the foundation of the Federal Republic in 1949 to the end of the 1960s has been characterized as 'two decades of non-reform'.[29] In federal politics the end of that period is formally marked by the accession to power in 1969 of the SPD/FDP coalition which had been preceded by a transitional 'Grand Coalition' (CDU/SPD, 1966–9). In terms of educational change the re-awakening of controversy is usually traced to Georg Picht's polemic writings of 1964.[30] As in France and Italy there was also some student unrest in 1967–8. Although not as dramatically focused as in France, the student movement had a disproportionate impact on West German public opinion, which had become accustomed to a high degree of consensus.

Against this generally quiescent background, the participatory systems in both socialist Hamburg and conservative Bavaria remained substantially unchanged until the end of the sixties. The 'legitimation' aims which had predominated when they were set up continued to predominate. There was little attempt even at 'cosmetic changes of rule' in the style of France in the 1970s, for the rather obvious reason that the government of neither *Land* felt under any real threat or pressure.

This absence of change is hardly surprising in Bavaria, with its authoritarian traditions, its apparently permanent CSU majority (maintained at about two-thirds of the total vote since the immediate post-war period), and its initial reluctance to install any system at all. Hamburg is a more puzzling, and a more instructive example. As we have seen, Hamburg's traditions were politically democratic and educationally progressive. In 1949, when Heinz Kloss published a passionate and well-researched plea for the schools of the new democratic Germany to be run by local *Genossenschaften* or cooperatives,[31] he had seen Hamburg as the obvious centre from which real change could flow. Reforms which could be achieved there with relative ease could be the precursors of a historic shift throughout Germany to replace bureaucratic control of schools from the top downwards by a more flexible and democratic style of control, which would correspond more closely to the *educational* imperatives.

Yet for all these high hopes the Hamburg system of teacher and parent participation remained obstinately conformed to the bureaucracy — admittedly a relatively humane and efficient bureaucracy, subservient to the city parliament, but still in Kloss's terms operating from the top downwards, and not even showing any very obvious evolution towards the aims of 'responsiveness'. Partly this was due to the dominance of the teacher unions in the post-1946 committees. Their essentially professional orientation turned out to be paramount. They saw their assembly as 'an organ of co-operation between experts',[32] essentially an information channel to and from the bureaucracy. For the relatively small numbers of parent representatives at *Kreis* and especially *Land* level the same was undoubtedly true. For most parents, however, the formal arrangements remained formal. An enquiry carried out in Hamburg in the late 1950s criticized the participatory structures as 'carrying a considerable deadweight inherited from old Utopias'.[33] There was a disturbing gap between what the system offered and what parents needed.

> The low level of interest in the school parent council becomes even clearer when it is realized that only 16 per cent of all respondents were prepared to stand for election as parent

representatives. By contrast the strong interest felt by parents in personal meetings with the teacher and in class parent meetings is quite plain.[34]

In Hamburg over the period 1946–69, so many of the factors were apparently favourable to the 1946 structures developing their own dynamic that one might have expected parents to formulate their own demands for change in the system: e.g., for the committees to become more 'responsive', perhaps by taking over a degree of financial control. Some more radical parent groups might even have tried to make more of a reality of the aims subsumed under the heading of 'overcoming alienation' by trying to make local schools more community-oriented and thus narrowing the gap between the rhetoric of the post-war period and the actual achievements of the schools. Various reasons can be advanced for the failure of the Hamburg participatory system to evolve towards a more flexible and open style of school management. One factor was probably the tripartite structure of secondary education, which tended to place the more active parents in the *Gymnasium* sector; they then became more or less committed to the defence of the *status quo*. No doubt there was some truth also in psychological generalizations — that people were too numbed by the traumatic experiences of war and defeat to undertake experiments in democratic participation, or that they were working too hard to rebuild their own fortunes and those of their country. More important in the long run, however, is probably the absence of any real threat to the SPD regime in Hamburg.

This analysis is borne out by the fact that the first major change in the 1946 system resulted very directly from the student unrest of 1967–8, which in Hamburg occurred in both universities and secondary schools. Although the new legislation was in a sense drafted by the SPD 'ruling elite', like the roughly contemporaneous French decrees, in a spirit of self-preservation, the style of the process of change was very different. The *Bürgerschaft* proceeded rapidly to pass a new 'School Administration Act' of 8 July 1968. This was regarded as a rather hasty tidying up of the 1956 Act, with the introduction of an element of student representation to meet the clamour from some older Hamburg pupils in 1967–8. Once the University Act had been passed in 1969, the *Bürgerschaft* initiated a more elaborate process of consultation and discussion which terminated in 1973 in a 'School Constitution Act'. Much of the argument centred on the need to preserve the pre-eminent authority of the parliament — or in the words of Gunter Apel, the Minister or *Senator*, addressing the Hamburg parents' assembly in 1971, 'it was a matter of working together to raise dams against radicalism and mob-rule; that was why it was so important for him that all democratic forces represented in parliament should assent to the Bill in its essential features.'[35]

The first article of the new Act stated: '(Education) is the responsibility of the city government (*Senat*) acting for Parliament (*Bürgerschaft*).' The new system was thus a clarification of the existing division of responsibilities rather than the radical change which some SPD rhetoric suggested. Entirely characteristic was the lengthy controversy over the election of head teachers. In 1919 this had happened by acclamation within the school council or soviet; in 1973 the parliament laid down elaborate procedures for the drawing-up of short-lists by 'wise men', for the involvement of teachers and parents at different stages of the process, for probationary periods, etc. These arrangements were interesting and principled, but as with the post-war evocations of the 1920 Act, to see them as the lineal descendant of 1919–20 is unrealistic and ahistorical.[36] It is not to impugn the sincerity of the city's legislators and other interested parties to suggest that the 1973 Act fell into the category of 'cosmetic changes of rule' and that 'legitimation' continued to be the predominant aim of the Hamburg arrangements. Given the effectiveness of parliamentary control in Hamburg, it could hardly be otherwise. Aims such as those grouped under 'overcoming alienation' and to a lesser degree 'responsiveness' could be realized only to the extent that parliament was prepared to waive some part of its authority. Yet in Hamburg much of the argument over the 1973 legislation centred on the undesirability, on grounds of democratic accountability, of removing basic responsibilties for education from parliament. In the last resort an elected parliamentary representative was felt to be chosen by the people in a sense that no parent representative could be.

In the Hamburg debates we see a clash between two conceptions of democratic participation, and the argument was often quite principled and rigorous. When we move south to Bavaria, however, we are in a world in many ways closer to what we have already seen in France and Italy — a more or less conservative regime, more or less permanently in power, functioning through a centralized bureaucracy over a wide area of territory and learning to use the movement towards parent participation to consolidate and extend its own power. The fact that the pace of change is more sluggish than in France or Italy indicates only that the threat to the powers that be in Munich has been less urgent than in Paris or Rome. We see also something of the same pattern we saw in 1948, when the Bavarian government installed *Schulpflegschaften* at the behest of the Americans — i.e., that change often flows more from pressures from without (in this case from Bonn) than from within.

The rather spectral system of mixed school committees set up in Bavaria in 1948 began to take on substance through the fifties and into the sixties. As in France, much of the reality of parent participation in Bavaria stemmed from parent associations, though these differed from their French counterparts in having been formed as a result of the existence of official committees, rather than predating them. The first of these associations to emerge was the *Landeselternvereinigung der Gymnasien in Bayern* (LEV), founded in December 1950 when a number of individual *Gymnasium* associations banded together. The initiative came originally from the Bavarian *Philologenverband*,[37] the union of *Gymnasium* teachers, which has throughout the history of the Federal Republic maintained an energetic defence of tripartism. The LEV rapidly acquired a monthly journal, *Die Schulfamilie*,[38] whose title underlined the cosy, non-conflictual, 'apolitical' nature of the association.[39] As the years went by the LEV was strengthened by the adherence of two other associations, one of them Catholic.[40] The LEV claimed, and claims to be entirely non-political. However, the very nature of its existence as a *Gymnasium* parents'association meant that it must support the central core of CSU education policy, the selective secondary system, even if individual members adhered to other parties. Frequent contributions to *Die Schulfamilie* showed how the *Philologenverband* used the LEV as a channel for its own views. The LEV also showed a deep seated reverence for the Ministry in Munich which throughout the seventies had a regular slot in *Schulfamilie* headed 'The Ministry Speaks'.

Underlying this relationship with the *Philologenverband* and the Ministry is the prestige of the *Gymnasium* as the crowning glory of Bavarian school education. Parents want their children to attend the *Gymnasium*, which has for many years taken an increasing proportion of the 10-year-old age-group, and they value it in its traditional form. Thus a separate association of *Gymnasium* parents soon proved to be a useful support to the Ministry's basic policy. In the face of pressure from the SPD or from Bonn to undertake structural reform, the CSU could point to the support of an independent non-political association of parents. Mild criticisms of Ministry policy simply underscored the independence of the LEV from Ministry control.[41]

As the LEV established itself in this role the Ministry came increasingly to see its usefulness, and to modify the school regulations to encourage a modest degree of controlled parent participation. The main vehicle for this was to be the *Elternbeirat*, or parents' consultative council, an elected council at school level. There was at this stage no basc of class representatives, nor any attempt to set up a unitary network of representative institutions at district or *Land* level as in most other *Länder*. The *Gymnasium* regulations may be taken as representative:

> It is the task of the Parents' Consultative Council to promote the close relationship of trust between school and home ... The activity of the Parents' Consultative Council is not intended to replace the direct link between parents and guardians and teachers ... The activity of the Parents' Consultative Council is honorary; there is no provision for compensation or expense ...

Parents were elected yearly, one for every fifty pupils in school. The head must sit with the council; the school doctor and individual teachers could also take part. The council must sit at least once a term.[42]

Characteristically, the *Elternbeirat* was introduced piecemeal. It was added to the *Gymnasium* in 1961 and to the *Realschule* in 1962. Not until 1966, in the context of a new *Volksschulgesetz* (Elementary School Act) was the council introduced in the *Volksschule*.

Thus by the second half of the sixties there were some kind of elected parent representatives in all Bavarian schools. The fact that there were basically three sets of regulations governing this activity — one for the *Gymnasium*, one for the *Realschule* and one for the *Volksschule* (i.e., for primary and secondary modern schools, which in rural districts were often still combined) naturally led to three basic parent groups.[43] The LEV for *Gymnasien* has already been described. The *Landeselternschaft der Bayerischen Realschulen* was founded in 1958. The fact that its office was in the archiepiscopal administrative building in Munich reflected the largely religious origin of most *Realschulen* in Bavaria. The association was in general less active than in the LEV. Its membership was corporate, not individual, and it acted basically as an information service for *Realschulen* throughout Bavaria, operating through duplicated *Rundschreiben* (newsletters) which were mainly edited versions of ministerial decrees and regulations. While it undoubtedly had a pressure-group function, it exercised it in a discreet and gentlemanly style — 'maintaining' (in the words of its own constitution) 'the *Realschule* ... promoting its general recognition and furthering its interests with vigour.'[44]

The third major association was less favourably viewed by the Ministry.[45] The *Bayerische Elternverband* (BEV), for parents of children in *Volksschulen* (primary and secondary modern) and special schools, was founded in 1968. Why was it so late to emerge? It may be the case — certainly the French and Italian evidence supports this interpretation — that parents in the less prestigious sectors of the system are less conscious of themselves as an identifiable grouping, less confident in confronting professionals and less skilled in organizing associations. The very large number of small schools was another complicating factor, increased in Bavaria by the administrative lumping together of primary and secondary schools and by the rural character of much of the terrain. An additional complication was the strong confessional involvement in village education which led to an inevitable fragmentation of parent interests: this was resolved only in the latter part of the sixties when Bavaria agreed a scheme of *Gemeinschaftsschulen* which guaranteed religious education in common state schools while removing most of the cost from the churches.[46] Finally, the *Elternbeirat* in the *Volksschule* began to function only in the autumn of 1967 as a result of the 1966 legislation. Thus the BEV cannot be said to have emerged in 1968 *because* 1968 was the year when people began to clamour for participation. Rather, it was the belated offshoot of a system of school government dating in spirit from the fifties and early sixties.

Had the BEV arrived earlier on the scene it might well have evolved as a 'non-political' grouping acting as an external support for the CSU, and this would certainly have been the case if it had accurately reflected the preponderance of rural and small-town *Volksschulen*. However, the very fact that it appeared on the scene in 1968 probably made it a focus of opposition to the Ministry. It was certainly marked in the early years of its existence by some lively and combative leadership, and by a predominantly urban base in Munich, Nürnberg and elsewhere. In addition, while *Gymnasien* and *Realschulen* had an established position to defend, the *Volksschule* was manifestly underresourced and had long suffered from a parental crisis of confidence, with an ever-increasing proportion of the age-group in *Gymnasium* and *Realschule*, and a dwindling *Hauptschule* sector. Thus the BEV, for the first time in Bavaria, focused a degree of parental discontent with the *status quo*, and introduced an interesting new element of organized dissent. The dominance enjoyed by the CSU in politics and the local media made it inevitable that dissent would be perceived as 'socialist', even though individual members might belong to the FDP or even the CSU itself. As early as 1970 links were forged with the main teachers' union in the *Hauptschule/Grundschule* sector,[47] and in due course these links were strengthened, as the teachers saw useful allies in the new parents' association. The sharpening of the educational debate in and after 1968 and the growing federal pressure for the comprehensive school strengthened the trend towards polarization.

Even to Bavaria 1968 brought minor unrest in universities and in the upper classes of *Gymnasien*. However, what was much more significant was the feeling that a *German* debate on educational matters was beginning to impinge on *Bavarian* reality. After 1968, and particularly after the appointment of Hans Maier as Minister of Education in 1971, government worked much harder to put over the CSU view of education. The contrast was frequently drawn by CSU spokesmen between orderly, commonsensical Bavaria and the supposed anarchy prevailing in other parts of the republic. Elsewhere changes were governed by political prejudice; in Bavaria, it was claimed, reform was gradualistic, non-political, inspired only by scientifically proven and professionally attested truth.

Into this picture the Bavarian model of parent participation fitted very neatly. Properly handled — i.e., restricted to the level of individual schools and given no substantive responsibility for actual decisions — parents were a guarantee of the non-political character of schools. Faced with the minor student problems of 1968, and the unpredictable threats from the new SPD/FDP regime in Bonn, the Ministry in Munich did not panic. It had no need to. By the early 1970s it had plainly realized that a degree of controlled dissent was actually an asset in establishing its democratic *bona fides*. Pressure for participation by older students was met in 1968 by setting up a committee for elected pupil representatives and a consultative committee or *Schulforum* which would bring together — at least in the *Gymnasium* regulations of 6 September 1968 — two representatives each of teachers, parents and pupils with the head teacher as chairperson. In this way potentially awkward resolutions from pupils would be forwarded to a committee in which a majority would be difficult to achieve.[48]

The next move was to tidy up the hotch-potch of different regulations governing schools which had gradually accumulated since the war. The redrafting was done within the Ministry rather than in a process of open democratic discussion leading to legislation, as in Hamburg in the early seventies, yet the underlying motivation was very similar in spite of profound differences in vocabulary and style. Minister Hans Maier stated in April 1973, in an address to the LEV, that what he wanted to emphasize through the new arrangements was

> expert advice and the proper interests of all involved . . . not a wrongly understood democratization of education. The constitutional responsibility for the school is a matter for the State which cannot be relieved of that responsibility. For that reason the draft draws boundaries for participation wherever there is a danger that it may be unable to fulfil its duty. . . .[49]

He went on to say that requests for legal representation of parents at district and *Land* level, for which the BEV had been pressing, would be refused, as parental involvement was essentially a matter of cultivating 'trust and co-operation' at school level. He also mentioned the problems that trade union involvement would be likely to cause at *Land* level.

The only parent association to dissent from this line was the BEV. The beauty of the CSU's 'divide and rule' dominance of the situation is shown in the annual report of the LEV for 1972–3, delivered by the chairperson, Margret von Pechmann, herself a member of the SPD:

> The LEV has nothing against parent representation at *Land* level being written into the law, but it would not wish to have to give up what it has achieved through its own work — its political and financial independence and the right to address itself . . . in its own right and directly to public opinion and to the state administration and the political machine. This independent position would be endangered if the LEV became simply a part of a committee set up by the state, in which it might easily be outvoted.[50]

Two years later a speaker at the annual general meeting of LEV voiced the *Gymnasium* parents' suspicion of 'Councils':

> Everybody knows that political forces are trying to change parliamentary democracy into a state of soviets (*Rätestaat*). . . . We are all aware that this 'state of soviets' is intended to become reality in a long march through our institutions and that the school, the 'institution of the future', is the first and most important of these institutions. This parent association is no nest of revolutionaries. It wants no truck with 'Parent Councils against the state', or with 'Social autonomy' in order to over-throw parliamentary government. It will certainly support this and any other government which uses its authority to protect the school against ideology.[51]

The fact that these revolutionary parents' councils did not exist anywhere in the republic is irrelevant: what is interesting is the success of the Bavarian system in incorporating independent parents into the CSU propaganda effort not only without infringing their independent status but by using their independence as a support for the regime. Clearly a system which permitted public opinion to be manipulated with such economy of effort was unlikely to be scrapped. When on 2 October 1973 a new set of 'General school regulations' was approved, to come into force on 1 August 1974, the three basic types of school retained their separate regulations, and no provision at all was made for elective councils at district or *Land* level.

Two years later another refinement of this mechanism was introduced — the *Elternsprecher*, or parent spokesperson. This was incorporated in a change in the *Volksschulgesetz* passed on the 23 July 1976, but legislation for other types of school was also promised. The new arrangements had the effect of pushing the electoral process down to *class* level and thus making it very likely that *Elternsprecher* would simply 'emerge' from a small group of parents, without the sort of campaign meeting necessary in a *school* election. The *Elternbeirat* would now be made up of all the *Elternsprecher* in the school.[52] All these changes can very properly be described as 'cosmetic', for they did not alter in the slightest the basically centralized nature of the system.

Although both the forms and the spirit of the formal structures in these two *Länder* are very different, it is suggested that at a deeper level they have both followed a similar pattern of development:

    (i)   both systems were established to strengthen the legitimacy of states which aspired to be democratic but had just passed through a traumatic period of authoritarian rule and foreign invasion;

    (ii)   in time both systems were gradually adapted, but in making changes both governments retained the initiative in their own hands and showed no signs of wishing to devolve substantial extra powers to schools or subregions.

In terms of the clusters of aims described in Chapter 1, *'legitimation' remained the central concern.*

We now move to consider two *Länder* in which, at least for brief periods, the traditional German 'administered school' seemed to slip out of the control of *Land* government and bureaucracy. Is it possible in these less regulated circumstances to see some development away from 'legitimation' towards one or more of the other three aims: 'responsiveness', 'overcoming alienation' or 'personal development'?

4.4   The Extension of Parent Power: Hessen

So far it has been suggested that the main motivation which led the governments of France, Italy, Hamburg and Bavaria to install systems of participatory involvement in schools was self-interested rather than idealistic: they were anxious to preserve the *status quo* rather than to alter it. Although some movement towards less bureaucratic and hierarchical modes of decision-making and control was discussed, especially in relation to Italy, any such moves are at so early a stage of evolution that assessment of their long-term direction must remain tentative.

The presumption is that in relation to both the origins and development of parent participation the 'general crisis' or 'legitimation' theory sketched in section 1.3 is so far broadly confirmed. It has been suggested that all four governments (three of which set up the new structures more or less reluctantly) eventually learnt not only to live with participation but to see some of its advantages and modify it to be a more effective tool for the manipulation of public opinion. In other words, if 'legitimation' really is central to parent participation, the success of the policy can be judged by a reduction of controversy and confrontation through its incorporation within official structures; ideally control will be *indirect*, as opposed to the more *direct* control of traditional systems.

As a certain level of controversy is inevitable in any democratic system, it is not clear how the intended 'reduction' of controversy can be measured. If reduction means 'less than would have been the case had the machinery of participation not been installed', then such comparisons over *time* are hypothetical and subjective. If reduction means 'less than in similar polities without the machinery of participation', then we are back with the basic problems of comparison in *space*: that circumstances are never exactly similar and circumstances alter cases. What seems clearer is that high levels of educational controversy with a strong element of lay (normally parental) involvement in polities which possessed the machinery of parent participation would suggest either that the legitimation theory was faulty or that the particular structures implanted were inappropriate, or both.

In this context two German *Länder* provide useful counter-cases to Hamburg and Bavaria. Both Hessen and North Rhine-Westphalia (NRW) have suffered noisy and rather destructive confrontations on educational questions in the 1970s. In each instance government attempts to manipulate public opinion failed miserably, and in each instance there were considerable reverberations beyond the borders of the *Land* concerned. One of those *Länder* (NRW) had a not very highly developed system of parent representation similar in some ways to Bavaria's. The other *Land* (Hessen) had moved further than any other West German state in shifting real power from politicians and bureaucracy to parents. Thus well-documented public controversy combined with different styles of participation should provide useful additional information to elaborate the necessarily over-simple picture derived from Hamburg and Bavaria.

The special position of Hessen goes back to its emergence as a new unit of government in the first year of the occupation. One of the preconditions for later developments in parent participation, and a stark contrast with the equivalent in Bavaria,[53] was the explicitly 'progressive' *Land* constitution of 1946.[54] Its democratic tone was partly a result of the influence of Erwin Stein, the first elected Education Minister of the new *Land*. He was CDU idealist with a strong commitment to revivify German democracy by reasserting the old verities of Christianity and classical humanism. As in Hamburg much of the early educational discussion in Hessen went into hammering out a form of non-denominational school, the *Gemeinschaftsschule*. Stein hoped that this would be a better way of forging an open society committed to basic democratic principles than a divisively denominational system. For this to happen it was essential that tolerance should be guaranteed. Thus article 56 of the Hessian constitution reads: 'The basic principle of all instruction must be tolerance. The teacher must in any subject consider the religious and ideological sensitivities of all pupils and must present ideological concepts in a neutral way....' In this context, parental views must be considered; article 56 continues:

> Parents and guardians have the right to participate in decisions on the general formation of educational policy.... The law specifies this more closely. It must make provision to ensure that the religious and ideological principles according to which parents and guardians wish their children to be educated are not infringed.

These normative statements indicate that in Hessen, as elsewhere, the original commitment to parental involvement was essentially 'legitimizing'. It was a way of coping constructively with a plurality of views, not a blueprint for any radical recasting of the traditional bureaucratic control of education. In fact through the 1950s elected parent representation in Hessen remained somewhat less developed than in Hamburg, being concentrated mainly at school level. Yet the official framework began to generate more informal parent groups which by 1952 had come together to form a *Land* parent council. By the mid-fifties, encouraged by the 'parent power' clauses in the Hessian constitution, parent groups began to test those clauses in the courts. The first clarification was negative. A case attempting to establish the rights of parents to require the authorities to construct a *Realschule* in their area led in 1957 to a judicial ruling that Hessian parents were *not* responsible for *Schulwesen* or *Personalwesen* — roughly the planning and construction of schools and the hiring and firing of staff.[55] Curriculum and the reorganization of secondary education, being more obviously entangled with ideologies and beliefs, were rather different. In 1957 parents from Frankfurt and Darmstadt queried the legality of curricula promulgated by simple ministerial decree, and on Ash Wednesday, 18 February 1958, the Hessian Supreme Court ruled in terms of the constitutional article quoted above that 'general formation of educational policy' was *illegal* without some form of parental participation. This precipitated a constitutional crisis which was also political, in that a *Landtag* election was due shortly. The parent council had had their plans for a new law ready since September 1956, the government had none; and after hasty discussions the *Landtag* voted overwhelmingly for what amounted to the parents' 1956 draft bill. The whole process was an admirable example of the successful application of legal pressure.[56]

The resulting Act of 5 November 1958 is still generally regarded as the most advanced legislation in this area in the republic. It aimed at 'joint decision' (*Mitbestimmung*) rather than 'joint operation' or 'joint administration' (*Mitwirkung, Mitverwaltung*) in the style of Hamburg or Bavaria. The crucial advance in Hessen was that parents were given not only an explicit oversight of curriculum (which in other *Länder* had been traditionally seen as a professional matter) but also a veto over changes which they might not approve.

> The agreement of the parents' consultative council of a school is required (i) for the adoption of school rules and organization within the framework of the general school regulations; (ii) for the overall planning of the curriculum of the school, if it is intended to depart experimentally from the general guidelines; (iii) for any measures for which such approval is specified by law or administrative regulation. The parents' consultative council of a school must be consulted before the head teacher decides on measures which are of general significance for the life of the school.[57]

Similarly at *Land* level an elective *Landeselternbeirat* must be consulted about

> (i) general decisions about educational aims and tracks through the system (*Bildungswege*), especially in educational planning and examination regulations, in so far as they affect school curriculum . . . ;

(ii) general decisions regulating uptake into tertiary education and transfers between schools;

(iii) general guidelines on the choice of texts and other aids;

(iv) general school regulations in so far as they affect the curriculum.[58]

The purpose of these provisions was to achieve consensus between the interested parties: 'Measures requiring parental agreement must be discussed in the parents' consultative council of a school with the aim of reaching an understanding.'[59]

In the event of deadlock a dispute between parents and a head teacher was to be referred to the *Schulaufsichtsbehörde* — perhaps the nearest English equivalent would be 'the Office'. In practice it would largely be officials who tried to settle the dispute, though they would certainly be very aware of the likely political reverberations. At *Land* level disagreements had to be referred to the Minister. In the last resort the Minister could impose his views on the *Landesschulbeirat* only with the express approval of the *Land* government, and thus ultimately of parliament.

The Act also laid upon the authorities (from head teacher up to Minister) a duty to inform parents about changes envisaged. It gave to parents the right to initiate changes of their own and have them discussed and considered through the official machinery. It made provision for parent representatives to receive adequate financial support: for example, members of the *Landesschulbeirat* were to receive travel costs, an allowance for every day away from work on council business, and hotel costs where necessary. The rest of the Act laid down the composition of the councils at various levels, voting procedures, etc.

The basic reason for these considerable changes was probably to be sought in the political culture of Hessen, which seems to have been consistently more open and adventurous than either Hamburg or Bavaria. This was reflected in the combativeness and *savoir-faire* of the parent groupings, the relative quiescence of the teacher unions, and the readiness of the politicians to accept the parental blueprint as a way off the hook. However, the radicalism of the 1958 Act must not be overdrawn. Firstly, the reasons for the extension of the previous arrangements were still firmly in the 'legitimation' area: the 1958 Act was adopted not for idealistic reasons but in order to defuse an embarrassing confrontation between government and judiciary. Secondly, as in Hamburg, the ultimate rights of the *Land* parliament were retained. Thirdly, the rights allocated to parents, though unusually explicit and extensive by comparison with other *Länder*, were contained within a stringent bureaucratic framework: the 1958 legislation established new procedures and channels of formal accountability. It was not concerned to dissolve the barriers between school and community but rather to control change, novelty and experiment. In terms of Table 4, the 'legitimacy' aims were still present (though the mutual distrust between government and governed was less than in most cases so far reviewed), but the widening of lay responsibility was into the area of 'responsiveness' rather than that of 'overcoming alienation'. The new structures are designed to improve 'responsiveness', particularly in relation to 'planning of school provision' (see list of functions at end of section 1.5).

This lack of radicalism is worth pointing out because it was the misfortune of these structures to be tested and brought into public attention in connection with the reorganization of the tripartite secondary system. The structures themselves thus became associated, especially in the 1970s, with the image of 'red Hessen'. In fact for most of the time, parent participation in Hessen was no different from parent participation in other *Länder*. It was run in an orderly way by minorities of heavily committed parents (usually middle-class, often teachers or ex-teachers) who would for themselves often lay emphasis on 'personal development'. In terms of the structures of participation, Hessen was after 1958 certainly in advance of other *Länder* in attempting more by trespassing on the traditional preserves of the *Bildungsbürokratie* — but the advance was hardly as dramatic as is sometimes supposed. That must be borne in mind as we consider parent involvement in two Hessian controversies.

4.5 Parent Power and the Reorganization of Secondary Education: Hessen

Hessian politics, through the vagaries of a variety of coalitions, had been dominated by the SPD since the 1950s, and the Hessian government had been one of the earliest to experiment with modifications to the tripartite system of secondary schools. In 1955 the first Hessian *Förderstufe* was introduced as an experiment. This was a two-year cycle of studies for the first stages of secondary education. Its most obvious effect was to delay for two years the secondary selection process: this occurred, in Hessen as in most German *Länder*, at the age of 10 after only four years of primary schooling. The basic curricular organization was round a common core (German, social studies and science) taught in mixed-ability groups. English and mathematics were to be taught in sets

(A, B and C). At the end of two years pupils would either move on to a comprehensive school (of which there were even by the mid-1960s almost none, even in Hessen), or receive a report specifying their suitability for the *Gymnasium*, the *Realschule* or the *Hauptschule*. Parents who dissented from their allocation would have the same rights to negotiate as they would have had under Hessian law two years before. By 1964–5 twenty-seven areas in Hessen were experimenting with the *Förderstufe*.[60]

So long as the *Förderstufe* remained experimental, so that parents could still opt for the tripartite system, it seemed generally acceptable, and the 1958 arrangements requiring parental approval for such changes proved to be a useful device for legitimizing change and spreading knowledge about it through the community. In 1969, however, a new left-inclined SPD administration, consciously seeing itself as a local spearhead of more general change, presented to the Hessian *Landtag* a new School Administration Bill which in due course passed into legislation. It provided for a gradual spread of the *Förderstufe* as the norm, and required parents to send their children to the *Förderstufe* in whose zone they lived. It would thus no longer be possible for parents to send their child across catchment zone boundaries to a traditional school which they preferred. By 1971–2, 39 per cent of all children in the relevant age-group were in *Förderstufen*; 136 schools had voluntarily inaugurated this mode of organization and in forty-seven schools it was compulsory for all students within the catchment zone.[61] It was at this stage that the official machinery of parent representation began to move into opposition.

Many of the parent representatives most closely involved in the decision to take the matter to the courts did so with reluctance, both because they valued the relationships built up under the 1958 Act over a decade, and because many found the basic ideas of the *Förderstufe* sensible and attractive. The crucial point, however, was compulsion which in the West German context was seen as an infringement of parental rights under the Basic Law. The case was brought by a group of parents from Hanau and district, and the chairman of the *Landeselternbeirat* played a central role. The issue was sufficiently important to be referred from the Hessian Supreme Court to the Federal Constitutional Court in Karlsruhe. The judgment delivered by the latter on 6 December 1972 stated that the *Förderstufe* was not as such unconstitutional — i.e., *Länder* had a right to change the structure of schooling if they thought fit. However, parents must be informed and consulted about changes affecting their children. Parental responsibility could not be restricted to one part of a child's life only, with another part reserved to professionals: 'The common educational task of parents and school, which has as its aim the formation of the single personality of the child, cannot be split into individual competencies. It must be fulfilled in joint activity which must be coherently co-ordinated.' In so far as the *Förderstufe* was a transitional form, the judgment continued, some degree of parental apprehension was understandable.

> It is the responsibility of the educational administrators to convince parents of the advantages of the *Förderstufe* as opposed to the traditional system and in this way to bring them to entrust their children to the *Förderstufe*. In a free state educational reforms which arouse controversy should not be carried through by compulsion but rather, introduced as far as possible, with the free co-operation of those concerned.... [62]

Hessen had infringed parental rights by requiring attendance at the *Förderstufe* while alternative provision was available elsewhere. Strict zoning could not therefore be legally enforced until the *Förderstufe* had been established in all parts of the *Land*.

In assessing the judgment it must be remembered that in the early seventies Hessen was very much in the forefront of the comprehensive movement in West Germany. This judicial reaffirmation of parents' rights, permitting the creaming off of many children into the selective system, was thus to have a considerable retarding effect on the not very vigorous moves in the rest of the republic towards the *Gesamtschule*. [63] From the narrower point of view of the parents' movement, the *Förderstufe* case drew attention to its potential political impact. Over a quarter of a century, and as a result of a variety of impulses, the *Länder* had constructed various forms of parental consultation; to some extent these were now to be manipulated by politicians.

4.6 Parent Participation in the Early Seventies: A West German Overview

The *Förderstufe* judgment was delivered in 1972. By then all the *Länder* possessed legally required systems of parent participation. [64] As the three examples already described demonstrate, these systems varied considerably in history, scope and details, but the necessity for some such arrangements was universally acknowledged. By the early seventies there was a stream of general pronouncements from federal coordinating bodies like the *Bildungsrat*, from political parties, churches and similar bodies, earnestly advocating a prudent extension of

131

democratic rights over schools to lay persons.[65] Parent involvement was seen as a necessary part of citizenship in a democracy. Its rationale was invariably drawn from the clauses in the federal Basic Law which have already been quoted. As in Hamburg, the student disturbances of 1967–8 (which often involved older secondary school pupils as well as university students) led in many instances to a revision or extension of parent rights — so that it sometimes seemed that parent participation was favoured because it was likely to block the wilder excesses of student participation.

In spite of sporadic complaints about the unrepresentative character of parent representatives and their narrow recruitment from the intelligentsia and bourgeoisie, parent participation was very much part of the machinery of West German education by the early 1970s. The fact that parents had 'arrived' was publicly demonstrated in 1972 when the Federal Ministry of Education and Science allocated its first annual subsidy to the Federal Parent Council. This had grown since the mid-1950s as a central grouping of *Land* parent councils and associations, and operated mainly through congresses and a monthly information sheet.[66]

Even more significant was the energy which many *Länder* now devoted to informing and influencing parent opinion. The *Länder* were big enough and rich enough to mount sophisticated information programmes on issues they believed important. The late sixties and early seventies saw local administrations funding leaflets, booklets, and even regular magazines for parents. These were attractively produced, often using advertising techniques. Hessen for example, produced a series of booklets on different aspects of the system, explaining innovations or existing curricula. Another series gave advice to parents on common educational problems such as spelling, drugs, left-handedness, etc. A pamphlet, illustrated with coloured cartoons, explained the participatory system to parents. It reproduced substantial extracts from the constitution and the relevant Acts of Parliament, and explained how parents were involved in working out new curricula.[67] In Hamburg, ministry officials with special responsibility for parent affairs helped to edit the *Hamburger Elternblatt*, an attractive monthly. In 1973 the Bavarian Ministry founded its own popular journal, *Schule und wir* (subsequently rechristened *Schulreport*): this appeared every two months and was distributed free to all parents through the schools.

These efforts to communicate regularly and effectively with parents were commendable and must in the long run raise the information level of the public at large about the complexities of educational policy. Nonetheless, it is obvious that administrations subsidize information which is on the whole supportive of their viewpoint. For example, the

Hamburger Elternblatt was published by the SPD-oriented GEW teachers' union, and was in a sense a by-product of the SPD establishment which runs Hamburg. *Schulreport* actively promoted the views of Hans Maier, the Minister who founded it.[68] By regularly describing the various experiments funded by the Bavarian Ministry, it consolidated the impression that Bavaria was in the forefront of educational progress and lent credibility to claims that, for example, the comprehensive experiment had proved to be a failure. Protests from the Left or from outside Bavaria were easily dismissed as extremist, politically biassed or unscientific; the shriller they were, the more the Ministry's position was reinforced. *Schulreport* was thus part of a complex network of information channels used by the Bavarian Ministry to shape public opinion on educational matters. The elegance of the system was that it did not depend on total CSU control for all information. In that sense the various official publications directed at parents were part of a wider scene to which parent associations and the formal machinery of parent participation also contributed.

The need to influence parent opinion was more acutely felt in the 1970s because for the first time in the history of the Federal Republic alternative views on education policy were widely canvassed and discussed. The *Förderstufe* judgment was the first skirmish in a long-drawn-out war over comprehensive reorganization. Because of the federal division of powers, which reserved education to *Land* governments, the 1969 SDP/FDP coalition in Bonn could only cajole and persuade — largely by providing federal money for comprehensive 'experiments'. In the face of that pressure, conservative-ruled *Länder* needed to persuade their electorates that the SPD proposals were subversive of traditional values, while SDP states needed equally to argue the inevitability and desirability of change. In this process of opinion formation parents and their councils and organizations had a central part to play.

Parents everywhere are naturally suspicious of plans to alter the education which they themselves experienced a generation before and which their own children are now receiving. West German parents had other reasons for caution. A majority of secondary school children were in selective schools — the *Gymnasium* or *Realschule* rather than the less prestigious and less well-resourced *Hauptschule*. Thus a majority of the more articulate parents had a vested interest in the *status quo*. In addition, the *Gesamtschule*, which was usually designed as a whole-day school, required a greater change in middle-class parental attitudes than in France or the United Kingdom where whole-day schooling is the norm. Parents who were used to having their children at home in the afternoons doing extensive homework often saw the comprehensive school as taking over a traditional part of their parental responsibility and as reducing desirable pressures on pupils to achieve. A booklet summarizing the advantages of the comprehensive school felt obliged to address the question: 'Does whole-day school destroy family life?'[69]

It is against this background of multiple resistance to change that we must place the structures of formal parent participation. By the early seventies the 'parental responsibility' clauses of the *Grundgesetz*, and the network of consultative committees in the *Länder*, had gradually built up a certain consciousness of a separate 'parent interest'. This made it natural for those seeking or resisting change to address themselves to parents — and to expect that many parents would be supportive of the existing system rather than proponents of change. And as the whole apparatus of parent consultation was seen as 'non-political', the parent interest had obvious potential in terms of an alliance with teacher associations anxious to promote a purely professional and equally 'non-political' line in defence of tripartism.

The *Förderstufe* case which had marked the first real set-back to the move away from differentiation had been fought responsibly, indeed rather reluctantly, by more or less official groups of elected parents operating an official system of committees and councils and presenting their case ultimately through the legal machinery. As the 1970s advanced, and educational controversy sharpened, the initiative slipped to some extent from official parent representatives of a mildly progressive frame of mind towards unofficial parent groups highly resistant to change. The high points of that shift, and of the failure of the official machinery to defuse controversy and extend consensus, were in Hessen in 1973–4 and North Rhine-Westphalia in 1978–9.

4.7   Two Styles of Parent Power in Conflict: Hessen

The Hessian *Förderstufe* case had highlighted the attempt to unify the curriculum in the first two years of secondary education, thus delaying irrevocable choices between the three parts of the tripartite system. Behind such partial measures lay the pressure, growing stronger in the Hessian SPD as the sixties progressed, to install the *Gesamtschule*, or comprehensive school — at first as an experiment, and later as the normal school for all children. Because the tripartite form of organization with its separate syllabuses for each type of school was written into the law, changes could legally take place only by official approval for specific experiments, or by altering the law. By the mid-sixties Hessian politicians and civil servants decided that it was time to revise curricula. There were at least three main motivations for the process of curriculum change initiated through the Wiesbaden Ministry in 1967. One was to reduce curriculum differentiation. The new curriculum was to be unitary. At secondary level the same guidelines would apply to *Gymnasium*, *Realschule* and *Hauptschule*; they would also cover the *Gesamtschule* as it became a reality, and would thus facilitate change. Another reason for curriculum change, particularly appealing to some SPD politicians, was the wish to implement through the schools a more explicitly libertarian and democratic approach to society. Schools were to promote a questioning critical stance in their pupils: they were no longer to be mere purveyors of inert knowledge. This linked up with a third strand of thinking, particularly strong among the planners in the Ministry: the wish to translate into German terms the American aims and objectives approach to curriculum planning, as urged by Professor Saul Robinsohn and others.

The immediate motivations for change did not include any particular pressure from parents, though it might be said that the 'establishment' of parent representatives (for example, in the *Landeselternbeirat*) was generally benevolent towards change and pleased to see Hessen take on a 'vanguard' position in educational innovation within the Federal Republic.

Discussion of these complex curriculum changes turned out to be protracted and difficult. It was further complicated by a cabinet reshuffle in late 1969 which brought a more directive and abrasive personality to the Ministry in Wiesbaden, Ludwig Friedeburg, who saw himself, and was seen by others, as the promoter of the ideas of 1968.[70] At last in the autumn of 1972 the new curriculum guidelines were published. Almost immediately they became the centre of a furious public controversy. The Hessian government was accused of using the schools to subvert the young to adopt a Marxist, even revolutionary ideology. Particular obloquy was heaped on the guidelines for German and social studies: German because of a supposed devaluation of traditional standards of speech and writing; social studies because geography and history were integrated and because the new guidelines inevitably touched on sensitive questions of value. The controversy was widely publicized in the press and in televised debates. Passions ran so high that some of these public forums were disorderly, even violent. The debate rapidly spread far beyond the borders of Hessen, which became the hapless focus of a nation-wide debate on the values underlying the comprehensive change.

The most furious phase of the controversy was sparked off by a

CDU pamphlet (*Marx Statt Rechtschreibung* — 'Marx more important than spelling') of January 1973. The CDU, which had its own reasons (notably the *Landtag* election due in 1974) for wishing to launch an anti-Marxist crusade, addressed its case largely to parents. The role of parents in the whole affair has not been much commented on, but was obviously crucial. We have seen that Hessen had set up the most advanced structures of formal parent participation in the Federal Republic. It was legally necessary for curriculum changes to be approved by the elected parents' committee at *Land* level. Parent representatives were involved in the working parties from 1967 to 1970, and the publication of the new Guidelines was agreed by the *Landesel-ternbeirat* in 1972, before the controversy exploded. As the public debate focused considerable disquiet among ordinary people about the proposed changes, the formal structures of parent participation could thus be said to be ineffective and unrepresentative and to have been assimilated into the Hessian 'establishment'. This view was argued by the *Hessischer Elternverein* (Hessian Parents' Association), an unofficial grouping with strong links with the CDU.

The reality is more complicated. What the formal participatory structures had achieved in Hessen since the mid-fifties was a general-ized expectation that parent opinion counted. Much of the day-to-day consultation was unpublicized and undramatic; but an awareness that it happened gradually percolated through to the population at large. It was reinforced by the widely publicized *Förderstufe* case in which judgment was delivered in December 1972, two months after the publication of the guidelines and a month before the CDU launched its pamphlet. For at least fifteen years the Hessian electorate had become used to seeing parents formally associated with schools and questioning teachers and administrators. Thus the failure of the formal structures to contain the 1973 controversy is a failure only if one sees the main aims of those structures as the consolidation of central government control, in this case from Wiesbaden. If, however, the aim is also or primarily to encourage public interest in and discussion of education, then the long-term slow impact of the formal system may be judged more positively. Much of the debate in 1973–4 turned upon the legitimacy of the central administration's actions, the extent to which proper con-sultative procedures had been followed, etc. That parental opinion was clearly used by political parties, and that this particular debate was confused and in some ways destructive was unfortunate. It remains nonetheless true that fundamental issues of value as they affect schools were aired and for a time engaged the attention of large numbers of people. Indeed, for a brief period it was almost as though the barriers between the 'administered school' and a passive and indifferent society broke down, and traditional alienation had dissolved. The paradox was that this happened in a reactionary rather than a progressive direction.

The parties drew the obvious lessons from the Hessian imbroglio. In Hessen itself education loomed large in the elections of October 1974.[71] The CDU became the largest party in the *Landtag* and the position of the FDP in the governing coalition was thus strengthened. Minister von Friedeburg duly disappeared from the political scene. Changes were made in the guidelines for German and social studies. A decent smokescreen to cover this tactical retreat was provided by stressing the importance of proper consultation of all shades of public opinion.

To politicians in other *Länder* and in Bonn, the Hessian affair was a vivid reminder of the explosiveness of the comprehensive school issue. For the CSU in Bavaria, for example, 'red Hessen' could be presented as an instance of political extremism riding rough-shod over parental commonsense and professional advice.[72] This was contrasted with the sober Bavarian style: a sprinkling of 'experimental' comprehensives, as called for by Bonn, which were duly weighed in the balance and found wanting.[73] Minister Hans Maier was then able to turn to groups like the LEV, who had a vested interest in the maintenance of selection, and reassure them that their gut feelings were 'scientifically' attested.

The controversy over the Hessian guidelines was a public recognition that the debate between meritocracy and egalitarianism had focused decisively on the schools. In terms of the structures of parent participation which had been developing undramatically for a quarter of a century, it marked a change in their significance. Although it was largely due to the formal committees and councils that the parent interest had a certain weight in the public consciousness, when the knives were out the argument moved very rapidly beyond the official structures into parliament and the media. At that point 'official' parents were hamstrung by their ambiguous loyalty to the system as a whole, which in a way they still legitimated, and the initiative moved inevitably to *unofficial* parent groups. Events in North Rhine-Westphalia in 1978–9 were to show how well this lesson had been learned.

4.8 Parents as a Conservative Force: North Rhine-Westphalia

Formal parent participation in North Rhine-Westphalia (NRW), established in an Act of 1952, was not as well-developed as in Hamburg or

Hessen. It was restricted mainly to the level of individual schools. As in Bavaria this had the effect of producing separate associations or confederations for each of the types of school: by 1971 this included a small association of *Gesamtschule* parents strongly critical of their longer-established *Gymnasium* counterparts.[74] A single *Land* consultative council achieved legal status only in the Act of 13 December 1977.[75] Even then this central consultative council was not the summit of an electoral pyramid, as in Hessen, but an assembly of representatives from parent associations, teacher unions, trade union councils, employers' associations, churches, etc. The NRW government (a coalition of SPD and FDP) had begun the seventies by presenting a draft Bill on *Mitwirkung*, to rationalize and update the 1952 Act in the spirit of the late sixties.[76] The basic system adopted was bipartite: equal representation of professionals on the one hand and parents and pupils on the other. The CDU's alternative bill was based on the tripartite principle: teachers would be in a minority — but their proposals did not otherwise differ in principle from the government's: both relied heavily on *consensus* being aimed at and achieved, spoke only of the *advisory* status of the committees, and confined the main weight of representation to the individual school. Yet by the summer of 1976 the CDU was arguing for a system by which parents would have a *veto* over important decisions at school level, to be overcome only by a two-thirds majority of the *Schulkonferenz*, or governing body.[77] Between 1970 and 1976, for the CDU at least, parents had come to be seen as a bulwark against extremism, a way of making change more difficult. The CDU's rhetoric stressed democratic participation and parental rights. Against this rhetoric the ruling SPD/FDP coalition argued the more traditional view that the *Landtag's* responsibility was primary, and that the school-based committees it was proposing were less for decision-making than for improved communication between parents, teachers and administrators — or to put it in the CDU's words, parents were to be reduced to 'voluntary assistants of the school administration'.[78] This meant that the NRW government maintained a traditional 'legitimacy' position on parent participation, while the opposition had shifted towards a restrictive version of 'responsiveness' — restrictive because the 'functional areas of responsibility', the 'advice on decisions at various levels' (Table 4) were to be defined in such a way as to block change. This shift was made easier by the fact that the formal system of parent representation in NRW was effectively confined to the individual school, so that it became quite difficult to define the parent interest in other than defensive terms.

The background to this debate about parent participation was the ever more strident argument about the comprehensive school. An SPD/FDP coalition had taken over the NRW government in 1966. In common with several other *Länder* at this time it had rapidly come to an arrangement with the churches whereby confessional schools were replaced by state schools with guaranteed provision for the teaching of religion (*Gemeinschaftsschulen*). It had also separated the *Volksschulen*, or elementary schools, into a separate four-year primary sector (*Grundschule*) and a secondary *Hauptschule*.[79] This was seen as the decisive break with a vertical system. The *Grundschule* would be the first stage of a new common horizontally organized (*stufenbezogen*) system. It was thus logical at the same time to test out the *integrierte Gesamtschule*, i.e., the more radical model of comprehensive school in which the traditional separate tracks were replaced by some mixed-ability grouping and a reduction of curriculum differentiation, especially in the younger age-groups. Seven of these schools were founded in 1969; thirty were projected and were achieved by 1978. All these were new institutions, so that the disturbance to existing interests was minimal. They also remained experimental and exceptional, so that no parent was obliged to send his or her child to the *Gesamtschule*.[80] It was, as Minister Jürgen Girgensohn claimed in 1977, a middle path between Hessen and Bavaria: 'a middle line between innovation by Act of Parliament on the one hand and the setting up of isolated experiments .. on the other.'[81]

The impetus of the energetic reform programme of the late sixties became increasingly difficult for the SPD/FPD coalition to sustain as the seventies advanced. The reforms of 1966–9 had been more or less consensual, and were widely seen as essential steps to modernization. The *integrierte Gesamtschule* was more divisive. As the arguments in Hessen were debated and absorbed, differences of emphasis appeared in the NRW coalition, with the FDP markedly less enthusiastic about comprehensive reform than the SPD majority partner. As the SPD was in an overall minority in the *Landtag*, its coalition partner's views had to be given serious consideration. Yet the SPD itself was by no means uniformly convinced of the virtues of the *integrierte Gesamtschule*. There was an obvious division of opinion between those who wished to proceed to a decisive remodelling of secondary education in NRW (such views were particularly strong in the teachers' union GEW and in urban areas[82]), and those who favoured a more gradualistic approach. Such people felt that the *integrierte Gesamtschule* should remain experimental and exceptional until it had proved its worth, and that various intermediate forms of comprehensive should also be tried out — notably the local version of the *additive Gesamtschule* (multilateral): the grouping of different types of schools on one site (*Schulzentren*).[83] The Minister of Education, Jürgen Girgensohn, had the unenviable task of defending the middle way against attacks from both Left and Right,[84] for the state of his own party, of the coalition and, in the wake of the Hessian controversy, of public opinion, all made it necessary to advance with great caution.

Meanwhile the CDU opposition had grown increasingly frustrated at its failure to topple the ruling coalition in spite of achieving a slight majority in votes over the SPD in 1970 — a majority which was increased in the *Landtag* elections of May 1975. In 1971 the CDU had advanced plans for a diluted form of comprehensive school to be known as the *Kooperative Schule*: three separate tracks would be maintained, but the curriculum would be substantially common in the first two years (10–12 — the *Orientierungsstufe*[85]), and there would be possibilities thereafter for the joint teaching of music, physical educaiton, etc. and for some sharing of staff and facilities. The CDU policy programme included the '*Koop Schule*' from 1971 till 1975.

By 1975 the political climate was quite different from what it had been four years previously. This was not just a matter of a shift of opinion, though clearly the Hessian confrontation had played its part. It was also a case of objective constraints on *Land* policy which had not existed in the early seventies. The 1973 oil crisis had, to some extent actually and certainly psychologically, brought to an end a period of apparently unlimited expansion. Cuts in public expenditure were universal, and the SPD was caught uneasily between its wish to extend and improve welfare facilities, including education, and its desire not to appear before the electorate as the party of profligate spending and high taxes. At the same time the NRW government was with increasing urgency having to plan for a declining school population. It was estimated that by the late eighties the number of pupils in school would be reduced by a third.[86]

All this helps to explain why when in May 1975 the SPD and FDP agreed on a 'coalition pact' for the coming legislature, they concurred on the least radical possibility on offer: the *Koop Schule*, which had already formed part of the electoral programme of the CDU opposition. The *Koop Schule* was not to be universally introduced, but simply to be on offer in areas (which would be mainly rural) where the three types of school could co-exist on one campus. This was, in other words, to be the *Schulzentrum*, which already existed in some districts, but placed on a regular footing through being legally recognized and regulated. There would be a common two-year *Orientierungsstufe*, but parents' rights to the choice of the *Gymnasium*, *Realschule* or *Hauptschule* track thereafter were absolutely guaranteed. The *Koop Schule* would be erected only after obtaining the consent of the local community. This was the minimal structural reform on which agreement could be expected. As Minister Girgensohn put it in an interview of 1977:

> The *Koop Schule* is anything but a 'revolutionary' change of our education system. For many communes it means a school which guarantees a full range of curriculum offerings in spite of falling rolls.... People should see the *Koop Schule* for what it is: a development of the traditional forms of school which corresponds to the needs of our time.[87]

If the SPD and FDP had imagined that stealing the CDU's clothes would have the effect of producing consensus in education they were badly mistaken. In fact the CDU began to move away from the middle ground. It needed a simple issue round which opinion could be polarized and which would show up the governing coalition as doctrinaire and incompetent. The *Koop Schule* turned out to be exactly what it wanted.

A critical factor in helping the CDU to select the *Koop Schule* as a campaign issue was the uncertainty with which the NRW government prepared and presented its legislation in 1976 and 1977.[88] It soon became apparent that nobody felt any great enthusiasm for the *Koop Schule*. On the left of the SPD, among supporters of the *integrierte Gesamtschule* and in the teachers' union most closely allied to the SPD (the GEW),[89] there was considerable dismay that the government was promoting a CDU policy. In such quarters the *Koop Schule* could have been sold only as a half-way house towards the *integrierte Gesamtschule*; yet to say that openly would have been unacceptable to the FDP whose support was crucial.[90] Thus the *Koop Schule* had to be sold as a pragmatic response to complex administrative problems, notably falling rolls. These arguments were worthy but difficult to follow and uninspiring; in the face of a sharp attack from the Right attempting to equate the *Koop Schule* with the *integrierte Gesamtschule* and with centralized and authoritarian rule from the Left, the government's arguments were further obscured by a welter of riders and disclaimers underlining the complex conditions to be met before such schools could be established, the guarantees for parental rights, etc. The more elaborately the government defended its proposals, the stronger grew the impression among a public with unclear ideas of what the new schools would be like that there was no smoke without fire, and that something underhand was being prepared.

The argument was initially pursued through the *Landtag* in

Düsseldorf. In the summer and autumn of 1977, however, the CDU, encouraged by local election successes earlier in the year, began to grasp the potential for extraparliamentary agitation. The mechanism for this was a provision in the NRW constitution allowing for a 'people's petition' (*Volksbegehren*). If a fifth of the electorate signed a petition against legislation, the offending law had to be referred back to the *Landtag* for reconsideration. If the parliament then persisted, the law had to be submitted to a referendum (*Volksentscheid*) at which a simple majority of the electorate would resolve the issue. The CDU decided in the summer of 1977 to mount a people's petition against the *Koop Schule*.[91]

It was in this campaign from October 1977 to March 1978 that the role of parental opinion as a conservative force was most clearly seen. In the argument hitherto, parents had received little real attention. The important decisions were made by politicians. However, it was now important for the CDU to present its anti-*Koop Schule* campaigns as in some sense 'non-political'. The initial launching of the campaign in July 1977 was the work of twelve associations, including parents' groups.[92] The network of the *Gymnasium* teachers, the *Philologenverband*, was particularly important with its offices and paid officials and its access to colleagues in other *Länder*. An agreement was reached in October 1977 that while the CDU would concentrate on the 'political' side — debates in the *Landtag* and the more virulent sort of polemic — a more consensual aspect should be given to the main part of the campaign. The campaign office was located in the premises of the *Philologenverband* in Düsseldorf.[93] It immediately began to collect support and money not only from NRW (including local employers[94]) but also through the *Philogenverband* network in other *Länder* as well. Clearly parental support was also vital, and because of the school-based character of parent participation in NRW, it lay readily to hand in the *Gymnasium* parents' association whose members could rapidly be mobilized in defence of the form of school attended by their own children. As in Hessen, there was also a smaller *Elternverein* of strongly conservative character which was in practice a ginger-group of the CDU though it claimed to be independent.

The people's petition campaign was conducted with vigour by the CDU, the *Philologenverband*, the *Gymnasium* parents' association and the *Elternverein*. As in Hessen in 1973–4, the press and television were heavily involved. A booklet issued by the *Philologenverband*[95] played a similar role to the CDU pamphlet in Hessen in setting the parameters of debate and provoked some considered responses.[96] Nonetheless, the general impression is of a debate less well focused on educational matters than in Hessen. This was partly because of the subject of the debate (the general structure of a minority of schools which did not yet exist) was less concrete than the universal curriculum change debated in Hessen, partly because it was vital for the initiators of the debate to push the argument to wider and more emotive issues than the modest tinkerings of the *Koop Schule*.

Perhaps the most vivid way of characterizing the campaign is to quote some of the posters used which evoke some of the central themes:

Our children are not guinea-pigs!

In a broadly planned manoeuvre the left coalition of SPD and FDP is creating a new education mess. In a roundabout way and piecemeal it intends to introduce the *Einheitsschule*. A first step is the *Koop Schule*. At the end of the road looms the pupil-processing plant . . . .

Our children must not become guinea-pigs for socialist experiments. Tomorrow as well as today parents must still be allowed to love their children. We will not hand them over to be moulded by alien forces.[97]

The case is even more schematic in a poster issued by a Mülheim parents' group:

Do you want there to be only one party? Then you won't need to vote (*wählen*) any more! Do you want there to be only one sort of school — and soon?
Then you won't be able to choose (*wählen*) any more![98]

Contrast these simple emotive appeals with the contorted argument of a poster on the other side:

Koop Schule: no cause for excitement

There is no reason to welcome the Act setting up the *Koop Schule* as a decisive advance in educational policy. The decisive advance in educational policy would be the introduction of the *Gesamtschule* as the norm in NRW. Equally there is no reason to conduct a campaign against the setting up of the *Koop Schule*: the characteristics of that campaign are bitterness, contradictory arguments and educational ideas left over from the day before yesterday. . . .[99]

Thus a campaign which was marked on the one side by emotive slogans which might have been used in the early fifties was met on the other by confusion, embarrassment and silence.[100] In fact the GEW and the *Gesamtschule* parents' association eventually refused to take part in the government's efforts to put over its own point of view,[101] and the initiative remained decisively with the opposition. In due course the booths were opened for citizens to register their signatures against the *Koop Schule* and long queues formed in the cold of February and early March. The result was a disaster for the government: 2.4 million signatures (20 per cent of electorate) were needed if the *Koop Schule* Act was to be referred back to the *Landtag*; in fact 3.6 million (29.9 per cent) were recorded. The main weight of support came from the rural areas which were in theory those which the *Koop Schule* was most likely to benefit.[102] There was also some evidence in the voting figures to suggest that church influence (especially Catholic) had had some impact on the voting.[103] On 13 April the Government, putting a brave face on its defeat — it was not after all a central part of SPD/FDP education policy, said Jürgen Girgensohn[104] — withdrew its legislation.

To the well-intentioned reformers of the SPD in NRW and elsewhere, the people's petition was a salutary reminder that education, dealing as it must with questions of value, can evoke great passion among ordinary people.[105] That passion can be manipulated by politicians all the more easily where parents are ill-informed. The cynicism of the CDU in NRW was demonstrated by its onslaught on the *Orientierungsstufe* as the thin end of the red wedge while the governing CDU just over the *Land* border in Lower Saxony was busy promoting it as a consensual reform.[106] Cynicism cannot be countered by merely technical arguments about falling rolls, still less by deliberately evading the question whether the *Koop Schule* was simply a stage on the way to the fullblooded *integrierte Gesamtschule*. A more open and honest fight from the government side might have produced a result which would have been more satisfactory to it. For that to have happened, the government would have needed to address itself more directly — as the opposition did — to the parent interest. It had failed to recognize that by the late seventies parents had become aware of themselves as a distinct group. Ten years earlier, when political differences seemed less acute, it had made little attempt to incorporate parents into the machinery of school government, so that when the storm broke it could not even turn towards the official committees and claim some legitimacy from them, as the Hessian curriculum planners did, or the Bavarian Ministry when it rejected the comprehensive school. Its conversion to a more effective information policy came only in early 1977, when it decided to publish a popular magazine for the parents of all children in NRW schools.[107] By then the initiative had passed decisively to the *unofficial* parent movement.[108] 'Parents' rights' had been defined as concerned with preserving the *status quo* and vetoing change. So ineffective had the official parents' committees been in even spreading information that the monthly journal of the NRW branch of the teachers' union GEW could complain in January 1981 that 'among parents the *Gesamtschule* is substantially unknown',[109] and in the autumn of 1981 the GEW launched a new popular magazine for parents (*Klasse*), thus confirming that the struggle for the school and its future had moved beyond formal participatory structures into the general political and pressure-group arena. All this meant that any evolution of the *official* machinery from its primary 'legitimation' function towards more open, community-oriented 'overcoming alienation' concepts of parent participation would be doubly difficult, as any change would now be fought by *unofficial* groups of parents and/or teachers.

4.9 Balance-Sheet

Drawing up a 'balance-sheet' for a country containing eleven distinct education systems is obviously more complicated than for countries where national legislation at least determines the broad framework within which parent participation evolves. In some ways the West German equivalent to such legislation was the parent rights clauses of the federal Basic Law; yet as we have seen even that was preceded by legislation in several states, was couched in extremely general terms and began to make a real local impact through court decisions only in the late fifties. In effect the Federal Republic constitutes a mini-comparison within itself. To make sense of its variegated development, we have to compare the four *Länder* described, then attempt some generalization about West Germany, and then compare that with other nations.

The first obvious difference between West Germany and the French and Italian examples already described is that German parent participation has a much longer history. While the first stirrings of parent interest in schools can be observed in France and Italy in the first years of the twentieth century, in neither case did parents achieve the broad base and legislative backing observed in Hamburg (and incidentally in Prussia and elsewhere). Even if we consider, as is argued in section 4.2, that the Nazi period was a decisive break, the importance of the immediate post-war period in the establishment and consolidation of new systems of parent participations means that Germany preceded France and Italy by roughly a quarter of a century.

Yet in spite of the great difference in historical circumstances, the aim of 'legitimation' seems to have been as critical in West Germany as elsewhere. In desperate situations, parent participation was an achievable means of rooting the fragile institutions of the new German society in the affections of the people. Some idealism went into that process, but it was the idealism of a minority of leaders, formers of opinion and drafters of constitutions rather than a spontaneous upsurge of tradition or of the people. Indeed, in one case (Bavaria), participation was installed to legitimize the new state to the American forces rather than to the people themselves. Thus the structures which had emerged in most *Länder* by the early 1950s resembled each other in their preoccupation with the *legitimation* of the traditional state machinery. Even the rhetoric of 'overcoming alienation' was absent from Adenauer's resolutely anti-communist state. The concern of administrators and politicians alike was to support the bureaucracy which was now subordinate to parliaments and had thus acquired a new democratic air; there was no practical interest even in the piecemeal devolution of decisions over finance or the curriculum which a shift towards 'responsiveness' would have necessitated.

Thus in all four *Länder* studied, the sole effective function attempted in the systems which emerged after the end of the war was the sixth: the improvement of school-community relations. In some *Länder* (Bavaria, NRW, Hessen) legally recognized parent participation was for a considerable time restricted to the school level only. Even in *Länder* with more developed systems such as Hamburg the potential of councils at class or *Land* level was not realized for some time. The reasons for this may be ascribed partly to the countervailing power of teachers; but the most important pressure for inertia was surely the spirit of the age, a deep-seated deference to experts (politicians, administrators, teachers) and a failure to value lay opinion other than expressed through periodic elections in which a variety of issues was aggregated through political parties. Paradoxically, the achievement of democracy strengthened the bureaucracy by making their powers derive from an elected body.

When change came, it came because the consensus began to crack. The changes in parent representation achieved in Hessen in 1958 were atypical, earlier than elsewhere, and more radical, because of a chance combination of circumstances; but they were typical in that the motivation for them sprang from a minority of parents who questioned the prevailing orthodoxy. The Hessian *Förderstufe* case was an early sign of growing dissent in the field of educational policy. As that dissent grew through the sixties and seemed to link up somehow with the student unrest of 1967–8, *Land* governments increasingly grasped the potential of parent participation as a means for containing and manipulating public opinion. The style of development was generally more considered and thoughtful than the clumsy conversions to participation observed in France and Italy; yet the basic motivation was quite similar.

Round about 1970 one begins to see some extension of the functions of parent participation, at least to the extent that in some *Länder* differences of opinion on education are acknowledged and compromises are sought. Although the crucial function of resourcing (function (iv)) remained everywhere reserved to traditional bureaucratic procedures, a *Land* such as Hamburg was beginning to involve class councils in considering function (i) (progress of individual pupils) and in Hessen primary school class council reports could be taken into account in deciding on secondary transfer.[110] In a similar spirit of cautious evolution school councils in Hamburg were to be concerned, in however remote and bureaucratic a style, in the selection of head teachers, though not of staff (function (iii)). Planning decisions (function (v)) necessitated some legitimation by councils at the levels of school, locality (*Kreis*) or 'political centre' (i.e., *Land*) — as, for example, in the dissemination of the *Förderstufe* throughout Hessen. Function (ii) (curriculum and internal organizations of the school) was still formally reserved to the political centre (the *Kultusminister* and ultimately the *Land* parliament) but in Hessen at least parents were beginning to be involved in curriculum change, albeit in a formal and marginal way. In terms of Table 4, a system based almost entirely on 'legitimacy' was beginning to edge gingerly and at different speeds towards 'responsiveness'.

The next stage was not, however, to be a gradual piecemeal evolution of formally recognized parent representatives towards a more satisfying and liberal interpretation of their role. Differences of opinion on important questions of value were too sharp for that. The mechanisms of parental involvement in the management of schools were in a sense the expression of an age in which consensus was fundamental, and dissent operated within a fairly restricted area. When, as with the comprehensive school issue, that area widened, the formal legitimizing systems established in the 1940s and prudently modified in the 1960s suddenly appeared outdated. The initiative slipped from more or less apolitical committees to unofficial parent groupings claiming to be apolitical but in fact used and sometimes created by political parties. By the time of the NRW people's petition, these new groups were veering towards 'overcoming alienation' ('emphasis on mass meetings and similar collective events to underpin formal representation; contribution of broader groupings (including political) encouraged at all levels; stress on community accountability . . .'). What was still unclear by the early 1980s was whether these ideas would ultimately be translated into durable forms of parent representation attempting to *subordinate* schools to community and family pressures, or whether the existing structures could evolve to achieve a more even *balance* in the management of schools between community and administration. Presumably this latter form of evolution would require Germans to adopt a more relaxed view towards differences between schools and particularly towards local variations in curriculum.[111] Functions (ii), (iii) and (iv) (curriculum, personnel and resourcing) will be the ones to watch as indicators of a more pragmatic trend, while the radical right seems likely to concentrate on functions (ii), (iii) and (v) (curriculum, personnel and planning) to ensure central political control of any change.

The critical difference between parent participation in West Germany on the one hand and the systems of France and Italy on the other lies in the nature of the political consensus. The West German systems erected in the aftermath of war were in a sense based on an assumption of dissensus: it was supposed that there would be considerable resentment of what was after all an imposed democracy, and an accompanying nostalgia for Nazism. In reality the regime was so discredited, the destruction so traumatic and the threat from the east so apparent that West German opinion seemed to consolidate with amazing rapidity and completeness in basic support of the Federal Republic. Thus the parent committees and councils were able to evolve in an atmosphere very distinct from that obtaining in France and Italy, where a stylized confrontation between Left and Right was built into the traditions and structures of those two states. It was much easier in Germany to see parents as 'unpolitical', and indeed the various types of parent committee were simply part of a widely accepted definition of education itself as being outside politics; these were the 'two decades of non-reform'.[112]

Although here and there there were signs of evolution towards 'responsiveness' and a less rigid and more pragmatic approach to central control, the real agent of change was the break-up of this consensus. It is at this point, when West Germany becomes *more like* France and Italy in having to cope with major differences of opinion on questions of value, that paradoxically the *difference* between the Federal Republic and its Latin neighbours becomes more apparent. The three systems of parent participation are similar in having been set up for reasons of legitimation. They differ in that while the French and Italian committees were rapidly and inevitably colonized by the traditional Left-Right groupings, time and circumstances conspired in Germany to permit the growth of more or less 'non-political' structures. When educational controversy sharpened, the official structures, manned by 'professional parents' (the phrase is derived, significantly, from West German parlance), suddenly found themselves outflanked by unofficial groupings; these tended to be on the political Right because the controversy hinged on moves towards more egalitarian forms of educational organization.

The implications for parent participation are profound. Until the early seventies the assumption was that structures established for 'legitimation' could and should evolve towards 'responsiveness' — i.e., that the traditional tightly controlled curriculum would become more open to change and adaptation at lower levels than the *Landtag*, and that official parent representatives would be helpful in legitimating and publicizing this shift in attitudes and power over schools. That was the rationale behind the Hessian Act of 1958 and the assumptions behind the Hessian curriculum changes which were first discussed in 1967. However, in a situation where a substantial body of opinion believes schools to be sufficiently important to want to control curriculum change quite closely, it is difficult to see that traditional systems of parent participation based on legitimation through extraparliamentary and apolitical channels have much function at all. There is a real possibility that polarization round the comprehensive issue may have frozen the West German parent movement at roughly the point reached in about 1970 — i.e., with systems distributed along a continuum ranging from the pure 'legitimation' phase (Bavaria) to structures where legitimation is somewhat diluted by elements of 'responsiveness' (Hessen). Change might be thought most likely at the Hessian end of the spectrum, yet a new Hessian Act of 1981 indicates no substantial advance in the 1958 Act, and some potentially conservative consolidation of parental influence over such matters as choice of textbooks. The spirit of these changes is indicated in the Minister's foreward to the booklet publicizing the new Act: 'I promise you that I will strive to reach the important decisions needed in our schools in consensus (*Konsens*) with parents, pupils and teachers.'[113]

All this suggests that the broad theoretical statement made at the end of section 2.7 as a result of the French case-study, and broadly confirmed in 3.6 after reviewing the Italian case, ought now to be further refined. There are three linked problems in the 2.7 statement, all relating to its second half in which the *development* of parent participation is characterized. These are: (i) the statement fails to highlight the importance of consensus in differentiating between systems; (ii) the idea of parent groups as 'information networks within which plans originate and evolve' now seems rather vague; and (iii) the idea of 'mismatch' between the aims of government and parent groups does not altogether fit systems where parent groups' and governments' aims may coincide or substantially overlap. The following revision is therefore suggested:

> The 'general crisis' theory provides the better explanation of the origins of parent participation, and of some of the factors (especially on the government side) controlling its subsequent development. There is some tendency for structures of parent participation to be used to legitimate looser and more pragmatic attitudes towards the control of curriculum and greater tolerance of differences between schools. This tendency is strengthened by the way in which formal committee structures and the parent groups which operate them naturally constitute information networks through which information flows from the formal school system into the community, and sometimes in the reverse direction also. There is thus an inbuilt pressure towards activities and interactions which can be explained and justified within the 'reformist' paradigm. There are, however, quite sharp limits to evolution towards a lessened emphasis on 'legitimation'. Those limits are set through the political system. They naturally differ from country to country. In polities where an inbuilt polarization of world-views is normal, parent groupings directly reflect the compromises reached from time to time at macro-level, so that in the last resort the system of parent participation is directly subordinate to the political system. In polities where a wide area of consensus is assumed, parent groupings operating the participatory machinery more readily see themselves as 'non-political', or as aggregating a variety of more or less mainstream views, and they may therefore find themselves in confrontation with other parent groups promoting a more ideologically simple line. In both cases, the reformist theory offers an adequate explanation of only one part of parent participation, whose origins and limitations are better accounted for by some variation of the general crisis theory.

This more elaborate variation of the hypothesis originally stated at the end of Chapter 2 can now be confronted with a fourth case presenting considerable basic differences from the previous three.

Notes

1 Legally Berlin is still administered by the Allied Control Commission. West Berlin operates, however, to all intents and purposes as an eleventh *Land* of the Federal Republic.

2 The report of the Hamburg Police President is reproduced in Appendix 30 (pp. 310–15) of WEBSTER, CHARLES and FRANKLAND, NOBLE (1961) *The Strategic Air Offensive against Germany, 1939–1945*, Vol. IV, London, HMSO.

3 LANGE, HERMANN (1947) *Aufgaben der Elternräte. Vortrag ... gehalten in der Arbeitsgemeinschaft Sozialistischer Eltern am 9. April 1947 in Hamburg*, Hamburg, SPD, Landesorganisation Hamburg, Arbeitsgemeinschaft Sozialistischer Eltern, p. 3.

4 PETERSEN, RUDOLF, *et al.* (1945) *Ansprachen von Bürgermeister Rudolf Petersen, Bürgermeister Adolf Schonfelder und Senator Heinrich Landahl*, Hamburg, Deutsche Hilfsgemeinschaft and J. Trautmann Verlag.

5 For details, see HEARNDEN, ARTHUR (1978) 'Education in the British Zone', in HEARNDEN, ARTHUR (Ed.) *The British in Germany: Educational Reconstruction after 1945*, London, Hamish Hamilton, pp. 11–45.

6 For a general description of pre-1933 *Reformpädagogik*, see SCHEIBE, WOLFGANG (1974) *Die Reformpädagogische Bewegung 1900–1932*, 4th ed., Weinheim and Basel. The community aspect is discussed on pp. 124–31. A summary of the antecedents of various forms of devolved school administration can be found in KLOSS, HEINZ (1949) *Lehrer, Eltern, Schulgemeinden*, Stuttgart and Köln, W. Kohlhammer Verlag, pp. 35–71.

7 LANGE, *op. cit.*

8 *Hamburger Lehrerzeitung*, 1/1, 1948, 3. A predecessor (the *Mitteilungsblatt*) had existed since 1946.

9 LÜBKERT, ERNST (1948) 'Vom ersten Hamburger Schulgesetz', *Hamburger Lehrerzeitung*, 1/9, pp. 1–4.

10 HERZER, A. (1959) 'Trizonale Tagung über Fragen der Schulverwaltungsreform in Wiesbaden am 10. und 11. Marz 1949', *Hamburger Lehrerzeitung* 2/2, p. 9–11.

11 The structures are discussed in greater detail in GLASS, THEO (1932) *Die Entstehung der Hamburger Gemeinschaftsschulen und die pädagogische Arbeit der Gegenwart*, Berlin, Neuland Verlag, and MILBERG, HILDEGARD (1970) *Schulpolitik in der pluralistischen Gesellschaft. Die politischen und sozialen Aspekte der Schulreform in Hamburg, 1890–1935*, Leibniz-Verlag.

12 A well-known novel describing this period in the Hansa city of Lübeck is Thomas Mann's *Buddenbrooks*.

13 MILBERG, *op. cit.*, pp. 59 ff.

14 KLOSS, *op.cit.*, p. 65. The main provisions of the 1920 Act are reproduced on pp. 66–7.

15 GLASS, *op. cit.*, p. 11.

16 HAMBURGISCHER STAATSAMT (1935) *Hamburg im Dritten Reich. Arbeiten der Hamburgischen Verwaltung in Einzeldarstellungen. Heft 1: Die Neugestaltung der Schule*, Hamburg, Staatsamt, p. 8. This is a report on the achievements of the new administration.

17 *Ibid.*, p. 12.

18 EILERS, ROLF (1963) *Die nationalsozialistische Schulpolitik. Eine Studie zur Funktion der Erziehung im totalitären Staat*, Köln and Opladen, Westdeutscher Verlag, pp. 75 ff.

19 LANDAHL, H. (1958) 'Elternhaus und Schule gehören zusammen!' *Hamburger Elternblatt*, March, pp. 2–3. *Schulsenator* Landahl was an influential figure in post-war Hamburg — cf. HEARNDEN, *op. cit.*, pp. 26–7.

20 For contemporary critiques, from an SPD viewpoint, see LANGE, *op. cit.* and KRAUS, F. (1948) 'Haben wir eine demokratische Schule?' *Hamburger Lehrerzeitung*, 1/4, pp. 3–7.

21 See VON MANGOLDT, H. and KLEIN, F. (1957) *Das Bonner Grundgesetz*, Berlin and Frankfurt am Main, F. Vahlen, pp. 264 ff. The 'parents' rights' compromise is discussed in English in GOLAY, JOHN FORD (1968) *The Founding of the Federal Republic of Germany*, Chicago, University of Chicago Press, pp. 196–8.

22 OSTERLOH, EDO (1950) 'Schule und Kirche nach dem Zusammenbruch 1945', *Kirchliches Jahrbuch*, pp. 372–422; here, p. 398; and ANON. (1949) 'Hamburger Schulgesetz endgültig angenommen', *Hamburger Lehrerzeitung*, 2/9, p. 1.

23 Directive No. 54 of the Allied Control Council, 25 June 1947, quoted in KLOSS, *op. cit.*, p. 73.

24 Described in detail in BUNGENSTAB, KARL-ERNST (1970) *Umerziehung zur Demokratie?* Düsseldorf, Bertelsmann Universitätsverlag.

25 For example, the constitution requires that girls shall receive special instruction in baby-care, the upbringing of children and home economics (Article 131(4)).

26 *Schulpflegschaften* originally emerged in Bavaria in the critical 1919 period (*Verordnung* of 28 August 1919). They were loose consultative bodies with representation from churches and the local community as well as parents. See SEUFERT, WILHELM (1968) 'Von der Schulpflegschaft zum Elternbeirat', *Blätter für Lehrerfortbildung / Das Seminar*, 20/1, pp. 68–74.

27 BUNGENSTAB, *op. cit.*, Ch. 5.

28 GÖLDNER, H.D. (1978) *Elternmeinung, Elternwille und ihr Einfluss auf die Schule*, Munich, Mineva, p. 248. This study, though biassed in favour of the Kultusministerium, contains a detailed description of the Bavarian system.

29 ROBINSOHN, S.B. and KUHLMANN, J.C., (1967) 'Two decades of non-reform in West German education', *Comparative Education Review*, 11, pp. 311–30.

30 PICHT, GEORG (1964) *Die deutsche Bildungskatastrophe: Analyse und*

Dokumentation, Olten and Freiburg im Breisgau, Walter-Verlag.

31 KLOSS, *op. cit.*

32 SCHARNBERG, RUDOLF (1972) *Die Hamburger Lehrerkammer — 1. Sitzung 5 Oktober 1953, 100. Sitzung 14 November 1962*, Hamburg, Lehrerkammer, p. 13.

33 KOB, JANPETER (1963) *Erziehung in Elternhaus und Schule — eine Soziologische Studie*, Stuttgart, F. Enke Verlag, p. 113.

34 *Ibid.*, p. 69.

35 PROTOKOLL (Minutes) *Hamburger Elternkammer*, 10 October 1971.

36 The details of the 1973 Act and its formulation over a period of years are documented in BILSTEIN, HELMUT and LANGE, ROLF (1973) *Politische Willensbildung im Parteienstaat: Analyse der vorparlamentärischen Meinungsbildung und des Entscheidungsprozesses in der Hamburger Bürgerschaft zum Schulverfassungsgesetz vom 12 April 1973*, Hamburg, Kuratorium für staatsbürgerliche Bildung. The position in Hamburg, Hessen and Bavaria up to the mid-seventies is summarized in BEATTIE, NICHOLAS (1979) 'Three patterns of parent participation in education: Bavaria, Hamburg, Hessen', *Compare*, 9/1, pp. 3–15.

37 PICKEL, SEPP (1970) '20 Jahre Landeselternvereinigung der Gymnasien in Bayern', *Die Schulfamilie*, 19/6, pp. 104–6.

38 Technically this is an independent journal, published by Manz Verlag, Munich, but in reality its readership is largely restricted to members of LEV.

39 This interpretation of the title is explicitly made in RAUSCHER, HERBERT (1970) 'Zusammenarbeit — Konflikt — Zivilcourage', *Die Schulfamilie*, 19/10, pp. 169–76.

40 The *Elternvereinigung der Katholischen Ordensgymnasien*; the *Landeselternvereinigung der Fachoberschulen*.

41 For an excellent illustration of this process in action, see the various speeches made on the thirtieth anniversary of the LEV, including one from Hans Maier (LEV (1980) 30. *Jahresbericht 1980*, Munich, LEV).

42 BAVARIA, STAATSMINISTERIUM FÜR UNTERRICHT UND KULTUS (1968) *Schulordnung fur die Gymnasien in Bayern, 1968*, Munich, Staatsministerium. The quotations and summary are all drawn from section 38.

43 In some ways these groupings resemble those in France prior to 1960.

44 *Satzung der Landeselternschaft der Bayerischen Realschulen e. V.*, 1973, section 2 (c).

45 There are several confessional parents' associations (one has already been mentioned as adhering to the LEV) but they appear to retain little real significance on the Bavarian stage, being small and localized.

46 Willy Hertlein, Chairman of the BEV from 1976 to 1978, states that the BEV originated from groups involved in discussions of the *Gemeinschaftsschule* (BEV (1979) *10 Jahre Bayerischer Elternverband*, Nürnberg, BEV/Verlag Fritz Osterchrist, p. 4).

47 The BLLV, or *Bayerischer Lehrer — und Lehrerinnenverband*. See

BEV, *op. cit.*, p. 5. There is a certain symmetry in the opposition LEV/*Philologenverband*, BEV/BLLV.

48 See RAUSCHER, HERBERT (1971) 'Das Schulforum', *Die Schulfamilie*, 20/9, pp. 154–7 for some discussion of this innovation. Reports from 141 *Gymnasien* are summarized.

49 MAIER, HANS (1973) 'Rede des Kultusministers Professor Dr. Hans Maier bei der 23. Jahresversammlung der LEV der Gymnasien in Bayern am 8. April 1973 in Bayreuth', *Die Schulfamilie*, 22/6, pp. 97–107; here, p. 104.

50 PECHMANN, MARGRET VON (1973) 'Bericht des Vorstandes', in LEV, 22 *Jahresbericht*, Munich, LEV, pp. 11–20, here, p. 19.

51 LEISNER, WALTER (1975) 'Die Schule und das Elternrecht', in LEV, 24 *Jahresbericht*, Munich, LEV, pp. 22–31; here, p. 31. The word *Rätestaat* has connotations of the short-lived Bavarian soviet republic of 1919 which was eventually suppressed with great violence.

52 Even the LEV was somewhat alarmed at this development — see KREMSREITER, JOHANNA (1977) 'Klassenelternsprecher', *Die Schulfamilie*, 26/2, pp. 27–8.

53 The Bavarian constitution specifies 'the highest aims of education' as 'the fear of God, respect for religious conviction and the dignity of man, a sense of responsibility and a pleasure in taking responsibility, helpfulness and openness to everything true, good and beautiful' (Article 13, (2)).

54 The summary which follows is based on KLOSS, *op. cit.*, pp. 74 ff; STEIN, ERWIN (1968) *Elternmacht — Möglichkeiten und Grenzen der Mitarbeit der Eltern in der Schule*, duplicated; and SCHLANDER, OTTO (1975) *Reeducation: ein politisch-pädagogisches Prinzip im Widerstreit der Gruppen*, Bern, H. Lang; Frankfurt am Main, P. Lang, esp. pp. 192 ff.

55 Judgment of Hessian Supreme Court, 19 December 1957.

56 This account is based partly on conversations with Frau Susi Hübsch on 13 February 1975, partly on KUTHER, HERMANN (n.d.) 'Elternrecht und *Mitbestimmung der Erziehungsberechtigten und den Landesschulbeirat*),

57 Act of 30 May 1969, modified on 18 March 1970 (*Gesetz über die Mitbestimmung der Erziehungsberechtigten und den Landesschulbeirat*), Section 9. This is a revision of the 1958 Act.

58 *Ibid.*, section 10.

59 *Ibid.*, section 22.

60 ENDERWITZ, HERBERT (1973) 'Die Orientierungsstufe in Hessen: ihre Möglichkeiten und Grenzen', *Gesamtschule*, 5/2, pp. 19–20.

61 *Ibid.*, p. 19.

62 Quoted from the *Landeselternbeirat's* duplicated response, dated 10/11 December 1972 (*Erklärung des Landeselternbeirats von Hessen zum Urteil des Bundesverfassungsgerichts vom 6 Dezember 1972 ...*). This account is based on that, on the Hessian decree of 14 March 1972 — *Richtlinien für die Förderstufe*, on the duplicated deposition (*Stellungnahme*) presented to the Constitutional Court by the *Landeselternbeirat* on 26 September 1972, and on conversations with individuals in the spring

of 1975, especially Frau Susi Hübsch.

63 On the consequences in the schools of Frankfurt am Main, see Bruining, Jeanet G. (1976) *Möglichkeiten und Grenzen der Realisierung von Bildungsreform durch bildungspolitische Entscheidungen; ein Vergleich zwischen der BRD und den Niederlanden*, unpublished Diploma-Arbeit, University of Frankfurt am Main.

64 The exact arrangements for the individual *Länder*, as they had evolved to the early eighties, are set out in Boppel, Werner and Kollenberg Udo (1981) *Mitbestimmung in der Schule*, Köln, Deutscher Instituts-Verlag, pp. 90–160. For more evaluative general accounts, see Schleicher, Klaus (1972) 'Elternhaus und Schule in der BRD', in Schleicher, Klaus (Ed.), *Elternhaus und Schule — Kooperation ohne Erfolg?* Düsseldorf, Schwann, pp. 33ff; *ibid.*, (1973) *Elternmitsprache und Elternbildung*, Düsseldorf, Schwann; Breckenridge, Ian (1981) 'Legalism and participation in school-government in West Germany', in Baron, George (Ed.), *The Politics of School Government*, Oxford, Pergamon.

65 A selection of such documents is discussed in Boppel and Kollenberg (1981) *op. cit.*, pp. 62 ff. The views of political parties can be studied *passim* in Michael, Berthold and Schepp, Heinz-Hermann (Eds.) (1974) *Politik und Schule von der Französischen Revolution bis zur Gegenwart*, Vol. 2, Frankfurt am Main, Athenäum Fischer, pp. 388–90.

66 *Bundeselternrat*, or BER: it first appeared in 1955 and was formally constituted in 1957. These comments are based on BER (n.d./1975) *Aufbau-Entwicklung — Beschlüsse des Bundeselternrates*, Ludwigshafen am Rhein, BER, on its newsletter (*BER-Informationen*), and on conversations in 1975 with Herr Karl-Horst Tischbein, then president of the BER, and Frau Erika Suthoff, of the special schools sub-committee. The most thorough historical acount (which is incidentally rather sceptical of the BER's usefulness) is in Mohrart, Dieter (1979) *Elternmitwirkung in der Bundesrepublik Deutschland. Ein Beitrag zur politisch-historischen und pädagogischen Diskussion*, Frankfurt am Main, Bern, Cirencester, Peter D. Lang, pp. 79–118.

67 The series were entitled *Bildungswege in Hessen* and *Schriftenreihe zur pädagogischen Information*. The former was free, the latter cost, in 1974, between DM 0,90 and DM 3,90. The pamphlet was *Welche Rechte Haben Eltern?* All were published by the Hessian *Kultusministerium in* Wiesbaden.

68 Willy Hertlein, Chairman of the BEV, describes it as a 'Propagandablatt für das Staatsministerium' (BEV, *op. cit.*, p. 11).

69 Gemeinnützige Gesellschaft Gesamtschule e.V. (1979) *Gesamtschulbrevier: Fakten gegen Vorurteile*, Ammersbek-Hoisbüttel, G.G.G., pp. 40–3.

70 'Without the unrest of 1968 I would never have become Minister' (McNeir, Clive (1981) 'Curriculum control', *Education*, 6 November, inset i–iv, here, ii). This is a brief account of Hessian educational politics

through the seventies. For a detailed account of the 1973–4 controversy, containing the references on which the following summary is based, see BEATTIE, NICHOLAS, (1977) 'Public participation in curriculum change: A West German example', *Compare*, 7/1, pp. 17–29.

71 See GEMEINNÜTZIGE GESELLSCHAFT GESAMTSCHULE (1975) *Gesamtschule 75, Bundeskongress Gesamtschule, 8–10 Mai 1975, in Wetzlar — Arbeitspapiere, Berichte, Materialien*, GGG, duplicated, *passim*.

72 A protagonist of the *Gesamtschule*, Joachim Lohmann, commented, 'The characterization of the *Gesamtschule* as a totalitarian socialist *Einheitsschule* is the stab-in-the-back legend of the seventies' (in GEMEINNÜTZIGE GESELLSCHAFT GESAMTSCHULE (1977) *Bundeskongress Gesamtschule 1977 — Referate — Berichte der Arbeitsgruppen — 19–21. Mai 1977 in Hannover*, GGG, duplicated, p. 13.

73 See SCHORB, ALFONS OTTO (Ed.) (1977) *Schulversuche mit Gesamtschulen in Bayern — Ergebnisse der wissenschaftlichen Begleitung 1971–1976*, Stuttgart, Ernst Klett Verlag. This report of the Bavarian *Staatsimtitut für Bildungsforschung und Bildungsplanung* was widely discussed in the educational and general press throughout the Federal Republic in 1977.

74 The *Gymnasium* parents constituted the *Landeselternschaft der Gymnasien in NRW*, the *Gesamtschule* parents the *Landeselternrat der Gesamtschulen in NRW*. In terms of the 1952 Act these were technically groupings of *Schulpflegschaften*, or school governing committees. They had no real legal clout.

75 The system is discussed in detail in PETERMANN, BERND (1978) *Gesetz uber die Mitwirkung im Schulwesen — Schulmitwirkungsgesetz*, Essen, H. Wingen.

76 The objections to the 1952 scheme are detailed in WEHNES, FRANZ-JOSEF (1973) *Mitbestimmung im Schulwesen für Lehrer, Schüler, Eltern*, Essen, Ludgerns Verlag, esp. pp. 84 ff. The relevant texts as they stood in 1971 are printed in the *Informationsbrief des Kultusministeriums NRW*, August 1971. (*Sonderausgabe*).

77 CDU 'Gegenüberstellung' of July 1976, reported in *LER Information Gesamtsschule NRW*, 37, January 1977. The *Landeselternschaft der Gymnasien in NRW* backed this viewpoint: see their *Mitteilungsblatt*, No. 95, January 1977, 'Die LE der Gymnasien zum Gesetzentwurf "Kooperative Schule".'

78 The phrase was used in the *Landtag* debate of October 1977, reported in *Landtag intern*, 31 October 1977, p. 3.

79 This was to have the incidental effect of making small rural schools even less viable as the population fell. This was to be one of the problems the *Koop Schule* was supposed to alleviate.

80 For a commentary on this period, from an SPD angle, see ROSE, H. PETER (1970) 'Die Rolle der Parteien in der Diskussion um die Bildungsreform', in EVERS, CARL-HEINZ and RAU, JOHANNES (Eds) *Oberstufenreform und Gesamthochschule*, Frankfurt am Main, Berlin, Munich, Diesterweg, pp.

133–45. The official government line is set out formally in LANDTAG NRW, Drucksache 8/1775, Antwort der Landesregierung auf die Grosse Anfrage 2 der Fraktionen der SPD und FDP . . . (*Landtag* document, 26 January 1977).

81 Speech made at Düsseldorf, 22 April 1977 (*Reden des Kultusministers Jürgen Girgensohn*, duplicated file in collection of *Landesinstitut fur Curriculumentwicklung*, Düsseldorf).

82 For a critique from a position considerably further to the Left than that of the government, see GEMEINNÜTZIGE GESELLSCHAFT GESAMTSCHULE (1974) *Gesamtschule 74: Bundeskongress Gesamtschule, 23–25 Mai 1974 in Kassel — Arbeitspapiere, Berichte, Materialien*, GGG, duplicated, pp. 238 ff.

83 See NRW decree, 13 December 1972.

84 See, for example, a speech made on 18 April 1975: 'Those who link the *Gesamtsschule* with utopian and extreme demands . . . do harm to the *Gesamtsschule*. They make it easy for the opponents of the *Gesamtsschule* idea to question it as a Utopia and to declare it politically undesirable . . .' (*Reden des Kultusministers Jürgen Girgensohn*, duplicated file in collection of *Landesinstitut fur Curriculumentwicklung*, Düsseldorf).

85 This was essentially the same as the Hessian *Förderstufe*.

86 VOLAND, CLAUS (1977) 'Schulkampf im Revier', *Die Zeit*, 28 October. The exact figures are 1975: 3,384,194 pupils; estimated number in 1990: 2,245,000 (NRW *KULTUSMINISTERIUM, Lehrerbedarf und Lehrerbestand*, Schriftenreihe des Kultusministeriums, 30, Sept 1976, p. 87) The figures are discussed in detail in KLEMM, KLAUS (1978) 'Erhaltung von Bildungschancen als Aufgabe regionaler Schulentwicklung', in BOHNSACK, FRITZ (Ed.), *Kooperative Schule*, Weinheim and Basel, Beltz, pp. 73–82.

87 FROMMBERGER, HERBERT, and GIRGENSOHN JÜRGEN (1977) 'Alles andere als revolutionär', *Schulmanagement*, 8/2, pp. 136–7; here, p. 137.

88 The *Koop Schule* was announced in the 'coalition pact' of May 1975. A bill was brought before the *Landtag* on 9 November 1976 and referred to the education and culture committee on 25 November. A revised version was submitted on 8 June 1977 and adopted on 22 June. (MARGIES, DIETER and ROESER, KARSTEN, (1978) 'Verfassungsrechtliche Aspekte der Kooperativen Schule', in Bohnsack, *op. cit.*, pp. 113–25. The third reading took place on 26 October 1977 and passed into law as the *Schulverwaltungsgesetz*. It was due to come into force on 1 August 1978 (*Landtag intern*, 31 October 1977).

89 GEW attitudes are clearly analyzed in its journal, *Erziehung und Wissenschaft*, December 1977.

90 As Minister Jürgen Girgensohn did on 26 June 1977: 'The *Koop Schule* is an interim stage on the way to the *integrierte Gesamtschule* as the normal school for all children in this *Land*' (quoted in *Landtag intern*, 4 July 1977). This statement was understandably used very frequently as proof of the duplicity of the government.

91 Interestingly the *Volksbegehren* idea had first emerged in the SPD in the spring of 1977 as a means of swinging public support behind the *integrierte Gesamtschule*, but had been vetoed by the FDP (ADELMANN, DIETER (1978) 'Wie der Koop-Apfel reifte', *Mitteilungsblatt des LER Gesamtschule*, 10, 9 March); also articles in *Westfälische Nachrichten*, 6 July 1977 ('Vermutlich kein Volksbeghren für integrierte Gesamtschule') and *Westfälische Allgemeine Zeitung*, 6 July 1977 ('Rau schliesst Volksbegehren für Gesamtschule nicht aus'). Lehmann's well-documented account suggests, however, that the CDU picked up the idea from the associations, including parents' associations (LEHMANN, HANS GEORG (1978) 'Schulreform und Politik. Der Konflikt um die Kooperative Schule und ihre Orientierungsstufe', Supplement to *Das Parlament*, 36, September pp. 3–23).

92 PIEPER, ALFONS (1977) 'Volksbegehren nun beschlossene Sache: zwölf Verbände gegen die Koop Schule', *Westfälische Allgemeine Zeitung*, 5 July.

93 VOLAND, *op. cit.*

94 PIEPER, ALFONS (1977) 'Koop-Schul-Gegner bestreiten Bitt-Briefe an Revierindustrie', *Westfälische Allgemeine Zeitung*, 27 August.

95 PHILOLOGENVERBAND NRW (1977) *Plädoyer fur das gegliederte Schulwesen*, Düsseldorf, Philologenverband NRW. The ideas of Josef Hitpass were frequently used; for a brief summary of his position, see HITPASS, JOSEF (1977) 'Die Kooperative Schule — eine Reform gegen die individuelle Lernforderung?' *Die höhere Schule*, 3, pp. 100–6.

96 For example, HERRLITZ, HANS GEORG (1978) 'Wilhelm von Humboldt ist nicht mehr gefragt', in Bohnsack, *op. cit.*, pp. 11–24.

97 Poster published by CDU (in the files of the *Landesinstitut für Curriculumentwicklung*, Düsseldorf).

98 Published by *Mülheimer Eltern-Initiative gegen die Kooperative Schule* (in the files of the *Landesinstitut fur Curriculumentwicklung*, Düsseldorf).

99 Issued by the GEW in 1977 and reproduced in *LER Gesamtschule NRW*, 47, 1, August 1977. Similar arguments on two fronts are presented at greater length in FELDHAUS, BERND, *et al.* (1978) *Kooperative Schule — Analysen, Arguments, Antworten*, Düsseldorf, Sozialdemokratische Gemeinschaft fur Kommunalpolitik in NRW e V.

100 On the Left there was some agitation for the *Gesamtschule* — a *Progressiver Elternverein* and an *Aktion 'Mehr Gesamtschulen in NRW'*; but as the campaign was focused on the *Koop Schule* these initiatives served mainly to confirm the view of its opponents that the *Koop Schule* was a stalking-horse for the *integrierte Gesamtschule*.

101 Private conversations. Obviously these groups did not wish to rock the boat by publicizing their opposition too shrilly. Nonetheless, at the height of the campaign (18 February 1978) the *Gesamtschule* parents issued a declaration (in files of *Landsinstitut*, Düsseldorf): 'The *Koop Schule* has nothing in common with the *integrierte* or *differenzierte Gesamtschule* in NRW. It is in our opinion neither an interim stage on the way to the

Gesamtschule nor an appropriate route to it.'

102 The figures are given in *Landtag intern*, 6 March 1978. In rural areas 37.5 per cent turned out to vote; in the towns only 20.5 per cent.

103 This is a complex question: both the Lutheran and Catholic churches had voiced misgivings about the *Koop Schule*. See SCHRADER, WILHELM (1978) 'Statistik zeigt: CDU und Kirche führten Volksbegehren zum Erfolg', *Westfälische Rundschau*, 13 April.

104 Speech in Winterberg, 7 April 1978 (*Reden des Ministers Jürgen Girgensohn*, duplicated file in collection of *Landesinstitut fur Curriculumentwicklung*, Düsseldorf).

105 See ROEDER, PETER M. (1978) 'Alternativen für die Hamptschule?' in BOHNSACK, *op. cit.*, pp. 57–71; esp. p. 57.

106 ANON. (1977) 'Hannovers CDU–Kultusminister verteidigt Orientierungsstufe', *Westfälische Allgemeine Zeitung*, 30 November. The Lower Saxony example was discussed in the *Volksbegehren* campaign, but seems to have carried little weight against the full-blooded 'red menace' argument.

107 See *Landtag intern*, 28 January and 13 June 1977. *S wie Schule*, along the same lines as *Schulreport* in Bavaria, began to appear in the autumn of 1977.

108 *Vorwärts* published several thoughtful analyses from the SPD viewpoint: notably HENTIG, HARTMUT von (1978), 'Die zweite Reform. 22 vorläufige Thesen zu einer möglichen Erneuerung der SPD — Bildungspolitik' (2 February); ADELMANN (1978) *op. cit.* (a reprint) (9 March); FRIEDEBURG, LUDWIG Von (1978) 'Die Bildungsreform steht noch aus. Hinter dem Rücken der Politiker' (6 April); GLOTZ, PETER (1978) 'Vor erstarrten Fronten' (4 May).

109 HESSE, FRIEDEL (1981) 'Gesamtschulpolitik ist Elternpolitik', *Neue Deutsche Schule*, 33/1, p. 8.

110 The procedures of the different *Länder* are usefully tabulated in HAENISCH, HANS and ZIEGENSPECK, JÖRG (1977) *Die Orientierungsstufe. Schulentwicklung zwischen Differenzierung und Integration*, Weinheim and Basel, Beltz, pp. 52–5.

111 MOHRART, *op. cit.*, p. 149, points out that this would in fact be a return to the relative simplicity of the *Reformpädagogik* tradition. His survey, although read after most of this chapter was written, confirms most of the generalizations made in this final section.

112 ROBINSOHN and KUHLMANN, *op. cit.*

113 HESSEN, KULTUSMINISTER (1981) *Elternrecht in Hessens Schulen: Gesetz und Wahlordnung*, Wiesbaden, Kultusminister, p. 7.

5   England and Wales

5.1   Background

The most obvious difference affecting the functions and 'feel' of parent participation in England and Wales as opposed to France, Italy and West Germany is the position of the individual school. In France, Italy and West Germany the popular perception of schools is that they are unmistakably institutions of the *state*. They are staffed by state employees and operate (for example, in matters of curriculum) according to state rules. Organized parental intervention of a more or less political kind may thus focus on altering the rules or on devolving some defined responsibility away from the state to the individual school; the 10 per cent of the curriculum handed over to school councils in France for school decision is an example of this style of thinking.

Parents and teachers in England and Wales, on the other hand, tend not to see the issues in such clear-cut terms. In their eyes the school already enjoys a substantial degree of autonomy. The role of the head teacher in shaping the atmosphere and policy of 'his' or 'her' school is generally acknowledged to be important. It is recognized that outwardly similar schools may differ quite sharply in their internal arrangements. The differences may affect important matters of curriculum and organization such as what subjects are offered or how pupils are grouped.

It is thus undeniable that autonomy exists — yet it is by no means as absolute or deep-rooted as is sometimes thought. Although frequently acclaimed as a time-honoured tradition, it is in fact relatively recent. Maclure suggests that it is an almost unintended consequence of the 1944 Education Act: 'The authority which was once vested in the Department went to the local authorities, which by default passed it to the schools, and it has now got all the ivy encrusted [sic] tendencies of tradition which has in fact got a very few years behind it. But everybody believes that it has always been like that, and must go on being like that.'[1] That may overstate the case in exaggerating the impact of the codes of practice issued by the Board of Education over the first four decades of the twentieth century, and in underestimating the importance of initiatives taken by individual heads and teachers in the period prior to 1944; but it is a useful reminder of the fragility of school autonomy as a principle.

In any case, school autonomy seems quite often to be more a matter of rhetoric than reality. It is sometimes pointed out that the only legally required subject is religious education, yet in practice there seems to be a large measure of agreement about what should be taught. This is reinforced by the expectations of parents and employers, and (particularly in secondary schools) of higher education. Those expectations are powerfully reflected in the syllabuses of the public examination boards whose certificates are to a large extent the currency of the system. Thus the constraints within which experimentation can occur are often tighter than observers from centralized European systems expect. Even highly innovative secondary schools such as Countesthorpe College or the Sutton Centre[2] have to tread a wary path, and, as we shall see, the William Tyndale affair pointed up some of the limits even of primary school enterprise.

More formally, the 'autonomous' school is part of a chain of command running from the Department of Education and Science (DES) through the local authority to the school. The chain is less well-defined than in France, for example: the transmission of authority is complicated and sometimes subverted by the influence of local education authorities (LEAs) whose legitimacy derives, like that of central government, from the electoral process. Nonetheless, the chain exists, and some would like to see it strengthened.

Perhaps the differences in administration between England and Wales and its continental neighbours are less of substance than of style; yet for parent participation the style is very important. For all the constraints placed upon school autonomy, the fact remains that compared with the cases already described, the English and Welsh system has considerable potential for being 'responsive' *before parent representation is added*. The lack of legal definition, and the diffusion of responsibility among school, LEA, DES and examination boards, produce a 'systemic context' in which incremental small-scale change can happen relatively easily. From the parental point of view something can often be done to remove points of friction by negotiating with a school or (more dramatically) by negotiating one's child into another school with a different policy or atmosphere. However, it should be noted that the very flexibility of these arrangements puts a premium on *individual* cooperation and negotiation, rather than on the *collective* handing over of defined tasks to parents as a group. The stress on 'responsiveness' defines the interaction between parent and school in a way which tends to make more formal quasi-political interpretations of parent participation appear odd or unnecessary.

This rickety but in some ways supple structure is the product of long consensus. The absence of clear definitions is part of that. If the sole curriculum element to which the 1944 Education Act devoted attention was religious instruction, that was because religion seemed at the time to be a contentious issue. For the rest, education, like many other aspects of the national life, was assumed to be a consensual activity. The teacher was seen as a professional who within that consensus could be entrusted to apply his expertise in, for example, classifying the three types of pupil who would attend the three types of secondary school. Change was assumed to be slow and to operate within the very broad parameters fixed by legislation. Disputes would be settled by reference to notions such as what 'a reasonable parent' might expect, or be expected to do. This style of thinking and jurisdiction was made possible by the English common law system with its stress on precedent rather than immutable definition, and ultimately by the avoidance of sudden political change. England and Wales differed from France, Italy and the Federal Republic not only in its legal and parliamentary systems, but also in having escaped the radical rethink imposed in those countries by the discrediting of national institutions in 1944–5.

To put this in the terms of section 1.2, there existed a high degree of 'legitimacy' in the institutions of England and Wales, and that included the schools. If therefore England and Wales is advanced as a test case for the 'general crisis' theory sketched in Chapter 1, one would expect that the adoption of parent participation as a means of achieving greater legitimacy would be slower and less complete than in the countries discussed in preceding chapters. This sluggishness might be increased by the relative 'responsiveness' of the system — i.e., its capacity for dealing pragmatically with minor frictions and dissatisfactions.

Another reason for the particular interest of England and Wales as a counter-case is that it focuses attention on the idea of *crisis* as the supposed trigger for attempts to secure legitimacy. What was the crisis in England and Wales? 1945 in Germany, 1968 in France and Italy are more or less obvious watersheds, when the legitimacy of the state was called into question to the point where some action was necessary to reassert it. On the other side of the Channel, the idea of crisis seemed more diffuse. Samuel Beer's recent analysis is particularly interesting because he presents a view of 'the British crisis' which is in many respects diametrically opposed to his opinions in 1965, when Britain seemed to him a model parliamentary democracy,[3] a classic 'civic culture' of the sort described and assessed by Almond and Verba.[4] What has intervened he describes as 'the collapse of deference'.

The case of England and Wales will require us therefore to look more critically at the idea of crisis. The connection between parent participation and crisis is less immediately evident, because less neatly focused on political crisis, than in the three countries already discussed. It may even be that the emergence and evolution of parent participation will throw some incidental light on the crisis itself — on the question of whether there is a 'general crisis', and if there is, what sort it is.

In its original formulation in Chapter 1, 'the general crisis' was presented as a crisis of 'ruling elites'. In England and Wales, as in the other three cases, there is some difficulty in specifying exactly who constitutes the elite, in spite of the longstanding British fascination with 'the Establishment' and the markers which are supposed to indicate membership of it — accent, schooling, etc. 'The ruling elite' is a sufficiently elastic term to take account of the institutionalization of opposed political viewpoints within the Westminster system. If 'crisis' has any meaning in that system, it must ultimately be a crisis of parliament, which is sovereign and supreme as a result of long historical development. Both Labour and Conservative parties have an equal interest in maintaining the *status quo*, which more or less guarantees the alternation of power. In evaluating the rhetoric of both sides in debate, one must remember that the system produces highly stylized oppositional stances but within a commonly accepted framework. On the other hand, the areas of accepted consensus are not altogether stable, and in education the last twenty years have seen an increase in dissensus and a corresponding diminution of consensus.

Finally, this chapter is entitled 'England and Wales' not 'The United Kingdom'. This is for reasons analogous to those advanced for concentrating on four West German *Länder* rather than on all eleven. The discussion would become impossibly complex if the separate arrangements for Scotland and Northern Ireland had also to be introduced.[5] Bell and Grant have pointed out that each of the constituent parts of the United Kingdom enjoys a somewhat different relationship with central government in London.[6] To some extent those different relationships are reflected in the development and style of school management in Scotland and Northern Ireland, and presumably also in the various Channel Islands and the Isle of Man. The decision to concentrate on England and Wales is for convenience and clarity, and reflects the fact that in population terms England and Wales constitute the largest single unit in the United Kingdom. This does not mean that the author regards Scotland or Northern Ireland as peripheral or uninteresting. Indeed there is obvious scope for a comparative study of the evolution of school management in all three territories. This would need to illustrate the interplay of local circumstances in the smaller terrritories with events in England and Wales — but that is not the focus of this study. One of the consequences of concentrating on England and Wales is a certain clumsiness in formulae such as 'English and Welsh', and a reluctance to use neater but vaguer phrases such as 'Britain' and 'British'.

5.2   Parent Activity before 1960

The 'reformist theory' presented in Chapter 1 suggests that 'parent participation is the product of experience of and commitment to democratic involvement', and 'is established earlier and more easily in politics offering more experience of democratic involvement.'[7] In several ways England and Wales constitute an excellent testing-ground for these hypotheses. Favourable circumstances include the following:

(i) *Democratic institutions*   The Reform Act of 1832 marked the beginning of a period of evolution in which the right to vote was gradually extended to wider sectors of the population, culminating in the enfranchisement of all women in 1928. Over a similar period local government was reformed and democratized, and eventually given substantial powers over education. The rule of law was respected. The press and the media were regarded as 'free' in the liberal sense. Associations and interest-groups were numerous and often lively. It has already been noted that for both Almond and Verba writing in 1963 and for Beer two years later England and Wales (or rather, Great Britain and Northern Ireland) appeared to be a model of 'the civic culture'.[8]

(ii) *Stability.*   Over the last century or more England and Wales differed from the three other countries presented in having avoided, for geographical and other reasons, the traumas of invasion and political revolution. Change was incremental and in a sense organic. Institutions responding to new needs were added piecemeal to the existing fabric of society, so that the overall pattern never received a radical shake-up.

This continuity was reinforced by a legal system which relied less on precise statutory definition than on the interpretation of custom and opinion. In Tennyson's words, Britain remains

> A land of settled government
> A land of just and old renown
> Where freedom slowly broadens down
> From precedent to precedent.[9]

(iii) *Institutions likely to encourage parent participation.* The general conditions of a liberal democracy, especially freedom of opinion and association, will tend to favour the emergence of interest-groups and pressure-groups, and therefore of parent groups, which can be expected to crystallize their demands for change into institutional and/or political form. England and Wales have another advantage in that structures of educational government have evolved which would appear likely to focus and encourage local interest and involvement. Between 1870 and 1902 schools were run by a patchwork of elected school boards; the elections were often contested and lively.[10] In addition, individual schools were often managed by boards of governors or managers.[11] While these were hardly democratic institutions in any modern sense, they had some potential for democratization and for the involvement of parents. Finally, the local education authorities (LEAs), set up in 1902 to serve quite small local areas, were obvious foci for pressure-group activity, with a potential for parent activity and influence which the centralized systems of early twentieth century France, Italy or Prussia could not match.

In the light of these apparently favourable circumstances, one might have expected that, as schools grew in number and importance, groups and associations would begin to cluster round schools and LEAs; that some of those groups would be parent groups; that in due course demands would be formulated for increased parental influence on schools; that such demands would need to be balanced against those of other groups, such as teachers; and that balanced structures of consultation and participation would be devised. In addition, one might expect that as the obstacles to such developments were evidently less than in the more or less centralized, turbulent or authoritarian polities of the inter-war period on the Continent, parent participation would evolve more rapidly — perhaps in the 1920s or 1930s, or even sooner.

In reality, as we shall see, the growth of parent participation in the sense defined in Chapter 1 ('the legally required association of parents with the schools their children attend through systems of elected

representatives and committees') emerged somewhat later and more
tentatively than in Germany, France or Italy. Thus our fourth example
requires us to ask a question which could not have been posed other
than in a comparative study. It is Sherlock Holmes's classic question
about the dog which failed to bark in the night. Why did a system with
so many apparent advantages, and with as active a parent movement as
anywhere else (considerably more active than France or Italy), fail to
generate a participatory system involving parents at a much earlier stage
than it did? What does that tell us about the 'reformist' and 'general
crisis' theories?

Certainly the looseness and localism of the English system encouraged a considerable level of organized parent activity from about 1890 to
1960. However, the key to understanding that activity is to realize that
it had little or nothing to do with parent participation as described in
Chapter 1. Of the four broad participatory aims delineated in section
1.2, only 'responsiveness' occasionally appears in the contemporary
literature, and then only in a hesitant and peripheral way. The parent
movement in this period was preoccupied with informing and educating
parents — and not about their rights but about their duties. It was run
by people who thought they knew something about children, schools
and parents, and who wished to *inform* others of their knowledge. Thus
the parent movement was dominated by experts, and essentially
didactic. 'The very idea of elementary education [wrote Findlay in
1923[12]] sprang from pity for poor folk who could *not* organize, could *not*
pay, could *not* realize what was good for their children. It is not
suprising, therefore, that the organizers of schooling from the first
compulsory Act of 1870 to the last of 1918 treated "the parent" as a
prospective enemy, to be coerced by threat of summons and penalty.'

Attitudes of this sort inevitably influenced the form and growth of
parent organization. Because the movement depended on the energy
and commitment of quite small numbers of informed people, and
because their information had to be transmitted through a system whose
natural local focus was the school, growth was naturally patchy and
discontinuous, proceeding through a series of 'waves' as particular
interpretations of the parental role waxed and waned. In other words,
the parent movement (or successive parent movements) never really
rooted itself in the popular consciousness, and was therefore never able
to grow organically in the style presupposed by the 'reformist' model of
participation.

The pattern can first be traced as far back as the late 1880s with
the emergence of the Parents' National Educational Union (PNEU),
founded by Charlotte Mason as the Parents' Educational Union in

Bradford in 1887, and launched nationally a year later as the PNEU with its own journal, the *Parents' Review*, published from 1890. The Union's founder described the initial purpose of the new organization as being to spread among parents the 'principles of physiological-psychology':

> What if these two or three vitalizing educational principles could be brought before parents? Ah, what indeed!... How could we, with sincere deference and humility, offer to parents the help of those few principles which seemed a very gospel of education, so far depending upon scientific discovery, that only within the last few decades has it been an open book.[13]

This 'gospel' was to be preached throughout society: 'The most desirable members are young, earnest-minded people, full of purpose for their children.... An important section of the society includes parents of the artisan class.... We should hope to touch less capable parents indirectly....'[14]

PNEU was highly successful in establishing a solid institutional backing for its ideas. Accounts of its early meetings in *Parents' Review* provide ample evidence of support from the aristocracy and especially the Church of England, for Charlotte Mason was a strong believer in the spiritual character of any education worthy of the name. The responsibility of the parent was divine in origin. 'The voice of parents is the voice of God,' said the Reverend H. Russell Wakefield, addressing the PNEU in 1899. 'The parent is the ever-watchful who only regards this handing a child to a teacher as the specializing [sic] that which he cannot manage himself....'[15] This high view of the parental role did not, however, mean that parents were expected to be in conflict with schools, nor had it anything to do with accommodating to a pluralism of parental views and values. Rather, both parent and teacher were subordinate to 'the gospel of education'. The 'House of Education' at Ambleside had as one of its main tasks the training of idealistic elementary school teachers (and incidentally governesses) who would in turn influence the parents of their pupils. This led naturally to the encouragement of parent associations — but of a certain type:

> Here Charlotte Mason's trained students could be of help by giving talks and leading discussions on such matters as habit formation and discipline, on nature work, the value of reading, or on some part of the term's work. These associations [of parents] were at work in the early twenties and were a step towards a liberal education for parents as well as children....[16]

There is much to admire in the idealism and organizational thoroughness of PNEU, and its constant resolve to engage with state education as well as with the governesses among whom Charlotte Mason's activity began: as early as 1890 one of the three rules for branches of the infant PEU was 'that as much work be done with the parents of the working as with those of the educated class.'[17] Yet by the time Charlotte Mason died in 1923, PNEU remained earnestly didactic. For all its high view of the parents' responsibility, and its labours in producing teachers who would be open and sympathetic to parents, the thought that the state school should seriously take account of differing parental values, or that the management of schools aroused complex political questions, was quite alien. Thus PNEU simply ignored existing institutions such as local education committees or boards of managers and governors and concentrated on parents as individuals rather than as social or political beings. Perhaps it was this basic ideological fixation which led to the withering away of PNEU as a potentially broad-based parent movement. As its original doctrine came to seem more and more dated, it had no independent vigour in local parent groups to ensure renewal and change. By the 1930s it had become a worthy but marginal association organizing correspondence education throughout the world, and with a few private schools following its methods.[18]

In the absence of any serious historical study, it is difficult to assess how strongly the PNEU and its ideas were responsible for the style of parent-teacher relations widely regarded as desirable between the two world wars. It is at least clear that that style was almost universally of a kind that Charlotte Mason would have understood and approved: idealistic and mildly progressive, individualistic and non-political, supportive of the school and anxious to cooperate with teachers — parent education rather than parent participation. The vocabulary and the underlying psychology were different, the idealism was more humanist than religious, but the spirit remained remarkably similar. The parent was to be influenced to collaborate with the school. If, as in the Hadow Committee's 1938 report on infant and nursery schools 'close relationships between teachers and parents' were commended, this was because 'by these means the good influences of the school pass into the home.'[19]

By the 1930s the predominant institutional link between parents and schools was the parent-teacher association, or PTA. This seems to have been much more common than the parents' association (PA), differing from the PTA in running its own affairs without any formal teacher involvement. Yet PTA or PA activity was restricted to a small minority of schools. An enquiry conducted in Nottinghamshire at the end of the 1939–45 war revealed that only 3 per cent of schools had PTAs;[20] and even when allowances are made for the disruption of associational activity caused by the war, it is clear from the tone of publications aimed at parents (such as *Home and School*, the monthly journal of the Home and School Council of Great Britain) that PTAs were the exception rather than the rule, and encountered considerable suspicion from teachers.[21]

A parent-teacher association is by definition based on the idea that parents and teachers are sharers of a common task, rather than separate interest groups whose opinions need to be reconciled in some quasi-political process. The contrast with France or Germany is instructive. Presumably the *lycée* parents' federation originally arose in France without teacher membership because teachers were so clearly defined as civil servants, with their conditions of service and curricula determined in Paris.[22] Presumably the original school-based associations rapidly banded together into a national federation because this centralized structure was so dominant. In the early years of the century in Hamburg, Social Democratic parents came together separately from teachers because they dissented politically from the *status quo* which teachers represented and defended, and this political separateness was confirmed and institutionalized in the 1920 legislation.[23] If England and Wales took another direction, that reflected two important differences. One was the relative autonomy of the local school, which facilitated cooperative arrangements between teachers and parents by giving schools sufficient freedom to sort out minor problems locally — provided they were essentially *individual* problems, relating to pupil progress, etc. Larger questions of *general* policy were not catered for, and this indicates the second major difference: the failure to view education in an ideological perspective, 'the habit' (to quote Fred Clarke in 1940[24]) 'of thinking in terms of concrete precedent rather than in terms of abstract principle (with all that this means for the preservation of continuity).'

These background factors help to explain the particular character of the PTA movement as it slowly developed from (say) 1920 to 1960. It was not simply that PTAs failed to notice the potential of boards of governors or local education committees as channels for parent influence, it was rather that they saw their job as being to *support individual schools* — even to reinforce them in an essentially non-political role. Model rules for PTAs issued by the Home and School Council of Great Britain in the late 1930s stated as the objectives of a PTA: 'The Association shall foster and support the welfare of the school by all legitimate means, but shall at no time interfere with the discipline of the school, nor with the work of the Headmaster and Staff.'[25] Associations formed with such aims in view are not even in embryo participatory groupings: there is no real concept of a *balance* of interests to be achieved, rather an *alignment* of school and home.

The practical effect of this approach at local level was that pragmatic *ad hoc* activities for informing parents about the progress of their children remained predominant; the Nottinghamshire enquiry showed this clearly.[26] PTAs were not necessarily seen as desirable by teachers or indeed parents, and as they were school-based they tended to be dependent on the enthusiasm of particular parents or head teachers. Thus their rise and fall was patchy and unpredictable and no real maturing of parental thought or gradual extension of parental activity along post-war West German lines were discernible. A 1955 study of PTAs in Leicester could have been written twenty years before.[27]

The failure to evolve new thinking was accompanied by weakness in national and regional structures. The Home and School Council of Great Britain was founded in 1930 as a national focus for several regional councils grouping local PTAs. Predictably it failed to grow into a strong centralized parent voice along the lines of the French federations because the real life remained at the level of the school. National coordination and financing remained difficult, and a substantial proportion of PTAs never affiliated to the Home and School Council. It survived the war but finally died from lack of funds in 1951.[28]

Quite apart from these difficulties, the Home and School Council, as reflected in its journal, *Home and School*, resembled the PNEU in being basically didactic. The editor wrote in 1938: '... the Council dare not ever forget that it believes in parent-teacher co-operation above everything else as the only way in which most people will come to realize that one method of bringing up children has been found wanting....'[29] The Council had in fact grown up under the wing of the 'progressive' New Education Fellowship, and *Home and School* (known till 1936 as *Parents and Teachers*) appeared from 1932 as a supplement to the NEF's *Education for the New Era*. The Council saw itself as the vehicle for promoting amongst parents the findings of the new psychoanalytic psychology. Susan Isaacs, a tireless worker for progressive ideas, and herself a psychologist of standing, wrote the monthly 'Readers' Questions' section in *Home and School*.[30] One consequence of this orientation was a preoccupation with younger children. Although the price of *Home and School* was reduced to twopence in 1938 in the hope of obtaining a wider readership, one suspects from the sort of questions asked and the general tone of this periodical that its clientele was largely middle-class mothers who had survived the years of infancy with the aid of Truby King and other child-rearing experts and now sought similar advice on the early years of schooling. In fact the 1930s seem to have defined 'the parent question' very largely in relation to *young* children. It is characteristic that the three Hadow reports (on infant and nursery schools, primary schools, and the education of the adolescent) refer to parents only at the infant/nursery and primary levels, as already quoted.

The fact that by the mid-fifties it was again necessary to revive a national coordinating body for PTAs in the guise of the National Federation of Parent-Teacher Associations is evidence that the good intentions and solid intellectual base of the parent movement in the 1930s were insufficient. There seemed to be no growth of parent consciousness, no feeling of a balanced responsibility between parent and teacher in which the parent too had something to offer. The phrases with which in 1957 the then Minister of Education, Lord Hailsham, greeted the new federation, could easily have been pronounced a generation earlier:

> Some head teachers have excellent arrangements for keeping in touch with parents without any formal organization; others feel the need for more formal arrangements.
>
> I am sure that the National Federation of Parent-Teacher Associations respect as much as I do the authority of the head teacher in the conduct of his school.
>
> Parents cannot run schools. This is the job of the head supported by his managers or governors ... what I hope the Federation is going to do is to encourage the fullest co-operation between home and schools, leaving the precise organizations to those on the spot.[31]

In a word, the PTA movement as it had evolved over half a century or more was not a precursor of parent participation in any modern sense. To attempt to view it as such is to ask questions which the participants themselves were not asking, i.e., to be unhistorical. The conditions (which we noted to be apparently favourable to the emergence of parent participation) in fact produced parent activity of a different kind. In relation to the parent scene in the 1960s and 1970s, the conceptual problem is thus to disentangle parent participation from these other longstanding forms of parent involvement. This is a bigger problem than in continental Europe where parent participation emerged from more obviously politicized cultures and for more directly political reasons.

5.3   The Sixties: A New Impetus?

When in 1967 the Plowden commission published its report, *Children and Their Primary Schools*,[32] the response of the journal *Where* was to hail the report as the first official recognition of the parent interest:

> For the first time here is an official report on education which gives great prominence to parents. This is a remarkable change. When the first issue of *Where* was published in the summer of 1960 the idea that parents should be recognized as partners of teachers was a little bizarre, and it has taken time to make the bizarre one degree less so. The mood has now altered. *Where* has reflected an underlying change in society, in a small way contributed to it. . . .'[33]

This 'underlying change' is now part of the received wisdom about the parent movement in England and Wales. Anthony Crosland, Labour Secretary of State for Education and Science from 1965 to 1967, made a similar point when interviewed in 1970: 'I think one of the most encouraging trends in the last few years has been the growth of an informed educational public opinion, manifested in bodies like CASE nationally and parents' associations locally.'[34] This 'change' and 'growth' are usually characterized with reference to three institutions originating in the early sixties: the magazine *Where* which, though not directed exclusively at parents, had a largely parental readership, and began to appear in the spring of 1960; the Advisory Centre for Education (ACE) with which *Where* was closely linked; and the Confederation for the Advancement of State Education (CASE), formed in 1962 on the basis of local associations which had emerged in 1960 and 1961.

   Where and ACE were offshoots of the 'consumerist' movement of the late 1950s, when a newly affluent post-war society produced the Consumers' Association; the Association published a highly successful journal called *Which*, containing tests of various competing products and recommended 'best buys'. *Where*'s title and format were modelled on *Which*, and it was launched in conjunction with a new education consumers' advisory service (ACE) which was chaired by Michael Young, the founder and chairman of the Consumers' Association. The aim of both ACE and *Where* was to provide the information which would make informed parental choice possible. *Where* was even rash enough in the early days to attempt a 'Good Schools Guide' by analogy with the *Good Food Guide*.[35] As with restaurants or vacuum-cleaners, informed choice was expected in the long term to improve the quality of the product. This consumerist approach was essentially *individualistic*, even if the choices of many individuals might in the long run be expected to produce *collective* shifts in policy.

Meanwhile CASE was emerging independently in various localities. The earliest 'Association for the Advancement of State Education' appeared in Cambridge in 1960 in an attempt to bring some parental pressure to bear to improve facilities in a primary school. Within a year two AASE candidates presented themselves in the local election; one was elected and became a member of the local education committee.[36] Other similar associations emerged almost simultaneously. A joint committee was formed in February 1962 and soon evolved into CASE, which from then on evolved as a rather loose 'confederation' of local associations.

Constitutionally CASE was quite distinct from *Where* and ACE, and published its own newsletter, *Parents and Schools*, but many activists read *Where*, which in turn included a fair amount of news of CASE activities, so that to view the two 'wings' as aspects of a single movement is not unfair. Yet whether considered separately or together, CASE, ACE and *Where* did not constitute a grass-roots movement for 'parent participation' in the sense defined in Chapter 1. In fact the historical perspective brings out the similarities with PNEU in the 1890s and the Home and School Council of the 1930s.

Brian Jackson, director of ACE in the early seventies, caught the tone of all three institutions exactly:

> At ACE our strategy has been to strive towards a favourable climate, then to amass a unique store of information and advice, and finally to address ourselves to the only group which could genuinely be partners in forging new attitudes and techniques. This has proved to be, in a broad way, the professional middle class. Our members, so far as we can judge, have exerted an influence out of all proportion to their numbers. They are the ones who read and argue, suggest and complain, act and take office. Some degree of the improvement — the increase in flexibility and humaneness of our education system — is undoubtedly due to their work.[37]

The aims were consensual ('to strive towards a favourable climate') and didactic ('information and advice'). They were also restricted 'in a broad way' to 'the professional middle class'. The basic stance was not dissimilar from Charlotte Mason's or Susan Isaacs', though there were differences in tone: less straight proselytism, more weighing of alternatives in the consumerist style. *Where* reflected various points of view and was in a sense accountable to its subscribers rather than to some more abstract 'gospel of education' or to the 'progressive' principles of the PNEU or the New Education Fellowship. This orientation made if anything for a *less* popularizing approach than its predecessors: 'ACE works at a fairly high level of literacy, numeracy (all those tables!) and general sophistication. *Where* is a subscription magazine, and despite repeated efforts, W.H. Smith's will not handle it for direct sale on their bookstalls. Inevitably, then, its audience is predominantly the professional middle-class.'[38] Perhaps W.H. Smith's policy was not the only obstacle to a more popularist appeal. Consumerism by definition presupposed the possibility of choice, and particularly in the early years of *Where* articles and readers' letters showed that many subscribers belonged to that minority of the population for whom choice meant choice between private schools, or between preparatory schools and state primary schools. The very phrase 'state education' in CASE's name implied almost a conscious choice of 'state' as opposed to 'private', yet the early years of *Where* indicated little ideological preference for one over the other. Although CASE itself moved more firmly towards a desire to engage with the working class, it never seems to have been particularly successful in doing so.

Behind these ambivalences lay a deep reluctance to embrace political commitments in the sense of overt engagement with the traditional Right-Left *party* debate. The Cambridge Councillor elected under the AASE banner in 1961 was an exception, not a portent; indeed her decision to stand as a 'non-political' *parent* activist was a mark of this concern to retain a sort of ideological purity. It should be remembered that many of the early subscribers to *Where* and members of CASE had cut their teeth in the PTA movement and continued to support and promote it. The early numbers of *Where* are full of advice on parent-school relations which is entirely along traditional consensual PTA lines: 'It is highly undesirable that an Association should attempt in any way to interfere with the way the school should be run, educationally, or what should be taught in it. . . . It is a good thing for the Association's constitution to contain a clause making it clear that the organization is not to be used as a commission for determining the school's educational policy.'[39] School managers should observe the traditional demarcation lines: 'When it comes to watching the teaching the manager should tread with great caution and proper humility. Unless he himself has taught, he cannot be expected to know about the technique of teaching.'[40] And the very first CASE group's 'most important advice . . . to anyone starting a similar group' was 'don't antagonize the LEA.'[41] All this reflects the continuing power of the idea of consensus and the debt which the national and local parent structures owed to the school-based PTA movement.

All this suggests that the *Where*/ACE/CASE movement was yet another manifestation of a sort of generational cycle of English parent activity, renewing itself in roughly thirty-year 'waves'. Yet there was one element of novelty, more apparent in CASE than in ACE or *Where*: the shift of focus from the individual school to the LEA. As CASE branches were normally organized to cover a single LEA, for the first time a pressure-group existed which corresponded to that basic unit of political decision about education. This was to give CASE the significance which led to its rapid promotion as *the* parents' association *par excellence*. However numerically small a local group might be, it could speak for an area and to *politicians* in a way which a school-based PTA never could. CASE and its allies filled a vacuum.

The real mushrooming in membership came in the early sixties: 2000 members of ACE (i.e., subscribers to *Where*) had risen to ten times that number by late 1965 and levelled out at 24,000 by 1968; thereafter, membership declined somewhat. CASE's membership, being essentially local, was always impossible to establish accurately, and fluctuated a good deal as local groups flourished and declined. But in a sense the numbers were much less important than the legitimation of the parent interest on a scale wider than the indiviual school. It was only a year after its foundation that CASE had established its credentials sufficiently to be invited to provide two of the members of the Plowden Committee, in addition to Michael Young, the Chairman of ACE. CASE at this stage was a relatively small and fluid organization, essentially middle-class and concentrated in the urban areas of the south of England.[42] Its acceptability to members of the ruling elite such as ministers arose, no doubt, partly from its character as a well-informed group of the liberal intelligentsia,[43] but much more from politicians' *need for some legitimizing parent group*. Only this can explicate Anthony Crosland's extraordinary statement (extraordinary because of the numerical weakness and patchy incidence of parent activism in the 1960s) that the fact the CASE and local parents' associations 'were almost wholly pro-comprehensive was a major factor in the dynamic that we got behind *Circular 10/65* in early years.'[44] In a word, parents became important as consensus declined; and in education consensus declined most obviously as a result of the comprehensive issue. Almost one might say that if CASE had not existed, it would have been necessary to invent it.

5.4 Preconditions of Parent Participation, 1965–75

In assessing the changes of the seventies which eventually led to legislation on the election of 'parent governors', it is important to recognize that as late as the mid-sixties the demand for 'parental participation' in the 'legally required' sense defined in Chapter 1 had hardly been voiced in England and Wales. The parent movement of the early sixties may have been more assertive, and was certainly better publicized, than its more school-oriented predecessor and partner, the PTA movement; but its main demand was at most for increased LEA 'responsiveness'. There was no suggestion in the pages of *Where* at this time that parents had an inalienable *right* to monitor or control what schools were doing. Schools were still seen as 'non-political'; parents *supported* them in that role and could do so more effectively if they were better *informed*.

The change in parental perceptions and objectives between about 1965 and 1975 stemmed much less from the internal debates of the parent movement (still very much a minority activity with few, if any, links with the party political machine) than from the political world itself. The first important decision was to introduce a comprehensive form of secondary education. Although this had no direct bearing on parent participation, it highlighted value conflicts in education which had lain more or less dormant since the early years of the century. The parent movement moved closer to educational management as it came to be seen as one way of validating difficult value decisions or defusing conflict.

Comprehensive education had been seen by the Labour party of the early sixties as a consensual reform — or at least as a reform which, if initially controversial, would rapidly come to be seen as commonsensical and even popular.[45] By 1963 Harold Wilson was presenting comprehensivization as the answer to 'educational apartheid' and as a contribution to scientific, technological and economic progress.[46] Partly to avoid conflict at a time when Labour's majority in parliament was minute, the reform was promulgated in a ministerial circular (10/65) which 'requested' local authorities to prepare and submit plans for going comprehensive, and gave them six alternative patterns of organization from which to choose. This polite and gradualistic approach gave Conservative LEAs considerable scope for resistance. By 1968 the Labour party was doing badly in local elections, so that one of the main bones of contention in national-local relations became comprehensivization.[47] In these circumstances parent opinion became more important than ever before, whether in supporting existing schools seen as threatened by comprehensivization, or in validating change. In the nature of things PTAs tended to fall into the 'defensive' category, and this enhanced the importance of groups like CASE — i.e., informed persons, readers of *Where*, who would on the whole be likely to favour a 'progressive' or pro-Labour line.

The late sixties and early seventies in England and Wales saw no decisive turning-point in the French or Italian style. Rather, there was on the one hand a gradual polarization or politicization of the parent movement (or at least of parts of it), on the other a slow recognition by local and national governments that, as parent opinion was potentially explosive and difficult to manage, it might be useful to incorporate it in some way in the structures of government and administration. This rethinking was assisted by the participatory *Zeitgeist*, by current views of the role of parents in socialization, and by the availability of time-honoured structures in the shape of boards of managers and governors: these factors were secondary rather than primary, contributory rather than determining.

Brief summaries such as the preceding paragraph give a misleading impression of tidiness and purpose. In reality, the evolution of opinion about parent participation was hesitant, uncertain and confused. That was true in the first place of the parent movement itself. In fact to speak of 'a movement', or of 'polarization' and 'politicization' is deceptive if it implies any degree of unity or certainty of aim. CASE was undoubtedly the best informed and most aware parent grouping in the sixties. By the mid-sixties it had formulated a national policy which included support for comprehensive schools and urged that parents should sit as of right on school governing bodies and local education committees.[48] Yet it originally declared its support for comprehensive schools only by a tiny majority at its annual conference, and remained officially non-partisan, claiming to represent members of all parties and of none,[49] and pursuing a variety of educational issues in addition to comprehensivization. Thus there naturally grew up round CASE other single-issue groups to promote more single-mindedly 'the comprehensive revolution', better provision of nursery education, etc.[50] In addition, the local focus of CASE groups, and the fact that detailed plans for going comprehensive had to be worked out locally, meant that CASE's contribution was indeed non-partisan and pragmatic, at least within the broad parameters of commitment to the comprehensive school.

CASE was in a sense the intelligentsia of the parent movement, its most politically conscious sector. Round it one must imagine a wide variety of other groups, especially PTAs. The numbers of parents in these groups, though not large,[51] were certainly much greater than those in CASE. In the late sixties and early seventies, though, the majority of them were concerned above all else with supporting and defending their own particular school, and thus moved into the political arena only reactively, in response to changes emanating from the local education committee.[52]

The protean and resolutely non-partisan character of the parent movement in England and Wales presumably explains why polarization was so uncertain. After all, the changes proposed in Circular 10/65 represented a considerable shift, a desire to distribute life-chances more equitably. CASE and other groups which approved of these changes naturally campaigned for them. One might have expected another group or groups to have emerged in opposition. There was one such group, the National Education Association (NEA), but it led a shadowy half-life in the penumbra of the Conservative party, with very limited membership and only sporadic local activity. The contrast with France or Italy is marked, and reminds us that the parent movement in England and Wales was part of a political culture which valued the preservation of a certain distance between political parties and pressure-groups.

This concern can also be seen in the evolving reaction of 'governing elites' — in this case local and national politicians. Parent participation in the sense defined in Chapter 1 was achieved by local experimentation over the 1970s which was then consolidated and extended by national legislation in 1980. In moving to involve parents in the government and management of schools, both local and national politicians were in part responding to a general climate of opinion. This was favourable to parents, but again in a non-partisan way.

In England and Wales participation did not first present itself as a *political* demand. It was not an urgent response to crisis, as in France, nor a conscious attempt to root state institutions in the popular consciousness, as in Germany. No doubt 'participation' was part of the general intellectual baggage of thinking people in the late sixties; there is some evidence of that in the deliberations of the Maud commission on local government,[53] or of the Weaver report which introduced an element of lecturer and student participation into the management of colleges of education,[54] and acted as a model for further education as well. Although student unrest in 1968 was slight when compared with France, Italy and West Germany, universities generally moved to strengthen arrangements for student involvement in the running of their institutions, though no university moved as far in the erection of tripartite structures as their continental counterparts.[55] However, such shifts were evidence only of a general climate of opinion which was more likely to result in a revaluing of the *teacher's* contribution to school management; the involvement of *parents* in the running of schools required a rather different leap of the imagination and a commitment to working out practicable structures. In 1966 the Inspectorate could only report rather vaguely that there was some feeling for 'stronger parental representation'.[56]

The extra impetus was provided to some extent by the sociologists. The link-up between sociological interpretations of the educational process and parent participation through the formal structures of the school was made by the Plowden report as early as 1967. A whole chapter was devoted to 'Participation by parents'.[57] The chapter was basically an exposition of the newly popular sociological perspective on the family:

> A strengthening of parental encouragement may produce better performance in school, and thus stimulate the parents to encourage more; or discouragement in the home may initiate a vicious downward circle. Schools exist to foster virtuous circles. They do this most obviously through their direct influence upon children. . . . Some schools are already working at the same time from the other end, by influencing parents directly, and the children indirectly through the parents. . . .[58]

Now this argument about how to break into the 'cycle of deprivation' had very little to do with parent participation in the sense defined in Chapter 1. It was still didactic in the style almost of the PNEU or the progressive PTA movement of the 1930s: experts were to intervene to assist parents in their parental practice. Yet in spite of that the attempt to spell out the importance of PTAs and desirable practices for encouraging home-school communication reinforced the sentiment that parents were a definable group, that they were important and that some form of institutional recognition of their importance could and should be realized; and in England and Wales that institutional recognition naturally took the form of a reformed board of governors. The Plowden Committee had access to the interim findings of a research unit on school management and government based at the London Institute of Education,[59] and duly recommended 'the appointment as managers of parents who have children at the school'.[60] Thus the *collective* representation of parents as a group became rather uneasily attached to arguments focused on remedies for the shortcomings of *individual* parents.

The formulation of concrete objectives of that sort was a necessary first step towards legally recognized parent participation, but had little purchase in reality until worked out in more detail. Although Plowden provided two and a half pages of discussion on the management of schools,[61] most of the working out of how parents might relate more creatively to school management was done at the local level in the late sixties and early seventies. Plowden's recommendations on parent governors were not taken up by central government at the time; the proposal which commanded most attention and support was for the establishment of 'educational priority areas' (EPAs) — defined zones, usually in inner-city areas, in which the vicious circle of educational and social deprivation was to be broken by increased resources and experimentation. Many of these EPA schemes made imaginative attempts to engage the interest and support of parents, and some of the earlier thinking of CASE and ACE was brought to bear outside the original middle-class catchment of those organizations: for example, an 'education shop' run in the Liverpool EPA was run by the local CASE secretary and modelled on an ACE experiment.[62] The Liverpool EPA scheme under Eric Midwinter was particularly concerned to involve parents and improve home-school relations, and a flair for publicity produced a flow of lively articles not only in *Where* and the educational press but in the general press as well.[63]

All this activity remained in what we might almost call the Mason-Isaacs-Plowden tradition. Although less patronizing and earnest than Charlotte Mason and her helpers, the theory of 'virtuous circles' assumed agreement on what constituted 'virtue': the basic aims of schools were consensual. The possibility of politicization on, say, the Italian model was there, and the presence of parents might pose awkward questions to the teachers. Yet although activists like Eric Midwinter might argue for a complete rethink of the curriculum for the inner city, there is little evidence that parents themselves were moving into the political area.

Meanwhile another strand of thought was evolving: discontent about the existing state of boards of managers and governors. The boards which had emerged from the 1902 Education Act and which had been remodelled in the 1944 Act had nothing to do with participatory democracy, and even less to do with parents. Although an amendment to the 1944 Education Act had been proposed to require the appointment of at least one manager as 'a representative of the parents',[64] the amendment was withdrawn after the government had expressed 'complete sympathy' but had pointed out that a parent representative would upset the balance achieved between voluntary and LEA representatives, etc. By the mid-sixties the governing bodies which emerged from the 1944 Act were widely seen by the few people interested in such matters as unrepresentative, inactive and ineffectual. In particular the practice of grouping attracted much criticism. Some LEAs fulfilled their formal duties to set up governing bodies by declaring the education committee itself to be the governing body of all schools in their area; or they set up a separate single committee for that purpose; or they grouped schools in particular areas under several umbrella governing bodies. Even when each school had its own separate governing body, governors were criticized as being largely or entirely political appointees, so that a governorship became an instrument of minor political patronage.

There was general agreement among those who discussed such questions that the *status quo* was indefensible. CASE argued before the Royal Commission on local government in 1966 that governing bodies were 'little more than an anachronistic formality. They still have some duties, however, and have a considerable potential which is seldom realized. For this reason we would urge that their membership, like that of the LEAs themselves, should be broadened, and their functions enhanced. . . .'[65] This view was accepted by the Maud commission which deplored grouping, and suggested that 'the local community interest' could be 'represented by effective managing and governing bodies'.[66] Although these recommendations were not taken up by government, they were rehearsed in assorted reports over the next few years, coming mainly from the teacher unions, whose main preoccupation was with increased teacher influence.[67]

It was, of course, easier to agree on negative criticism of an existing institution than on positive moves forward, and one of the features of discussion at this stage was its unspecific character. In CASE's words quoted above, functions should be 'enhanced' — but what those enhanced functions were to be was left unclear. Again, this lack of clarity reflected the emphasis placed by the system as a whole on consensus. Support was more likely to accrue to something vague than to something precise and therefore objectionable. Sharper definition was to be achieved gradually in two ways. One was the evolution of the comprehensive debate, especially in its impact on parents. The other was the establishment of a National Association of Governors and Managers (NAGM).

NAGM was founded in 1970. It was in effect one of those single-issue groups mentioned earlier in this section which tended to cluster round CASE whose interests remained wider and more various. In its early stages its membership was very largely people who had become interested in school government through their membership of CASE, but felt the need of a more focused campaign to achieve a needed reform. It was strongly influenced in its foundation by Tyrrell Burgess, an imaginative and energetic academic somewhat in the style of Michael Young. NAGM moved quickly to recruit members among existing managers and governors. Its obvious usefulness to a group of locally influential people who might be described as 'pillars of society' soon gave it a rather more 'establishment' image than CASE, and the consensual nature of the reforms it promoted allowed it to preserve a notable 'non-political' stance. This did not, however, prevent it from undertaking some effective lobbying, both locally and nationally. In this its sober image and its ability to speak the same language as 'the ruling elite' was helpful, and NAGM must certainly take a good share of the credit for getting school government on to the agenda in the first half of the seventies.

Meanwhile, and much more controversially, the comprehensive issue had continued to evolve. The significance of that evolution for the parent movement lay in its increasing preoccupation with parental choice of secondary school. To see why this was so, it is illuminating to contrast the position in England and Wales with its continental counterparts. The relative autonomy of individual schools and the power of head teachers in appointing staff and modifying the curriculum; the existence of a considerable sector of religious schools largely funded by the state; the existence of a large and often prestigious fee paying system in parallel with state schools — all these had traditionally fostered the attitude among concerned parents that one of their most important functions was *choice* of the right school for their child. Especially in its early years, *Where* reflected that attitude very clearly. Thus one of the more telling arguments for the comprehensive school was that it would *increase* parental choice by removing the rigid selective process at 11+ and replacing it by more humane and flexible guidance procedures within the single comprehensive school — the 'grammar school for all'.

This traditional preoccupation with choice was sharpened by the circumstances in which the comprehensive change took place.[68] These might almost have been deliberately calculated to maximize anxiety among parents. LEAs were required by Circular 10/65 to consult parental opinion — a clause which was inserted as a result of CASE pressure.[69] In practice this meant that a fixed time was specified (three months) within which parents who objected to a proposed change in character in the school attended by their children could register a formal written protest with the Minister. The protest could be from an individual or a group, but obviously group submissions would carry more weight. This procedure put a premium on *defence* of the individual school and therefore of the *status quo*. Most schemes involved the amalgamation of existing secondary schools. Grammar schools of good repute which attracted considerable parental support became for that very reason more difficult to close. The political differences between local authorities and national government were quite easy to exploit with 'non-political' parental support. Conservative authorities could delay submission of their schemes to the Labour Secretary of State, or draft them in such a way that selection was preserved in some more or less covert way (e.g., by zoning arrangements), or draft them so that they would be rejected by the Secretary of State, with more delays and more chance of heading off unwelcome change until the return of a more sympathetic central government. Sure enough, when a Conservative Secretary of State (Margaret Thatcher) took over in 1970, she at once removed the requirement to 'go comprehensive' — but now it was Labour authorities which had to submit schemes designed to appeal to the new government's commitment to 'parental choice' (loose zoning arrangements, provision of single-sex schools, etc.). Some schemes were rejected, or more usually accepted only in part, with former grammar schools preserved side by side with former secondary modern schools. Although former grammar and secondary modern schools might now share the label 'comprehensive', old social divisions were often preserved by accidents of geography, with former grammar schools serving owner-occupied suburbs and former secondary moderns situated in council estates.

This complex and variegated chequerwork of change was at its height for about ten years from 1965. It had a threefold impact on the parent movement. Firstly, it greatly increased the awareness among parents of themselves as a separate group whose views had a right to a hearing. Secondly, it brought before many parents, in a vivid and personal way, the complexity of educational politics. Thirdly, it made politicians (and, rather more slowly, teachers) realize that parents had a certain political clout, and were more comfortable to have with you than against you.

The realities of the new situation were revealed in a number of court cases, of which the most celebrated in the immediate post-1965 period were two cases at Enfield. In one, a group of parents took out an injunction against the London Borough of Enfield for attempting to enforce comprehensive reorganization without complying with the consultation clauses of the 1944 Act.[70] The authority's defence turned on the interpretation of 'ceasing to maintain', but was not upheld by the Court of Appeal. This defeat was a reminder to LEAs that their electoral mandate had to be exercised within the provisions of the existing law, and that parents could use the legal system in a way familiar enough in the Federal Republic or the USA, but rather novel in the less litigious polity of the United Kingdom. The second case involved a single school, Enfield Grammar School.[71] A change in its articles of government was required in order to permit it to take a non-selective intake. The Secretary of State allowed only five days for objections to the changes to be made, and the court ruled that this amounted to a denial of statutory rights. The embarrrassment caused by this case led to the passing of the 1968 Education Act which widened somewhat the discretion exercised by the Secretary of State in determining what constituted a change of character in a school.

Buxton's judgment was that 'little of substance' was achieved by the Enfield litigation.[72] In strict legal terms that may have' been so. Politically, however, the reverberations were considerable. Kogan's assessment was more positive:

> Parents were showing that they could organize themselves both politically and forensically. . . . Parent power was now able to move from talking and pamphleteering about the general issues of standards and participation, as such bodies as the Confederation for the Advancement of State Education had done for some years, towards taking expensive, technically sophisticated and politically tough actions against elected councils and the DES.[73]

In a rather similar way to the Hessian *Förderstufe* judgments of 1957,[74] the 1967 Enfield cases were a sort of coming of age for what Kogan calls 'parent power'. Yet in Hessen the statutory incorporation of parents into school management at all levels followed at once. In England and Wales it was to take another thirteen years to achieve that recognition in national legislation. The difference flowed in large measure from the diffusion of power throughout the English and Welsh system, but it related also to the extreme reluctance to define the parental role in collective terms. The idea of a balanced partnership among parents, schools and LEA was implicit in the Enfield judgments, yet what was explicitly highlighted in the cases was the individualistic 'parental choice' aspect of parent-school relations. This tension was to run right through the seventies as first local authorities and then central government attempted to involve parents more closely in the running of schools.

5.5 The Establishment of Parent Participation at Local Level, 1970–80

The chronological account of the evolution of the parent movement from 1890 to 1970 presented in the preceding three sections of this chapter has implicitly refuted the 'reformist' theory of parent participation as sketched in Chapter 1. For various reasons eighty years of parent activity failed to produce (or even devote much thought to) 'the legally required association of parents with the schools their children attend through systems of elected representatives and committees' (see section 1.5). From about 1970 the picture began to change as first local authorities, then the national government, began to incorporate parents into existing schemes of school government. This change did not appear to be 'the product of experience of and commitment to democratic involvement'; if it had been, it would presumably have evolved much more gradually since the beginning of the century. Did the 'general crisis' theory provide a more satisfactory account of the change? To answer that question, it is necessary first to ask what the crisis was.

The least satisfactory answer relied heavily on the *Zeitgeist*. It was asserted that a 'spirit of participation' was abroad in the world towards the end of the sixties, and that people were seeking closer involvement with the institutions of the modern state, which they now perceived to be remote or impersonal.[75] This explanation was unrevealing. It blurred the differences between forms of participatory activity in different societies and places. Because it was ahistorical, it gave no reasonable basis for thinking about the future.

In the narrower focus of England and Wales, 'crisis' was a common term in the political and moral discourse of the late sixties and the seventies. Often the word was used loosely to indicate the writer's subjective concern that change was proceeding too fast, or in the wrong direction. Certainly this period was one when many people felt a sense of general turmoil, of modernization sweeping away much that was valued and loved, of a sharpening of debate to a point where violence began to take over. Yet these *perceptual* responses were again unrevealing, however strongly they may have been experienced by individuals. They suggested the need for objective analysis, but did not assist in making it.

Less simplistic explanations concentrated on the deepening economic crisis and on the incapacity of the machinery of state to overcome it. As the initiative for incorporating parents into the structures of school government came much more from 'the machinery of state' than from the parents themselves, this seems, *prima facie*, to be a more promising approach. It will be argued (i) that the inauguration of parent participation was in the first instance an attempt by local authorities to increase public support for schools which had to some degree forfeited it; (ii) that national legislation was then introduced as a diversionary tactic by a government whose capacity for taking more substantial initiatives was severely limited; (iii) that therefore the part played by the economic and social crisis in provoking both local and national initiatives was indirect but real; and (iv) that the diversionary and rather artificial character of parent participation in England and Wales was revealed by the erosion of the collectivist aspects of the 1977 Taylor proposals and the reassertion of more traditional individualist interpretations of the parental role.

By 1978, two years before national legislation on this matter, a *Where* survey showed that out of eighty-nine respondent LEAs, seventy-eight had some form of parent representation on school managing and governing bodies.[76] In less than a decade, through a large number of local decisions, the abnormal had become normal. What factors led to this change?

The first broad set of factors has already been described in section 5.4. It might be called 'parent awareness' — awareness by some parents that they constituted some sort of definable interest-group, and awareness by some local politicians that that was the case. That awareness had been greatly stimulated in the debates over comprehensive reorganization. However, sections 5.2–5.4 have also made it clear that parent awareness was not at all the same thing as parent participation in the sense defined in 1.5. The general idea that parents had an 'important influence on children's education and that their cooperation in the process of education ought therefore to be obtained predisposed politicians and others to look favourably on schemes for linking parents with schools, and to think that they might be popular; it did not *produce* parent participation, however. The restricted nature of parent interest in formal elections and committees was demonstrated not only by the history described in 5.2–5.4, but by the difficulties experienced by LEAs in inaugurating their new participatory systems — very low voting figures at elections of parent representatives, unfilled vacancies on governing bodies, etc. Parent awareness defined the issue in overwhelmingly individualist terms. It was a necessary condition of parent participation, but not a sufficient one.

More urgent reasons for the introduction of parent participation flowed from the difficulties of local government in this period. Ashford, in a provocative comparative study of local government in France and Britain,[77] has argued that relations between national and local governmen in Britain are rigid and incoherent, and that the reasons can be understood only in a historical perspective:

> Britain places an enormously high value on adversarial politics at the national level. Britain first developed democratic political institutions, and the critical importance of adversarial politics is rooted in seventeenth and eighteenth century struggles with the monarchy. It was essential to British democracy that statutory law be the supreme law of the land and that discretionary authority be kept to an absolute minimum. The institutional solution was to assert the power of the Cabinet and Parliament over all other forms of authority, and in many respects this remains the underlying institutional constraint on British local government, as on many other political institutions in Britain.[78]

The difficulties and shortcomings of local government were certainly a constant *leitmotiv* of educational politics throughout this period. The Maud commission of enquiry on local government sat from 1966 to 1969. Its report was then discussed under Labour and Conservative governments, and its recommendations were drastically altered. New larger units of local government were eventually inaugurated in 1974. Even so, the debate was far from settled, and less than a decade later the Conservative government went into the general election of 1983 pledged to abolish the metropolitan counties. A 1982 review of a wide range of writing on the issue as it affected education concluded:

> Support for a strong system of local government with a substantial degree of discretion is widespread. Yet the margin of discretion is being reduced by measures taken as part of the Government's economic strategy. . . . The wider issue, though, concerns the whole future of local government as an integral part of Britain's political and administrative system. The changes of recent years might lead to a permanent reduction in the role and influence of local government. . . .[79]

In more concrete terms, the experience of most local authorities over the seventies was that of (i) being remodelled into new, larger and more impersonal units and (ii) being subjected to increasing financial constraints. The 1974 local government reorganization reduced 163 local education authorities in England and Wales to 104. These changes were often accompanied by the internal adoption of corporate management procedures which were felt by many councillors and local government officers to reduce their capacity for flexible response. The financial constraints were largely external: they flowed ultimately from the nation's poor performance in the international trading system, but were transmitted to the local level through central government pressure to promote or maintain some national economic strategy, through modifications of the rate support grant, the imposition of cash limits, etc.

In these circumstances, local authorities naturally sought to undertake cheap, achievable initiatives which they thought would be popular, and they looked for such initiatives particularly in situations where some degree of political threat was felt. Thus the third element which facilitated policies of parent participation was often a local political upset, or a wish felt by a local party to achieve a slightly broader base in popular support. That feeling of insecurity was often the trigger mechanism in instituting new forms of parent representation.[80]

One of the earliest and best-publicized schemes of parent representation was that adopted by the City of Sheffield in 1970.[81] This innovation was part of the local Labour party's response to the shock of losing control of the City Council in 1968 after forty years of almost uninterrupted Labour rule. A new policy on school managing bodies was worked out in a brief period of opposition and implemented when Labour returned to power again a year later. An important group of Labour politicians was anxious to consolidate in the affections of the people the comprehensive system Labour had inaugurated before its temporary loss of office. Another important contributor to the innovation was an active local group of CASE. By the late sixties it had established its credentials as a channel for concrete ideas of parent participation to flow between the educational intelligentsia and the local political establishment, and the national secretary of CASE, Barbara Bullivant, happened to live in Sheffield. Once the idea of elected parent representatives had been 'sold' to the Labour party, it was rapidly implemented and soon became nationally known — partly through the CASE/ACE/*Where* network in general and Mrs Bullivant in particular, and partly through the LEAs' network. The Chief Education Officer for Sheffield, Mr G.M.A. Harrison, provided a steady flow of articles in *Education* on the Sheffield experiment, was in demand in the early seventies as a speaker at conferences and working parties and was eventually nominated to the Taylor committee, which discussed parent participation as a national issue.

The Sheffield system had two main components: firstly, it gave to every school its own separate governing body, and thus ended the practice of 'grouping'; secondly, it reduced the political representation on those governing bodies to a minority, and introduced elected representatives of parents, teachers and non-teaching staff, and representatives from local community, religious and voluntary organizations.

The rhetoric stressed the first three aims listed in section 1.2: responsiveness, legitimacy, and personal development:

> The emphasis will be more and more on partnership rather than edicts being handed down from on high. It will be exhilarating, exciting and interesting to see every school with local knowledge of both needs and abilities, engaging in a democratic process of helping the children to integrate in an expanding, interdependent social grouping. Thousands of people who have always wanted to play some role in education and who have felt that they could never do so, will now have their chance .... [82]

However, after studying the workings of the new system, Bacon laid greater stress on the legitimacy aims of what he called 'the leaders of welfare bureaucracies': 'Firstly the need to maintain their authority. Secondly, the need to maintain the stability and security of their organization. And thirdly the need to justify their continued claims upon the wider sources of society.'[83] In other words, the deeper purposes were those of 'legitimation' (1.5), or in Bacon's terminology 'the engineering of client consent'.

Bacon's view of the origins of the Sheffield innovations is also significant:

> ... most of the pressure leading to school board reform did not emanate from the community at large, but sprang from three fairly identifiable though closely related sources. Firstly, a district branch of the metropolitan intelligentsia which was primarily employed in, or indirectly involved with, the local educational industry, and which had formed local branches of such nationally organized pressure groups as the Campaign [sic] for State Education and the National Association of Governors and Managers. Secondly, a group of administrative officials who were dissatisfied with the city's extremely centralized system of organizing its educational service.... And finally, a group of local politicians....[84]

Such groups constituted what this study has described as 'a ruling elite' (1.5).

Liverpool provided a more complex example of the introduction of parent participation. This city differed from Sheffield and some of the big urban areas like Leeds and Manchester in having had for many years a relatively complete system of governing and managing bodies for individual schools. Apart from some grouping of schools (e.g., boys' and girls' schools serving the same district), it was accepted as normal that each school should have a separate body of governors rather than be controlled by large formal committees serving several schools or even all the schools in the city. Parents appeared on these governing bodies from time to time, but there was no attempt to require schools to appoint a parent governor as such until 1973. In the local elections of May 1972 a Labour administration had taken over from the Conservatives and had rapidly pushed through a plan for the comprehensive reorganization of secondary schooling throughout the city.[85] As a result of this it was also necessary to submit to the Department of Education and Science new rules ('instruments and articles of government') for the government of the new schools, many of which were amalgamations or drastic remodellings of existing selective schools. A single parent governor was included in these schemes, to be elected by a PTA or PA or, where schools had no such associations, by a parents' meeting convened by the head teacher. The term of office was to be three years. The reasons for this innovation were various. In part they were idealistic: there was a genuine feeling that the new schools should be 'community schools'. In part the reasons for change were more pragmatic, ranging from a desire to swing local support behind the new schools to the need to 'sell' the comprehensive scheme to the Conservative Secretary of State, Mrs Margaret Thatcher. It was partly to appeal to her preferences for 'parental choice' that the Liverpool scheme was drawn up to permit a great deal of choice (as between large schools and small ones, single-sex schools and mixed ones), and an element of parent representation seemed to be a logical extension of this. A single parent was not a very radical change in the existing system, and represented the smallest possible shift in that direction. The working party on secondary reorganization contained both individuals who were heavily involved in CASE and NAGM and therefore strongly committed to change, and councillors who tended to view parent governors with suspicion as a dilution of the councillor's traditional authority as the elected representative of the people. Thus the minimal shift of 1973 represented a compromise.

The new system was short-lived. It rapidly threw up some minor anomalies: the role and functions of parent governors had been insufficiently defined, and there was some feeling that to use PTAs as a base for parent representation was awkward — that it handed over public office to what might amount to a clique. However, these problems might have been dealt with administratively had there not been another change of political power. In May 1974 the Liberals took control of the city. Their victory was sudden and surprising and aroused much national interest. Parent representation — and more generally community representation — was of interest to the Liberals in two ways. They saw themselves as a 'new broom' moving in to sweep away the entrenched attitudes of the two-party system. They also saw themselves as 'populists', and much of their electoral success derived from their readiness to consult the people at grass-roots level and try to solve their problems in a non-ideological way. They relied heavily on local newsletters in which they publicized their campaigns for new pedestrian crossings, better rubbish disposal, etc.

The Liberals needed policies which would produce visible change at no expense for they were committed above all else to holding down the rates. They also needed policies which would not provoke the Labour and Conservative councillors to unite against them; although they were the largest group on the council, they were in an overall minority. An extension of parent and/or community control of schools had obvious attractions. It was in accord with their basic populist philosophy and unlikely to produce rifts in the variegated coalition of interests which had brought them to power. It would dilute the existing Tory/Labour domination of school governing bodies, which amounted to an instrument of minor party patronage. It was likely to cost little or nothing. In the summer of 1974 a working party was set up to reconsider the articles and instruments of management and government in Liverpool schools. It consisted of councillors of all three parties, representatives of the teacher unions and of NAGM and CASE. A wide range of documentation was submitted to the working party, both local (reports from CASE and NAGM) and national (accounts of what other local authorities had already done, extracts from *NAGM News* and Home and School Council publications, etc.).

Most of the discussion focused on methods of obtaining 'community' representation on governing bodies, and on the procedures for electing two or three parent representatives per school in annual elections (the previous scheme had been triennial) to be held at the start of the autumn term. The basic question of principle as it affected parents — that parent representation should be extended and strengthened by standardized electoral procedures — was never really in doubt. In other words, by the mid-seventies that had come to seem almost self-evidently a desirable objective for an LEA which thought of itself as progressive. This was also evident during the political discussions of the working party's recommendations: there was no dissent from the idea of increased parent representation on governing bodies strengthened by selection through an annual electoral process. What disagreement there was concerned the mechanics and expense of election; this swelled up again when the first elections (held in September 1975) produced small numbers of voters and a considerable number of vacancies, but the problem was handled not by questioning the basic idea but by pragmatic improvements to the electoral process: clearer letters to parents, simpler school-based procedures, less formal nominations meetings, etc. By 1975 every Liverpool school had one or more parent representatives on its governing body (the number depended on the size of the school) — or at worst a vacancy waiting to be filled by a parent.[86]

Although little in-depth research has been done on the circumstances in which local authorities implemented schemes of parent representation in the 1970s, these two examples permit some tentative generalizations about:

(i) *the extreme variability and complexity of local conditions*. This means that counter-examples — e.g., of LEAs which implemented parent participation simply because the chairman of the education committee thought it was a good idea — can probably be found. But the complexity of LEAs and of the total political system in which they operate probably means that examples of the Sheffield or Liverpool type are much more usual. The absence of concerted national pressure on this wide variety of local situations makes the relative uniformity of response rather striking.

(ii) *the importance of the comprehensive issue* — magnified by the tendency of the political system to produce swings against national governments in local elections. It seemed as if from 1964 to 1970 Conservative local authorities were in a state of embattled resistance to centrally decreed change, while after 1970 Labour authorities were busy trying to frame reorganization schemes to circumvent a government with a commitment to preserve 'good grammar schools'. In such circumstances politicians looked for support to 'non-political' groups such as parents. The role of parent groups tended to be reactive, even though in reacting they were often quite influential.

(iii) *the predominance of 'legitimacy' in the aims of the new schemes* for electing parents to governing bodies. Although 'responsiveness' featured in the rhetoric, there were virtually no changes of function to accommodate the presence of parents on governing bodies. As in France or Italy, innovation was simply added on to the existing system. Nor was there any real attempt to secure an effective parent input at LEA level, in spite of the greater suitability of the English and Welsh devolved system for such an innovation, as compared with its counterparts in continental Europe.

(iv) *the growing importance of public awareness*. The importance of the Sheffield scheme as a well-publicized working model has been mentioned. From the early to the late seventies there was a sort of bandwagon effect among LEAs (LEAs more than parents, for LEAs were the decision-makers in this matter), of which the creation of a national committee to review the working of governing bodies was both an effect and a cause.

5.6 Legitimizing Parent Participation at National Level, 1975–80

The Education Act of 1980 marked the moment at which parent participation became a statutory requirement in England and Wales. The Act was, however, only the culmination of several years' attempts to embed developments at local level in national legislation. The three main stages in that process were (i) an abortive Education (Parents' Charter) Bill (debate on second reading 25 April 1975); (ii) the committee of enquiry on the management and government of schools (Taylor Committee; announced in Parliament 27 January 1975; appointed April 1975; report published September 1977); (iii) an abortive Education Bill (debate on second reading 5 December 1978), drafted in the final phase of Mr Callaghan's Labour government, and aborted when parliament was dissolved four months later.

As we have seen in the cases of Sheffield and Liverpool, parent pressure was not a central factor in local change. Similarly, the national debate did not concentrate on the parental role alone, and had to be seen in the perspective of much broader issues. This was revealed most obviously in the fact that none of the legislation discussed in parliament between 1975 and 1980 was focused exclusively on the parental issue. It must also be recognized that the second half of the 1970s was seen by many people as a period of crisis and difficulty. The continuing economic problem was dramatized and deepened by the oil crisis of 1973. Successive governments failed to cope convincingly with rising unemployment, and the limits set by economic decline to social welfare policies were an object of bitter debate and repeated industrial confrontation. Throughout the seventies Northern Ireland continued to present insoluble problems of public order, and, as apparently powerful movements emerged in Scotland and Wales to renegotiate their relationships to Westminster, it was possible to argue seriously about 'the break-up of Britain'.[87] In terms of party politics, the seventies saw the rapid alternation of Conservative and Labour governments. The growth in the Labour party of a well-publicized and effectively organized radical left-wing was balanced by the take-over of the Conservative party by the radical right under Margaret Thatcher,[88] so that it is reasonable to talk of a polarization of national politics.

The generalized feeling of crisis to which all these events contributed was more diffuse and prolonged than the neatly focused 'May events' which shook France in 1968. In essence, however, the motivation which led to the national introduction of parent participation was similar. In situations where the uncertainty level is high and relationships between governments and electorates seem strained, it becomes important to be seen to be doing something progressive, consensual and cheap. This is the process already seen at local level in Sheffield and Liverpool. In the national debate sporadically conducted from 1975 to 1980, this underlying reality was reflected in several features which otherwise appear inexplicable:

(i)   the fact that the dynamic for legislation seems to have come almost entirely from inside 'the ruling elite', with little evidence of strong grass-roots pressure for change;

(ii) the highlighting in the debate of the parent issue, and the corresponding playing down of the balancing proposals for teacher participation;

(iii) the failure to engage with the question of the functions of the new governing bodies, which were simply grafted on to the existing system;

(iv) the reinterpretation of proposals implying some collective parental input in favour of more individualistic interpretations of the parental role;

(v)   the repeated presentation of the parent participation question in conjunction with other educational issues, so that it was never clearly discussed as a way of modifying existing authority structures (cf. (iii)).

(vi) the preoccupation with the low cost of the proposals.

All these features marked the dominance of the legitimacy aspect of parent participation.

The terms of the national discussion were in many ways established in the debate in the House of Commons on 25 April 1975.[89] A Conservative MP, Mr William Shelton, proposed an Education (Parents' Charter) Bill. The phrase 'Parents' Charter' had emerged in the early seventies as part of the Conservative party programme. A strengthening of parental rights in the face of the supposed incursions caused by the imposition of comprehensive schools had been part of the Conservative platform in the election narrowly lost by the Conservatives on 28

February 1974. However, Mr Shelton aimed firmly at the middle ground. His concrete proposals were the establishment of appeals tribunals to which parents would be able to submit disputes with LEAs over the allocation of their children to secondary schools; the inclusion of at least three parents on the governing bodies of schools, to provide a channel for 'satisfactory consultation' which would, however, exclude the curriculum; and the provision of information about schools so that parents could choose sensibly. Mr Shelton made it clear that he had no intention of imposing parental views on the professionals: 'It has been reported in the newspapers that the purpose of the Bill is parent power. That is nonsense. It is nothing to do with parent power. It is merely to tilt the balance slightly towards parental rights, and perhaps slightly away from local education authorities.'[90] He also pointed out that he had consulted widely before drafting his bill; that none of the associations he had contacted had objected to it; and that in certain particulars he had retreated from his own personal preferences (for example, he would personally favour governing bodies being made up of 50 per cent of parents, and would prefer some degree of parent involvement in curriculum matters).

Perhaps because of this stress on consensus, little attempt was made in the debate to delineate clearly the reasons for the changes proposed. The most persuasive and extended arguments related to parents' perceptions of schools — their 'concern' over low standards in schools was to be alleviated by increasing the element of choice, and this would have a double effect, in reducing parental discontent and in improving the standards of schools. A cursory bow in the direction of the sociologists was made in a brief mention of the American Head Start programme and its supposed success in involving parents. Mr Norman St John Stevas made a more ambitious claim for the long-term effects of the measures proposed as a reflection of a change in parental attitude, and a contributor to further attitude change:

> It is one of the paradoxes of the twentieth century that as society grows more affluent it loses its sense of community. Parents are no longer content to be treated as cyphers, as some kind of painful prerequisite for children, and as nothing else. They want to be listened to, and they want to exercise the most creative function that most human beings have, which is to bring up another generation and influence them for good in the future.... This Bill could have a profound effect on basic attitudes. After all, the law is a creative instrument as well as a

reflective one. It reflects consensus sometimes in a community, but in other cases it can create new attitudes....[91]

However, the tone of the argument was characterized less by this intervention than by Mr Shelton's pragmatic, middle-of-the-road emphasis on improvements being possible without offending anybody or incurring any expense: 'What can we do? In these days, one immediately adds a rider by asking "What can one do about this which will not cost much money?" In the country's present economic situation it is not sensible to make suggestions and recommendations which will cost a great deal.'[92]

Opposition from the Labour government was half-hearted and focused largely on the issue of parental choice of secondary school. Mr Ernest Armstrong, Under-Secretary of State for Education and Science, asserted that this was a front for evading the comprehensive issue, and that in a comprehensive system choice occurred rationally and gradually within schools. The issues of parental representation and the provision of adequate information were hardly discussed, and the Bill was eventually talked out. In spite of that the questions ventilated in the debate were to keep on surfacing over the next few years and were eventually to find their place in legislation.

The Parents' Charter debate took place in April 1975. The formal first reading of William Shelton's Bill took place on 27 November 1974, and the establishment of a committee of enquiry on the management and government of schools was announced in Parliament on 27 January 1975; it seems very likely therefore that in the short term the Labour government was prompted by a desire to steal some of the Conservatives' clothes. Its wish to pre-empt the initiative in this matter was no doubt reinforced by the fact that in the new parliament no party had an overall majority, so that the government was dependent upon Liberal support or acquiescence. Predictably, the terms of reference of the Taylor Committee hardly suggested a radical commitment to grass-roots participation. As it began work in the spring of 1975, its remit was: 'To review the arrangements for the management and government of maintained primary and secondary schools in England and Wales, including the composition and functions of bodies of managers and governors, and their relationships with local education authorities, with head teachers and staffs of schools, with parents of pupils and with the local community at large; and to make recommendations.'[93] This specification, in conjunction with other government statements, implied that the basic machinery of the education system would be left unchanged. George Baron, himself a member of the committee, commented: 'What was sought was a revitalising of one element in the school system without the disturbance of the others. This analysis is supported by an examination of the membership of the committee, which reflected a delicate and symmetrical balance of interests.'[94]

As the committee sat (from the spring of 1975 to the spring of 1977; the report was delivered to the Secretary of State in June) it was inevitably affected by two highly publicized events in the world of educational politics: the William Tyndale affair (maximum publicity July 1975 to autumn 1976) and the Great Debate (from the Prime Minister's Ruskin College speech of October 1976 to the Green Paper of July 1977 [95]). Both these events focused on, and fed, exactly that public concern about education which Mr Shelton had asserted in the Commons debate: 'If we could have all schools of a single, magnificent uniform level, parents would feel much less concern.'[96]

The sharpening of concern about standards tended to shift the emphasis from a generalized concern with what parents *as a group* could contribute to the running of school towards the question of how parents *as individuals* could choose 'good' schools and, having chosen them, monitor their standards. The Taylor Committee had been set up to answer the first set of questions; implementation of its proposals became increasingly entangled with the second set.

The William Tyndale affair managed to focus doubts about progressive methods of teaching, educational standards and public control. As the Taylor report commented rather mildly. 'We had not . . . previously found such a concentration of so many of these issues in a single school over such a relatively short period.'[97] Though the school's plight was clearly untypical, and rendered more so by the involvement of some rather unusual teachers and parents, and their readiness to turn to the press and television, William Tyndale school became for a period a national symbol of educational crisis. In the words of the right-wing *Daily Express*: 'The exposure of the teaching methods and appalling results at William Tyndale School, London, has alerted parents everywhere to the need to find out what is going on in the classroom.'[98]

The immediate cause for this 'exposure' was a disagreement over methods, exacerbated by poor personal relationships and mishandling by a new head teacher. As the problem swelled, the normal procedures of the Inner London Education Authority (ILEA) conspicuously failed to defuse the situation. Eventually the only way of retrieving the position seemed to be a long and elaborate judicial inquiry, conducted by Mr Robin Auld, QC, whose report must surely constitute the most elaborate account of such an incident ever compiled.[99] The report probes particularly the question of who, legally and actually, is responsible in the event of the breakdown of 'efficient education' as specified by the 1944 Education Act. The answer is clearly the Authority: '. . . However unpalatable and whatever the practical, policy or political difficulties in choosing a solution, if inefficient or unsuitable education is being provided at the school or insufficient regard is being paid to the wishes of parents of pupils at the school, the Authority must do something about it.'[100] The managers too have a role, delegated by the authority — 'the "oversight" of the conduct and curriculum of the school in consultation with the headteacher.'[101] But, as Auld points out, 'It is difficult to know in practice what this responsibility of "oversight" by the unqualified over the qualified can amount to.'[102] The William Tyndale inquiry, taken together with the *Express's* comment about parents now being 'alerted . . . to the need to find out what is going on in the classroom', placed a clarification of the responsibilities of managers and governors high on the political agenda.

Similar issues were raised in the highest quarters when the new Prime Minister, James Callaghan, decided to make education one of the themes of his ministry. The 'Great Debate' which he launched in the autumn of 1976 was designed to clarify the aims of the entire system.[103] The idea was that very broad general aims should be agreed in a series of regional consultations which would involve all sectors of society. These explicit aims would then facilitate the evaluation and updating of the system. In retrospect, the 'debate' looks remarkably like a diversion from deeper problems.

> The 'Great Debate' of the late 1970s about education was occasioned, not by inherently educational problems, but by economic failure and by a desire to find its explanation in aspects of British society that could not be controlled by received techniques of economic management. The debate was, in other words, a further symptom of crisis in the expansionist perspective which had accorded education such an important role in the creation of economic and social well-being.[104]

Whatever the Debate's origins, the desire for clarity and explicitness about aims and lines of responsibility predominated in the rhetoric both of the Tyndale inquiry and of the Great Debate. This would lead one to expect a similar clarity from the Taylor report, claiming as it did to have absorbed the lessons of the William Tyndale inquiry.[105] Revolutionary proposals were neither expected nor delivered. 'The overwhelming majority of witnesses agreed that the present pattern of school government should be continued.'[106] Thus the committee decided 'to reform . . . present practice and procedures within the existing arrangements.'[107] Having decided on that basic principle, and asserted the view that each school should have its individual governing body, the committee addressed itself in some detail to the membership of those governing bodies. It recommended a division of representation according to four categories: school staff, parents, LEA and the 'local community'. Each category would have equal membership, though the exact numbers would vary from a total of eight for a 100-pupil primary school to twenty-four in a large secondary school with 1500+ pupils.[108] The report then turned in a series of chapters to the critical question of what these representatives would actually do.

Firstly (Chapter 5), they would form part of a more open and democratic style of management in which heads would consult staff rather than direct them, and in which pupils and parents would be encouraged to form their own organizations and contribute their opinions freely to the formulation of school policy. The governing body's role here appeared to be that of monitoring and tactful prodding — the governing body should '*invite* the headteacher to submit his general proposals' (5.12); '*be empowered to authorise* the establishment of a school council' (5.18); '*ensure* that parents have access' (5.23); '*satisfy itself* that adequate arrangements are made to inform parents' (5.28).[109]

Chapters 6, 7 and 8 were devoted to curriculum, finance and appointments — i.e., to functions (ii), (iv) and (iii) of the list of functions placed at the end of Chapter 1 of this book. These were obviously critical issues if any real shift in power were to take place.

On curriculum, the report proposed a procedure for keeping aims and methods under continuous review. An appendix gave examples which indicated that the committee expected governing bodies to consider not just the obviously contentious issues (sex education, religious education, etc.) but such central questions as the introduction of the ITA reading system or primary school French or changes in school policy on Welsh, or far-reaching organizational questions such as mixed-ability grouping, pastoral care systems or careers teaching.[110] The report did not overlook the fact that all this would require considerable strengthening of local advisory services.[111]

Chapter 7, on finance, urged increased devolution of financial powers to the individual school. While overall responsibility must remain with the LEA, governing bodies could exercise some influence over the proportion of expenditure (admittedly a small one, because 'the greatest part of any school's expenditure is on salaries and wages . . .'[112] controlled by the school. This could happen through a system of governing bodies approving and monitoring annual estimates.

Chapter 8 recommended that governing bodies should be equally represented on the selection committees for head teachers with LEA representatives, and that as far as practicable governing bodies should be principally responsible for the selection of deputy heads and other teachers.

None of this represented revolutionary change — any real shift of *power* within the system — and certainly no shift of power to parents, who were to be present on the new governing bodies only as the parental quarter. It represented rather a clarification, regularization and updating of the more defensible arrangements arrived at by many LEAs in the mid-seventies. If even this minimal programme were to be effective in transforming the atmosphere for the better, as Taylor hoped it would, it would need to be translated rapidly into clear legislation, with adequate resourcing and sensible publicity. In reality, public attention was directed towards the new arrangements in a sporadic and ambivalent way; overall resourcing was diminished, not augmented; and above all the essential outlines of the Taylor proposals were blurred and distorted by three years' debate before they reached the statute book.

The resource problem loomed quite large in the immediate debate on the Taylor report. To start with, it interfered with imaginative publicity. To the National Union of Teachers (NUT), 'Mr Taylor revealed that he had wanted to produce a man in the street's guide to the Taylor report at a cost of between 25p and 50p. But HMSO had feared this would damage sales of the full report which sells at £3.25.'[113] The issue of the costing of the proposals was widely argued, the Society of Education Officers maintaining that the report's estimated costs should be doubled.[114] This argument was all the more damaging in being conducted at a time of great financial stringency when teachers could see it as a choice between resources for governing bodies and resources for teachers' jobs. The unfavourable financial position meant that when the Taylor proposals were eventually translated into some sort of reality, the style of their implementation was parsimonious in the extreme. For example, the electoral process was not conducted through the local or even national media. Rather, children brought home from school duplicated letters describing complicated adoption meetings to be held at school to elect persons whose function often seemed obscure. Training schemes for new governors were run on a shoestring, if at all, and the additional advisory backing which Taylor recommended as a necessity if governing bodies were in any real sense to monitor the curriculum remained a dream.

Further, and deeper, problems stemmed from the arguments which preceded and shaped the 1980 Education Act. The Taylor proposals were considerably diluted in the course of that argument, in ways which suggested that from the viewpoint of both governments concerned (Labour and Conservative) parents were a less powerful influence than teachers and LEAs. The NUT General Secretary denounced the Taylor report immediately after publication as 'a busybodies' charter'.[115] This hostility was followed up in May 1978 by a more considered report,[116] which concentrated particularly on the supposed weakening of teachers' responsibility over the curriculum and discipline. However, the Association of Assistant Mistresses (AAM) took an almost exactly opposite point of view,[117] and the NUT's fulminations probably contributed rather little to the rational argument, but quite a lot to identifying the whole area of the functions of governing bodies (roughly Chapters 6 to 9 of the Taylor report) as controversial. Probably the impact of the LEAs, working through their associations, was weightier, though less publicized. They were concerned to retain a degree of local control over the new governing bodies which were now inevitable. Their arguments therefore focused on the importance of local flexibility, and on the practical difficulties in implementing the proposals on, for example, finance.

To these pressures it was necessary to add the extra complication of national politics at this time. From March 1974 to May 1979 the Labour government had no overall majority, and was often dependent on Liberal support; hence the attractiveness of more or less consensual reforms such as the strengthening of school governing bodies and the recognition of the parental interest — hence also the tendency to fight shy of potential conflict. Yet at the same time as the government experienced a certain pull towards the middle ground, the Conservative opposition under Margaret Thatcher was shifting towards the right, and discovering a useful source of political discontent in people's resentment over the comprehensive issue. By the late seventies a large majority of the nation's children of secondary school age was in comprehensive education. For many parents the comprehensive school was now the *status quo*, and a full frontal assault on the comprehensive idea would have been politically unwise. However, there remained considerable local resentment about zoning arrangements. These sometimes determined that a child should attend a local school rather than a more distant school its parents would have preferred — sometimes because it was a former selective school which, they felt, retained something of its former ethos. In this way 'parental choice' became a potent way of coding a wide range of parental discontents, most of which had surfaced in the William Tyndale affair, the Great Debate, etc.; and 'parental choice' inevitably became attached to the debate about governing bodies, even though choice of secondary school and procedures of consultation in changing the character of schools (functions (i) and (v) as indicated at the end of Chapter 1) had not been mentioned in the Taylor report.

It is against this political backdrop that successive government retreats from the Taylor report must be seen. True, the consensual core remained unaltered — that each school should have its own governing body, and that parents and teachers should sit alongside LEA representatives — but two substantial shifts were to reduce the participatory potential of the new committees. The first and most obvious was a sidestepping of the whole question of functions. When the Labour Education Bill was debated in December 1978, Shirley Williams, the then Secretary of State, announced that her consultations had revealed no general agreement on the powers of governing bodies. These would therefore simply be left unspecified.

> Most people [she said], in my view rightly, see the nature of the relationship between the governing body and the school as something organic which is individual to each school. Where the relationship works, it does not need any over-elaborate delegation of statutory powers, and where it does not work no amount of formal statutory power will increase its usefulness or its influence.[118]

The refusal to specify powers meant (as in France and Italy, though the rhetoric of late-seventies pragmatism had a different ring from that of the late sixties) that existing mechanisms of control would continue unchanged. The 'right people' would ensure that — the phrase is that of the next Secretary of State, a Conservative, Mark Carlisle, batting on exactly the same wicket a year later as he introduced the Conservative successor to Shirley Williams' aborted bill:

> I accept that we have not attempted to set out the powers of governing bodies, any more than the previous government did, and I accept that the reason why we have not done so is that we believe that if we get the right people on the governing bodies it is up to them to exercise their powers as they feel so to be right.[119]

The second major shift away from the Taylor recommendations was on membership of governing bodies. Taylor had urged a four-way representation of parents, staff, LEA and 'the wider community'. This fourth category would consist of 'people with experience of the external forces and influences at work on the school'.[120] Much discussion centred on how these persons were to be identified. There was also considerable disquiet from the LEA side about their losing control of individual schools for which legally they were responsible, and about the potential for conflict between governing bodies and LEAs. Thus the 'wider community' representation, and the allied question of whether it was right to allocate half of the membership of governing bodies to parents and teachers, came under heavy fire from the LEAs. This was already apparent in Shirley Williams' reactions: she reserved her position on 'the wider community', and made no specific recommendations on proportions of membership. A year later Mark Carlisle had advanced to precise proposals: the Conservative Education Bill did not include community representation, and defined teacher and parent representatives as minima (two elected representatives in each category — one in very small schools). LEAs were at liberty to permit more non-LEA representation if they wished, but the full Taylor proposals were now to be permissive rather than required, and a patchwork of local schemes was preferred to a single uniform network. This was obviously a victory for the LEAs' lobbying. 'We accept,' said Mark Carlisle in presenting his bill, 'that the majority responsibility for running schools must rest with the LEAs. Therefore, it is right that they should be free to decide the correct type of governing body for their individual schools.'[121]

But the evolution of opinion was not simply a dilution of the original proposals into forms which would make them more easily assimilable by the existing system, it was also the admixture of other elements relating to parental choice. Both the abortive Labour Bill and the succeeding Conservative Education Act which passed into law on 3 April 1980 laid considerable stress on attempting to make more of a reality of parental choice of school — especially secondary school. The 1980 Act eventually required that, subject to considerations of cost, parental wishes should be considered in choice of secondary school; that adequate information should be provided by schools to permit informed choices to be made; and that a formal appeals procedure should be set up, so that parents aggrieved by an LEA's decision on the allocation of secondary places could refer their case to an independent tribunal. None of these matters had been dealt with by Taylor, yet all of them loomed large in the debate, and gave it much of its emotional tone. Even more than the Shirley Williams Bill, Mark Carlisle's Education (No. 2) Bill was a collection of separate items of legislation, including as well as these 'Parents' Charter' provisions, an assisted places scheme to provide scholarships in independent schools, and legislation on school meals and school transport. It was these other items which attracted controversy and attention, and which were in due course modified in the House of

Lords amid considerable media discussion. By contrast, the provisions on governors and managers eventually passed into law almost unnoticed. There could be no clearer illustration of the consensual character of parent participation than the way it eventually became a national requirement, packaged together with other more partisan issues, as though to lend them respectability.

5.7   The 1980 Act: National Legislation in Local Context

The 1980 Act did not represent a neat divide like the 1968 decrees in France or the *Decreti Delegati* in Italy. It built on, and extended, changes which had been occurring for at least a decade. Different conditions in 104 local authorities also make generalization hazardous, as does the almost total absence of research. All this makes it difficult to attempt anything more than an impression, which must range backwards into the seventies as well as forwards into the eighties.

The most obvious novelty inaugurated by the 1980 Act was the appeals tribunals to which parents could apply if they felt aggrieved at the overriding by an LEA of their choice of secondary school.[122] The new procedures began in the autumn of 1982, and demonstrated in a highly concrete way the limitations upon parental choice. The most obvious problem was that the number of places available in schools regarded as desirable was necessarily small. As one parent member of a local panel put it:

> Since the oversubscribed schools were already committed to accept pupils up to their full capacity before any appeals were considered, we were talking before we even saw any appellants about only a handful of places. Half a dozen, perhaps, would not seriously affect efficiency, perhaps up to double that number if one assumed a small drop-out among those already offered places. I am sure that most of those who appeared before us would have considered the whole affair a sham had they known how long the odds were . . . .[123]

To this intrinsic problem of reconciling the wishes of individual parents with the efficient running of a system was added the failure of the legislation to give any teeth to tribunals. Power was still reserved to the LEA. The appeals tribunal could only make recommendations which the LEA could turn down. The parents could then appeal to the Secretary of State, but clearly in so cumbersome and stressful a process the dice were loaded against the parents. The Advisory Centre for

Education commented in September 1982: 'Whilst Ministers' rhetoric continues unabated — describing the provisions of the 1980 Act as 'genuine participatory democracy' — the Government may not have calculated for the practical consequences of their token measure.'[124]

In terms of the definition of parent participation round which this study is structured, these appeals tribunals were not in any case a manifestation of 'the legally required association of parents with the schools their children attend through systems of elected representatives and committees' (see section 1.5). Yet the link between parental choice of secondary school and parental presence on governing bodies is revealing of the deeper meaning of the 1980 Act and of the debate which led up to it. Parental choice tended to dominate that debate, while the idea of parent governors was generally accepted without comment (see 5.6). However, as the parent member of an appeals panel quoted above pointed out, the tribunals which appeared to *add* to parent power were in fact a *subtraction* from the sort of power which mattered:

> How much better the time processing appeals could be spent if there were a tradition of routinely enquiring why certain schools were not chosen, discussing both problems and remedies more openly, dispelling prejudice where it has no foundation. How much better to put all that effort into making sure parents have more say in schools, since in the end it is the knowledge that they have no influence which makes them feel that choice is the only right worth having.[125]

Perhaps the linking in one piece of legislation of the parental choice provisions and of reformed governing bodies for all schools had a double effect. On the one hand the uncontroversial reform of governing bodies (with the parental presence an emotive but ill-thought-out selling-point) helped to smooth the passage of the more controversial 'parental choice' innovations. On the other hand, the parental choice clauses, both in debate and later when translated into institutional form, acted as a distraction from the more important business of thinking through what governing bodies, and parents, really ought to be doing. Whether this linkage was thought out in some Machiavellian way by 'the ruling elite' is dubious; it seems more likely that it emerged from a confused desire to appear to be doing something 'participatory' without actually changing existing power relationships.

This discussion would lead the disillusioned observer who has already read the case-studies of France, Italy and West Germany to have rather low expectations of the new governing bodies or of the impact on them of the parental presence. Sure enough, we find many of the criticisms already voiced in previous chapters emerging in England and Wales as well. LEAs were slow in implementing the provisions of the Act, which were immediately mandatory only for new schools: by the autumn of 1983 only about a third of LEAs had revised their arrangements,[126] and this piecemeal implementation of the national scheme meant local confusion among parents about what their status and rights really were. In any case the national guidelines left large areas open to local interpretation. The 1980 Act specified that parent and teacher governors should be elected by secret ballot, but left the frequency of elections to be determined by LEAs. For example, the Inner London Education Authority opted for a four-year period of office, while Liverpool held annual elections. The advantages of the longer period were held to be (i) that parents were treated on the same footing as all other governors, and (ii) that time was necessary for a board to learn to work together as a team. The disadvantages were the reduction in accountability in representatives elected for a long period, and the disenfranchisement of some parents whose children arrived in a school shortly after an election.[127]

Behind these practicalities lurked questions about the status of parent governors as opposed to that of the LEA nominees who outnumbered them. Was a parent eligible to become chairperson of the board? The legal answer was 'yes', but the practical answer seemed often to be 'no', and this was particularly the case when elections were for a year only. How could parents become as practised and confident as other governors (e.g., local councillors) in using formal committee procedures? To be effective, parent governors needed to communicate regularly with their electorate — but how in practice could they do so? To what extent did conventions about the confidentiality of official business (sometimes interpreted very rigidly) inhibit or prevent such communication? Was there anything a governing body, or a parent governor, could do to improve the monitoring of whatever finance was controlled by the individual school?[128]

It is too early to evaluate in any full sense the workings of the new governing bodies, still less of the contributions made to them by the parent element. Conditions vary greatly from LEA to LEA, and within an LEA from school to school. However, the impression derived from talking to governors, parent governors and informed observers is that what has been set up is exactly as promised in the parliamentary debates of 1978 and 1979: i.e., the 'new' governing bodies have simply been grafted on to power structures which remain unchanged. That is surely the meaning of the persistent refusal to define their functions, and the source of many of the problems faced by parent governors as they try to find a role. Even well-intentioned adminstrators tend to be sceptical of the new structures,[129] and parent enthusiasts feel a sense of disillusion at the gap between aspiration and actuality.

This general disappointment must be balanced against the undoubted stimulus given to an increased flow of information from schools to parents. The Act required schools to provide prospectuses, and some schools used the opportunity for an imaginative rethink. Even where prospectuses were more humdrum, the long-term effect seemed likely to be educative — both for schools (which had to open their operations to some sort of public scrutiny) and for parents (who had to evaluate information, especially about secondary schools).[130] At national level, too, there was a crop of books of varying degrees of technicality to enlighten lay persons about their new responsibilities.[131] Although the rash of new parent magazines which accompanied the 1975 legislation in Italy was absent in England and Wales, that absence was to some extent compensated for by a much greater flow of information at the level of the local school than had been the case only a few years before, and an evolution of teacher attitudes away from automatic hostility to parental 'meddling'.[132] The idea of 'accountability' began to be explored and developed beyond its original narrow definition: are the exam results good?[133]

The information issue reminds us that the elected parent governor was really quite a small part of a much wider evolution. The danger of a study such as this one is that in seeking to highlight one aspect of a multifaceted scene it may distort the complexity of experience. As an antidote, let us now consider briefly the *evolution* of the parent movement in the broader sense in one place (Liverpool). (The *origins* of the parent governor system in Liverpool have already been described in 5.5.) This focus should help us to view parent participation in the narrower sense against its background, to ask questions about the connections between the two, and to consider how things may develop in the future.

Throughout the seventies and into the eighties Liverpool was fertile ground for parent associations and parent activity. The fact that from 1974 to 1983 no political party had an overall majority in the city council not only left a power vacuum in which external pressure-groups could increase their influence, but also meant that important decisions (for example, about school closures) were repeatedly postponed, to a point where crises in educational administration became urgent and comprehensible even to uninformed observers.[134] During this period formally organized parent activity flowed through four main channels:[135]

(i) *PTAs and PAs.* From the late sixties onwards, these gradually became more acceptable and numerous, while remaining essentially school-based and non-political. They were sometimes dominated by head teachers. They frequently provided nominees for the parent representatives on governing bodies. The link between the school-based PTAs and city-wide parent organizations seemed a reality only at moments of crisis, e.g., when a new reorganization plan had to be combatted.

(ii) *CASE.* Liverpool CASE had been established in the mid-sixties, but its membership was always small and somewhat dominated by the local intelligentsia. It had strong links with the university and tended to be concentrated on the southern, more middle-class area of the city. Nonetheless, in the first half of the seventies it probably had a greater impact than its membership might suggest as being the only organization in the county sector articulating parental views (see 5.5). It then withered away and was eventually formally dissolved.

(iii) *LACPAPA* (Liverpool Association of Catholic Parents and Parents' Associations). This group emerged in 1971 in direct response to plans from the Catholic authorities to reorganize Catholic schools into a three-tier system. (Liverpool is unusual in that about 40 per cent of secondary school places are in catholic schools, so that the LEA is in effect responsible for two fairly evenly balanced but distinct systems.) The failure to achieve any agreed reorganization plan until 1983 gave LACPAPA unusual vigour and continuity. Schools and parents felt under continuous threat as various schemes were formulated, discussed and rejected, and both the archdiocesan authorities and the Catholic teachers' associations from time to time felt the need to secure parental approval.

(iv) *LASPA* (Liverpool Association of Parents Concerned with Education). CASE gradually declined in the mid-seventies and was replaced by LASPA, a more overtly populist group which had the declared intention of getting representation from ordinary parents in all parts of the city, not just in the more prosperous southern districts. LASPA was formed as a result of an initiative from LACPAPA. Confronted by the LEA's refusal to consult with them on the grounds that there was no equivalent body in the county sector, LACPAPA invited non-Catholic PTAs to a meeting to discuss the problem, and invited them to form a city-wide organization of their own. For a time LASPA seemed to be highly successful in mobilizing parent activity throughout the city, but perhaps became over-extended. So much work was generated that the relatively small leadership could hardly cope with it, and more recently LASPA has shown a tendency to become another south Liverpool-oriented organization. It has, however, been very successful in attracting funds for imaginative initiatives in the field of parent-school relations. In 1982 it secured finance from a charitable trust for a part-time worker to investigate and encourage the work of parent governors, and in 1983 it won a national competition organized by *Woman* magazine and Stork margarine and now runs a 'community education bus'. 'As well as providing information on all kinds of educational activity, and encouraging people to be active within their own immediate communities, the bus will provide a referral service to people with specific problems concerning their own or other children's education.'[136] LASPA is a registered charity, which means that its political activities are severely constrained.

In addition to this parent-initiated activity, the LEA itself initiated in 1979 a 'Parent Support Programme' in a number of inner-city schools (mainly, but not entirely, primary). A 75 per cent grant from central government has funded parent centres (one or two rooms) in schools and the appointment of 'teacher keyworkers' and 'outreach workers'. Their tasks are to build up relationships between parents and between the school and parents, and in a flexible and open way to stimulate and coordinate any activities, educational or otherwise, which seem appropriate. The idea is that these paid workers should be facilitators, and should not impose upon parents some official model of what they ought to be doing. The results of the programme, in encouraging a wide variety of relationships and activities, and in increasing parental confidence, trust in the school and willingness to support their own children in learning, appear to have been positive. [137] This scheme, which is aimed at 'social priority' schools and at under-privileged families, is a reminder of the persistence and vitality of the 'Plowden strand' in thinking about parents.

All the activity so far described remained strictly within the normal legal bounds. All the parent organizations mentioned claimed to be non-political. Although from time to time critical of the policies of particular parties, they tried hard to retain a non-partisan and 'respectable' image. Yet the nature of Liverpool's planning problem (a dramatic decline in population producing a clear need to close large numbers of schools), and the longstanding political failure to grasp the nettle of school closures, produced a situation in which the picking off of individual schools seemed the only way forward. This in turn generated real resentment among parents in the poorer areas in which most closures took place, as they saw 'their' schools (almost the sole remaining social institutions) being removed. The latter part of the seventies and the early eighties saw sporadic outbursts of parent resistance, culminating in 1982–3 in the occupation by parents of two schools (one secondary and one primary) under threat of closure: an extra-legal tactic which eventually forced the acquiescence of the Secretary of State himself.

All this activity was interesting, and in some ways impressive, and would hardly have been predicted ten or fifteen years previously. It had a good deal to do with a growing consciousness among parents that they did constitute an indentifiable group. It had, however, rather little to do with 'parent participation' in the sense of 'the legally required association of parents with the schools their children attend through systems of elected representatives or committees'. Action in defence of individual schools, whether resulting in extra-legal action or not, seems to have been spontaneous and reactive, with the parent governor network an irrelevancy and the city-wide parent associations distancing themselves from activities which they often saw as anarchic and irresponsible. In any case, LACPAPA and LASPA, although counting a number of parent governors among their members, remained essentially associations of individuals rather than officially recognized bodies on the model of Hessen or Hamburg.

While, therefore, there is evidence of a changed consciousness among some Liverpool parents since about 1970, it would be unwise to be euphoric about the impact either of LACPAPA and LASPA, still less about the official structures of parent participation. In the first place, all this variegated activity affects only a small minority of parents. Secondly, neither LACPAPA nor LASPA would claim to have solved the problem of running mass organizations of parents. Both are heavily dependent on quite small and predominantly middle-class leaderships who tend to live in south Liverpool. They are therefore subject, as CASE was, to a kind of cyclical waxing and waning as initiatives undertaken become too burdensome to be carried by the leadership. Finally, and most importantly from the angle of this comparative study, there is no evidence that all this activity is producing change in the distribution of real power through the system. Gill Mullen's enquiry into the experiences and opinions of Liverpool parent governors throws up the same problems and criticisms that we have already noted in continental Europe.[138] Repeated attempts by LACPAPA and LASPA to secure parent representation on the Education Committee have been of no avail. An elaborate agreement about forms of consultation with parents in reorganization was reached between the parent organizations and all political parties, yet it was simply ignored by the Labour party when it at last achieved a majority in May 1983. LEA initiatives in the first year of the new elected parent governors to provide some sort of training were not followed up, and parent governors frequently voiced feelings of neglect and isolation. By the summer of 1983, when this chapter was written, all parent activists consulted were highly sceptical about 'parent participation' as defined in Chapter 1.[139]

5.8 Balance-Sheet

Chapter 4 ended with the promise that England and Wales would present 'considerable basic differences' from France, Italy and the Federal Republic. These differences meant that some of the goals which attracted and motivated parent activity in continental Europe had long been taken for granted on the other side of the Channel. For example, there already existed a degree of local and school autonomy. Predictably, this was accompanied by a high valuation placed upon individual choice of school, so that the preoccupation with 'parental choice' distinguished the English and Welsh scene from its continental counterparts. Another important source of difference arose from the fact that Britain had enjoyed a long period of social and political evolution uninterrupted by revolution or invasion. This continuity endowed the institutions of the state with an unusual degree of legitimacy. It also favoured the 'natural' growth of parent activity over about a century without state intervention or assistance.

For these reasons England and Wales constitute a kind of test-bed for the 'reformist' theory of parent participation sketched in Chapter 1. If the basic mechanism underlying 'participation' is that 'people learn to be democratic by being given opportunities for democratic activity', then we should expect to find in England and Wales an earlier awareness of the importance of formal links between parents and schools, an earlier experimentation with devices (such as parent governors) for strengthening those links, and a gradual extension of those devices throughout the system. Instead we find a parent movement whose interest in collective or pressure-group activity remained negligible because of a fixation on individualistic interpretations of the parental role *vis-à-vis* the school, and which had little real impact on the style and character of formal parent participation when it was eventually introduced by the 'ruling elites'.

The evolution of the English and Welsh parent movement since the 1880s appears paradoxical. Why was it so tardy and tentative in its advocacy of parent participation? why, when parent governors were eventually introduced by local government in the 1970s, was its role more reactive than initiatory? The explanation lies primarily in the much greater prestige enjoyed by political and social institutions in England and Wales, as compared with France, Italy or West Germany. Parents really did tend to interpret problems they encountered as being susceptible to individual solutions rather than as symptoms of some wider conspiracy. Schools really did seem to be non-political. This tradition of trust began to crumble only in the 1960s as the comprehensive issue highlighted extensive value conflicts. A renewed emphasis on the rhetoric of school autonomy served in part to shore up that trust, and the stress on parental choice which was built in to the structures of parent participation approved by Parliament in 1980 formed part of that bid for legitimacy.

That the legitimation hypothesis (at least as it affects the *origins* of parent participation) appears to hold in a system so different from the other three discussed is important. However, the English and Welsh example also throws up more clearly than the other cases the difficulty of distinguishing among parent participation, parent activity and parent awareness. The focus of this study is on the first of these terms, as defined in Chapter 1. In France, Italy and West Germany it is easier to regard the three terms as overlapping to such an extent as to be coterminous. In France, for example, organized parent activity outside the federations is slight, and the annual routine of the parent federations has been directed since the late sixties to operating the official machinery of parent participation. It is easy to forget that parent awareness — the consciousness among parents that they are a separate group and have certain rights and duties *vis-à-vis* their children — may exist independently of all this organized, more or less official activity.

In England and Wales the balance between these three factors is very different. Sections 5.2 and 5.3 (the history of the parent movement) and 5.7 (especially the description of Liverpool) illustrate a situation in which there is a good deal of parent activity and a growing parent awareness, but in which parent participation has featured only recently and plays only a subordinate part.

Thus one of the questions which needs to be asked about parent participation in England and Wales is whether it will grow in importance — whether in concrete terms the elected parent governor will become a more effective focus for parent activity and parent awareness. The evidence for change in that direction is not encouraging, but the parent governor as a socio-political experiment in participation is so new that judgments about trends can hardly be made at this stage. All one can say is that in terms of the potential functions delineated in Chapter 1, the new post-1980 governing bodies, of which parent governors are a small and subordinate part, seem to have done no better than their continental counterparts. Although they have considerable potential as channels for 'communication' between the school and its clientele, that potential has been actualized only rarely. Their ability to 'advise' and 'ensure' (i.e., to keep some sort of check on a school's standards and purposes) is severely limited by existing professional attitudes and responsibilities, and by a lack of imagination on both sides, so that even the vision of the Taylor report seems utopian. As for 'deciding', the realities of economic decline and the concern of both central and local government to control the public purse make school autonomy even less of a possibility than ten years ago. Although parent participation in England and Wales may appear more relaxed and less bureaucratic than in continental Europe, that does not make it any more real as participation. In all decisions of any weight or importance, governing bodies are involved in Pateman's 'pseudo-participation': parents and others are being persuaded 'to accept decisions that have *already* been made by the management'.[140]

If this fourth case highlights the relationship between parent participation, parent activity and parent awareness, then similar questions need to be asked in retrospect about the other three cases. In societies which differ from England and Wales in having lower levels of spontaneous and loosely structured parent activity, does the initiation of parent participation promote parent activity or parent awareness or both? This question will be discussed further in Chapter 6.

Such questions pertain to the *development* of parent participation. As this enquiry has proceeded, it has become apparent that it is easier to talk about the origins of parent participation than about its development. To describe and assess factors leading to a definite innovation is relatively straightforward; to delineate trends in complex situations which for the most part have had little time to work themselves out is more difficult. Bearing that in mind, let us turn now to the summary of the theoretical position presented at the end of Chapter 4. Does our fourth case suggest that any further revision is needed?

There are two points at which revision is required if the summary is to take proper account of England and Wales. It has been argued that the pursuit of legitimacy in England and Wales, whether by local authorities or by the Department of Education and Science, took a rather different form from in continental Europe. The problem was not so much to raise low levels of legitimacy by innovating in a progressive sense (e.g., by legislating for school autonomy) as to divert back to the schools the trust and confidence which supposedly they previously enjoyed. The progressive aspect of parent participation as a balanced and mutually educative partnership between parents and teachers was played down, and the more individualistic models of parental control and parental choice were highlighted.

The second insight provided by England and Wales but neglected by the summary relates to the relationship between parent participation, parent activity and parent awareness, briefly discussed above.

To incorporate these insights the following revision of the summaries gradually elaborated through each of the preceding case-studies is suggested. This compressed statement will form the basis for more extended discussion in the final chapter.

The 'general crisis' theory provides the better explanation of the origins of parent participation, and of some of the factors (especially on the government side) controlling its subsequent development. In systems where the day-to-day practice of education is perceived as being under centralized bureaucratic control, there is some tendency for structures of parent participation to be used to legitimate looser and more pragmatic attitudes towards the control of curriculum and greater tolerance of differences between schools. As the loosening of central control is an important motivational force for parents and teachers, parent participation is often presented by governments as a step in that direction. On the other hand, in systems which already allocate some degree of autonomy to individual schools, this 'progressive' factor is less evident, and parent participation represents an attempt by governments both to attract support from pre-existent parent groups, and to control potentially troublesome clients. In neither case, however, are such policies pursued by governments with vigour or consistency or even with any very clear idea of their manipulative aims. Thus parent participation tends to develop in directions unforeseen by those who originally approved it, as from time to time parent groups combine with other interests to define and achieve some particular goal. This unpredictability is strengthened by the way in which formal committee structures and the parent groups which operate them naturally constitute information networks through which information flows from the formal school system into the community, and sometimes in the reverse direction also. An increased flow of information tends to produce an increased level of general parent activity (whether connected with parent participation or not) and a greater awareness in the community of parents as an identifiable group. The precise interplay of participation, activity and awareness differs from place to place, but in general there is an inbuilt pressure towards activities and interactions which can be explained and justified within the 'reformist' paradigm. There are quite sharp limits to evolution towards a lessened emphasis on 'legitimation'. Those limits are set through the political system. They naturally differ from country to country. In polities where an inbuilt polarization of world-views is normal, parent groupings directly reflect the compromises reached from time to time at macro-level, so that in the last resort the system of parent participation is directly subordinate to the political system. In polities where a wide area of consensus is assumed, parent groupings operating the participatory machinery more readily see themselves as 'non-political', or as aggregating a variety of more or less mainstream views, and they may therefore find themselves in confrontation with other parent groups promoting a more ideologically simple line. In both cases, the reformist theory offers an adequate explanation of only one part of parent participation, whose origins and limitations are better accounted for by some variation of the general crisis theory.

Notes

1 Quoted in KOGAN, MAURICE (1978) *The Politics of Educational Change*, Manchester, Manchester University Press, pp. 62–3. On this theme, see also WHITE, J.P. (1975) 'The end of the compulsory curriculum', in UNIVERSITY OF LONDON INSTITUTE OF EDUCATION, *The Curriculum: The Doris Lee lectures*, London, University of London Institute of Education. of Education.

2 See WATTS, JOHN (Ed.) (1977) *The Countesthorpe Experience*, London, George Allen and Unwin, and chapters on Countesthorpe and Sutton in MOON, BOB (Ed.) (1983) *Comprehensive Schools: Challenge and Change*, Windsor, NFER-Nelson. The difficulties at Sutton are interestingly chronicled in FLETCHER, COLIN (1978) 'Assessing school performance: The background of an inquiry at Sutton Comprehensive School', *British Educational Research Journal*, 4/2, pp. 51–61.

3 BEER, SAMUEL H. (1982) *Britain against Itself: The Political Contradictions of Collectivism*, London, Faber and Faber. For his earlier view, see

BEER, SAMUEL H. (1965) *Modern British Politics: A Study of Parties and Pressure Groups*, London, Faber and Faber.

4 ALMOND, GABRIEL A. and VERBA, SIDNEY (1963) *The Civic Culture: Political Attitudes and Democracy in Five Nations*, Princeton, N.J., Princeton University Press. In this context consider ALMOND, G.A. and VERBA, S. (Eds) (1980) *The Civic Culture Revisited: An Analytic Study*, Boston, Mass., Little Brown, especially the essay by DENNIS KAVANAGH, 'Political culture in Great Britain: The decline of the civic culture'.

5 On Scotland, see the admirable survey by MACBETH, ALASTAIR, *et al.*, (1980) *Scottish School Councils: Policy-Making, Participation or Irrelevance?* Edinburgh, HMSO. On Northern Ireland, see DEPARTMENT OF EDUCATION FOR NORTHERN IRELAND, (1979) *Report of the Working Party on the Management of Schools in Northern Ireland* (The Astin Report), Belfast, HMSO.

6 BELL, ROBERT and GRANT, NIGEL (1977) *Patterns of Education in the British Isles*, London, Allen and Unwin.

7 See section 1.5, Table 3.

8 ALMOND AND VERBA (1963) *op. cit.* and BEER (1965) *op. cit.*

9 TENNYSON, ALFRED, 'You ask me why'.

10 The *raison d'être* of these boards was to fill in the gaps left in denominational provision. They proved to be the spearhead of a more secular style of education. In one perspective, school board elections conferred legitimacy on innovation. In another, they represented central government allocating to local boards issues that were too contentious to be resolved nationally.

11 See GORDON, PETER (1974) *The Victorian School Manager: A Study in the Management of Education 1800–1902*, London, Woburn Press.

12 Quoted in GORDON, *op. cit*, p. 174.

13 KITCHING, MISS (1899) 'The history and aims of the PNEU', *Parents' Review*, 10, pp. 441–34; here, p. 412. Miss Kitching was one of Charlotte Mason's earliest disciples. This article is the transcript of a speech in which she claimed to be using Miss Mason's words: '"I" and "we" refers in every case to our founder' (p. 411). Miss Mason was probably ill: she suffered from the same persistent Victorian ill-health as Florence Nightingale, whom in some ways she resembled.

14 *Ibid.*, p. 414.

15 WAKEFIELD, H. RUSSELL (1899) 'The parent in the educational system', *Parents' Review*, 10, pp. 502–13; here, pp. 508 and 510.

16 CHOLMONDELEY, ESSEX (1960) *The Story of Charlotte Mason, (1842–1923)*, London, Dent, p. 143. Most of this discussion is drawn from this source and from a sampling of *Parents' Review*. A serious historical study is needed.

17 CHOLMONDELEY, *op. cit.*, p. 30.

18 This judgment makes no attempt to assess the impact of PNEU on mainstream education, particularly at the primary level, or on teacher

education. It may have been considerable.

19 BOARD OF EDUCATION (1938) *Report of the Consultative Committee on Infant and Nursery Schools* (Chairman, Sir W.H. HADOW), London, HMSO, p. xxiv. In a similar vein the Board had advised in its 1927 *Handbook*, 'Teachers who view their work as a whole will avail themselves of every opportunity for bringing about an intimate relationship with the home' (BOARD OF EDUCATION (1927) *Handbook of Suggestions for Teachers*, London, HMSO, p. 22).

20 WALL, W.D. (1947) 'The opinions of teachers on parent-teacher co-operation', *British Journal of Educational Psychology*, 17/2, pp. 97–113.

21 WALL's survey (*ibid.*) gives ample evidence of this.

22 See section 2.2.

23 See section 4.2.

24 Quoted in SIMON, BRIAN (1974) *The Politics of Educational Reform, 1920–1940*, London, Lawrence and Wishart, pp. 295–6.

25 ANON. (1938) 'More news from parent teacher groups', *Home and School*, 3/4, pp. 66–7; here, p. 66.

26 WALL, *op. cit.*

27 STEPHEN, ALAN (1955) 'Parent-teacher associations', *Journal of Education*, 87, pp. 488–91.

28 For example, it collaborated with the teachers' associations, the National Council for Social Service, etc., in setting up in May 1944 a committee for parent-teacher cooperation whose sole discernible activity seems to have been the promotion of the Nottinghamshire enquiry (WALL, *op. cit.*).

29 ANON. (1938) 'Editorial', *Home and School*, 3/5, pp. 73–4; here, p. 74.

30 Susan Isaacs was involved in a wide variety of progressive educational activities: see GARDNER, D.E.M. (1969) *Susan Isaacs*, London, Methuen Educational. Her advice to parents is gathered in book form in ISAACS, SUSAN (1948) *Troubles of Children and Parents*, London, Methuen; brief articles published in *Nursery World* from 1929 to 1936 under the reassuring pseudonym of Ursula Wise.

31 Quoted in JONES, JACK A. (Ed.) (n.d. 1970?) *Bridging the Gap: Thoughts on Parent-Teacher Co-operation*, Home and School Council/NFPTA, p. 4.

32 DEPARTMENT OF EDUCATION AND SCIENCE (1967) *Children and their Primary Schools: A Report of the Central Advisory Council for Education (England), Vol. 1, The Report*, London, HMSO.

33 YOUNG, MICHAEL and JACKSON, BRIAN, (1967) 'An open letter to all ACE members', *Where*, 30, pp. 4–5; here, p. 4.

34 In KOGAN, MAURICE (Ed.) (1971) *The Politics of Education: Edward Boyle and Anthony Crosland in Conversation with Maurice Kogan*, Harmondsworth, Penguin, p. 176.

35 ADVISORY CENTRE FOR EDUCATION (1967) *Good Schools Guide* (*Where*, Supplement 10).

36 ANON. (1961–2) 'Cambridge Association for the Advancement of State Education', *Where*, 7, pp. 12–13.

37 JACKSON, BRIAN (1971) 'A message from ACE's Director', *Where*, 54, pp. 37–40; here, p. 37.

38 JACKSON, BRIAN (1969) 'A message from the Director: Who does ACE serve?', *Where*, 44, pp. 134–5; here, p. 134.

39 ANON. (1961) 'Parent-teacher association', *Where*, 5, pp. 15–16; here, p. 16.

40 PEASE, MICHAEL (1962) 'How to be school manager or governor', *Where*, 10, pp. 10–11. This passage is italicized in the original.

41 ANON. (1961–2) 'Cambridge Association for the Advancement of State Education', *Where*, 7, pp. 12–13; here, p. 13.

42 These points are quite frequently made in *Where*. The Brian Jackson quotation above is only one of many.

43 Cf. Edward Boyle: 'I'd received the first deputation of CASE and I'd been much impressed by them', (KOGAN (1971) *op. cit.*, p. 133).

44 KOGAN (1971) *op. cit.*, p. 176. Suspicions are further raised by the very doubtful veracity of the first part of this statement ('CASE ... pro-comprehensive').

45 For the background, see RUBINSTEIN, D. and SIMON B., (1969) *The Evolution of the Comprehensive School 1926–1966*, London, Routledge and Kegan Paul; FENWICK, I.G.K. (1976) *The Comprehensive School, 1944–1970: The Politics of Secondary School Reorganization*, London, Methuen.

46 See FENWICK, *op. cit.*, p. 128.

47 KOGAN, MAURICE (Ed.) (1971) *The Politics of Education*, Harmondsworth, Penguin Books, p. 191. It should not be overlooked that some Labour authorities were far from enthusiastic: see FENWICK, I.G.K. and WOOD-THORPE, A.J. (1980) 'The reorganization of secondary education in Leeds: The role of committee chairmen and political parties', *Aspects of Education*, 22, pp. 18–28.

48 CASE submission to Royal Commission on Local Government: ROYAL COMMISSION ON LOCAL GOVERNMENT IN ENGLAND (Maud Commission) (1969) *Written Evidence of Private Citizens, Ratepayers' and Residents' Organisations and Other Witnesses ...*, London, HMSO, pp. 354–69.

49 And incidentally split from time to time by quarrels between the strong personalities who tended to predominate at the top. For a characteristic dispute, see ALLARD, JOHN (1974) 'Will CASE weather the comprehensive storm?' *Education*, 144/15, p. 417, and the reply by the National Secretary in *Education*, 144/20, 1974, p. 598.

50 For example, the Comprehensive Schools Committee, the Pre-School Playgroups Association, etc. From time to time *Where* included publicity for these groups, which often ran their own newsletters and magazines for subscribers.

51 In the late sixties the chairman of the NFPTA guessed that about 400 PTAs were affiliated to the National Federation, and that this represented about 1 per cent of all schools in the country. He considered that a large number

of schools had unaffiliated PTAs, but even so this could have represented only a small minority (HUGHES, T.E. (1968) *The Origins and Development of Parent-Teacher Associations in a Selected Group of Primary Schools*, University of Liverpool Diploma in Education dissertation, p. 16).

52 This reactive stance can be traced already in the late forties: see SARAN, RENE (1973) *Policy-Making in Secondary Education: A Case Study*, Oxford, Clarendon Press, pp. 159–75. A more unified and better resourced national movement, along the lines perhaps of the French *Fédération Cornec*, might have helped to give a wider vision to PTAs. However, 'Inter-organisational distrust and jealousy prevented the Home and School Council becoming, as in Michael Young's vision, a co-ordinated parents' movement ...' (ALLARD, *op. cit.*). My own feeling is that the failure was rooted in the *structures* of educational government and administration, rather than in *personal* disputes implicit in phrases like 'distrust' and 'jealousy'.

53 ROYAL COMMISSION ON LOCAL GOVERNMENT IN ENGLAND (Maud Commission) (1969) *Report*, London, HMSO.

54 DEPARTMENT OF EDUCATION AND SCIENCE (1966) *Report of the Study Group on the Government of Colleges of Education*, (Weaver Report), London, HMSO.

55 See MACRAE, DONALD (1975) 'The British position', in SEABURY, PAUL (Ed.) *Universities in the Western World*, New York, Free Press, pp. 176–80.

56 ROYAL COMMISSION ON LOCAL GOVERNMENT IN ENGLAND (Maud Commission) (1967) *Written Evidence of the Department of Education and Science*, London, HMSO, p. 39.

57 CENTRAL ADVISORY COUNCIL FOR EDUCATION (ENGLAND) (1967) *Children and Their Primary Schools*, London, HMSO, pp. 37–49.

58 *Ibid*, p. 37.

59 Their findings were later published in BARON, GEORGE and HOWELL, D.A. (1968) *School Management and Government*, London, HMSO.

60 CENTRAL ADVISORY COUNCIL, *op. cit*, p. 415.

61 *Ibid.* pp. 414–16.

62 PULHAM, KEITH (1970) *The Great Exhibition 1970: An Account of a School-Community Experiment*, Liverpool, Liverpool EPA Project Occasional Paper. For the original experiment, see MARCH, LINDSEY (1966) *The Education Shop: A Report on a Social Experiment*, Cambridge, ACE.

63 For a more thorough account, see LOVETT, TOM (1970) *The Role of School Managers in Educational Priority Areas*, and MIDWINTER, ERIC (1970) *Home and School Relations in Educational Priority Areas*, both Liverpool, Liverpool EPA Project Occasional Papers.

64 PARLIAMENTARY DEBATES (Hansard), 5th Series, vol. 397, Columns 2299–2305 (Education Bill in committee, 9 March 1944). Mr E. Harvey proposed the amendment in entirely non-political terms: 'I think from all quarters of the committee there has come an expression of appreciation of

the parents' part in the education of the child ...' (Col. 2299).

65 ROYAL COMMISSION ON LOCAL GOVERNMENT IN ENGLAND (Maud Commission) (1969) *Written Evidence of Private Citizens, Amenity, Ratepayers' and Residents' Organisations and Other Witnesses ...*, London, HMSO, p. 358.

66 ROYAL COMMISSION ON LOCAL GOVERNMENT IN ENGLAND, *Report, op. cit.*, pp. 10, 16.

67 RANK AND FILE (n.d. 1971?) *Democracy in Schools*, London, Rank and File; NATIONAL ASSOCIATION OF SCHOOLMASTERS (1973) *The Government of Schools*, Hemel Hempstead, NAS; NATIONAL UNION OF TEACHERS (1973) *Teacher Participation*, London NUT.

68 For a useful general account, see FENWICK, *op. cit.*

69 KOGAN (1971) *op. cit.*, p. 190.

70 Bradbury v. Enfield London Borough (1967) — reported in TAYLOR, GEORGE and SAUNDERS, JOHN B. (1976) *The Law of Education*, 8th ed., London, Butterworth, pp. 261–2.

71 Lee v. Secretary of State for Education and Science (1967) — reported in TAYLOR and SAUNDERS (1976) *op. cit.*, p. 262. The same plaintiff had previously brought a case against the Borough.

72 BUXTON, R. (1973) 'Comprehensive education: Central government, local authorities and the law', in FOWLER G. *et al.* (Eds) *Decision-Making in British Education*, London, Heinemann/Open University Press, p. 117.

73 KOGAN, MAURICE (1978) *The Politics of Educational Change* Manchester, Manchester University Press. pp. 84–85.

74 See 4.4.

75 A characteristic contemporary statement of this view was REICH, CHARLES A. (1971) *The Greening of America*, London, Penguin. This book posited a worldwide shift through successive modes of 'consciousness'.

76 SALLIS, JOAN. 'Current practice in school government' *Where*, 143, 1978, pp. 295–300. There were 104 LEAs in England and Wales, so that even if the 15 who failed to respond made no provision for parents, the majority making such provision was substantial.

77 ASHFORD, DOUGLAS E. (1982) *British Dogmatism and French Pragmatism: Central-local Policymaking in the Welfare State.* London, G. Allen and Unwin.

78 *Ibid.*, pp. 355–6.

79 BUSH, TONY (1982) *Rhetoric and Reality: Relationships Between Central Government and Local Authorities*, London, Society of Education Officers, p. 11.

80 Cf Anne Corbett's blunt reply to the Taylor committee's question: 'Are governing bodies necessary?' — 'Yes, because there is no consensus about what schools should do ...' (CORBETT, ANNE, (1976) *Whose schools?* London, Fabian Society, p. 17). Absence of consensus produced the feeling of insecurity which in turn produced a felt 'need' for governors in some shape or form. Compare Caroline Benn's views on a parallel but

potentially more explosive device, the referendum (BENN, CAROLINE. 'Referenda — do they help or hinder decision-making?' *Education*, 139/16, 21 April 1972, pp. 374–5).

81 The Sheffield changes are described in detail in BACON, WILLIAM (1978) *Public accountability and the schooling system — a sociology of school board democracy*. London, Harper and Row.

82 BACON, *op. cit.*, p. 52.

83 *Ibid*, p. 182.

84 Ibid, pp. 191–2. The 'C' in 'CASE' stands for Confederation, not Campaign.

85 In all this account only 'county' or 'state' schools are referred to. The LEA also controls a large catholic sector which was unaffected by these changes. Another complicating factor is much smaller Anglican and Jewish provision. In these respects Liverpool is untypical.

86 This account is based mainly on the author's own experience, as he was a CASE representative on the 1974 working party.

87 This was the title of a much-discussed study, written from a broadly Marxian perspective: NAIRN, TOM, (1977) *The break-up of Britain: crisis and neo-nationalism* (London, NLB, 2nd expanded edition, London, Verso, 1981). Parliament was preoccupied with 'devolution' for several years: certainly from the White Paper of September 1974 to the referenda of March 1979.

88 An exemplary statement of the educational preoccupations of this Conservative right wing can be found in BOYSON, RHODES (1975) *The Crisis in Education*, London, Woburn Press.

89 HANSARD, 5th Series, Volume 890, 1974–5, columns 1944–75.

90 *Ibid.*, column 1946.

91 *Ibid.*, column 1966.

92 *Ibid.*, column 1946.

93 DEPARTMENT OF EDUCATION AND SCIENCE AND WELSH OFFICE (1977) *A New Partnership for Our Schools* ('Taylor Report'), London, HMSO, p. 1, para. 1.1.

94 BARON, GEORGE (1981) 'Political parties and school government in England and Wales', in BARON, G. (Ed.), *The Politics of School Government*, Oxford, Pergamon, pp. 81–103; here, p. 90.

95 For references to the William Tyndale affair, see footnotes 98 and 99. There is a succinct summary of 'The Great Debate' in FENWICK, K. and MCBRIDE P. (1981) *The Government of Education*, Oxford, Martin Robertson, pp. 218 ff. For a full contemporary account of the Ruskin College speech see *The Times Educational Supplement*, 22 October 1976. The Green Paper's full title was DEPARTMENT OF EDUCATION AND SCIENCE AND WELSH OFFICE (1977) *Education in Schools, A Consultative Document*, London, HMSO.

96 HANSARD, 5th Series, volume 890, column 1946.

97 DEPARTMENT OF EDUCATION AND SCIENCE AND WELSH OFFICE, *op. cit.*,

p. 3, para 1.10.

98 ELLIS, TERRY, *et al.* (1976) *William Tyndale: The Teachers' Story*, London, Writers and Readers Publishing Co-operative, p. 157.

99 INNER LONDON EDUCATION AUTHORITY (1976) *The William Tyndale Junior and Infants Schools: Report of the Public Inquiry Conducted by Mr Robin Auld, Q.C. into the Teaching, Organization and Management of the William Tyndale Junior and Infants Schools, Islington, London N.1*, London, ILEA.

100 *Ibid.*, p. 270.

101 *Ibid.*, p. 271.

102 *Ibid.*

103 The speech he made at Ruskin College on 18 October is reported in *The Times Educational Supplement* of 22 October 1976, and reproduced in full in *Education*, 148/17, 1976, pp. 332–3.

104 GRAY, J., MCPHERSON A.F. and RAFFE, D. (1983) *Reconstructions of Secondary Education: Theory, Myth and Practice since the War*, London, Routledge and Kegan Paul, p. 105.

105 DEPARTMENT OF EDUCATION AND SCIENCE AND WELSH OFFICE, *op. cit.*, 2.3, para 1.10.

106 *Ibid.*, p. 14, para. 3.6.

107 *Ibid.*, p. 13, para. 3.2.

108 *Ibid.*, p. 35 (Annex to Ch. 4).

109 *Ibid.*, pp. 39–44 (my italics).

110 *Ibid.*, pp. 215–22 (Appendix G).

111 *Ibid.*, p. 58, para. 6.42.

112 *Ibid.*, p. 64, para. 7.7.

113 ANON. (1978) 'Taylor report: Warm welcome from the Labour party ... but NUT gives the chairman a roasting', *Education*, 151/2, pp. 22–3; here, p. 23.

114 ANON. (1978) 'Taylor: Why the Committee's costings are wrong', *Education*, 152/4, p. 76. The Taylor costings are on p. 108 of the report (para. 13.15): they estimate an annual expenditure by LEAs of £4.3 millions.

115 ANON. (1977) 'Reactions to Taylor', *Education*, 150/14, pp. 198–200.

116 NATIONAL UNION OF TEACHERS (1978) *Partnership in Education: The NUT Commentary on the Taylor Report*, London, NUT.

117 ASSOCIATION OF ASSISTANT MISTRESSES (1978) *The Management and Government of Schools: The AAM Response to the Taylor Committee of Enquiry*, London, AAM.

118 HANSARD, 5th Series, Volume 959, 1978–9, column 1230.

119 HANSARD, 5th Series, Volume 973, 1979–80, column 33.

120 DEPARTMENT OF EDUCATION AND SCIENCE AND WELSH OFFICE, *op. cit.*, p. 30, para. 4.27.

121 HANSARD, 5th Series, Volume 973, 1979–80, column 31.

122 A fuller account would need to note the elaborate arrangements flowing from another Education Act in 1981 to define the rights of parents whose

children were deemed to require special educational provision. For a summary, see NEWELL, PETER (1983) *ACE Special Education Handbook*, London Advisory Centre for Education. In some respects, these 1981 arrangements are more concrete and educationally appropriate than those provided for in the 1980 Act: see RUSSELL, PHILIPPA (1983) *Children's Needs and Parents' Rights: — New Influences in Provision*, London Centre for Studies in Integration in Education.

123 ANON. (1982) 'School choice: "You can't have what isn't there."', *Where*, 182, pp. 5–6; here, p. 6.

124 ANON. (1982) 'Choice: ACE comments', *Where*, 181, p. 8. Rather similar comments are made from the administrator's point of view in SLOMAN, PETER (1983) 'Rights and whims — how parental choice works', *Education*, 161/15, pp. 289–90.

125 ANON. (1982) 'School choice . . .', *op. cit.*, p. 6.

126 HANSARD, 6th Series, Volume 33, 1982–3, column 377.

127 For the arguments on both sides, see ANON. (1982) 'Parent elections: How often?', *Where*, 179, pp. 22, 30; and letters from Joan Sallis and Eric Midwinter in *Where*, 180, 1982, pp. 11 and 24.

128 On these and allied matters, see SALLIS, JOAN (1982) 'Parent governors: their status', *Where*, 180, p. 30; and 'Who controls the school fund?', *Where*, 184, 1983, p. 30.

129 See, e.g., BUSH, TONY and KOGAN, MAURICE (1982) *Directors of Education*, London, George Allen and Unwin, pp. 45–7, 139–40, 207.

130 See, for example GIBSON, R. (Ed.) (1980) *Teacher Parent Communication: One School and Its Practice*, Cambridge, Cambridge Institute of Education; SOUTH WEST HERTFORDSHIRE PRIMARY HEADTEACHERS' GROUP (1979) *School and Society: Teachers, Parents and Schools*, Watford, South West Hertfordshire Teachers' Centre. Although the 'good practice' recorded in such local publications often predated the Act's formal requirements, it was presented to others as an example to copy. As with governors, the Act thus set an official seal on changes which were already occurring. ACE provided a 'Prospectus planning kit'.

131 For example, various 'Governors' Handbooks' issued by ACE; BAGNALL, NICHOLAS (1974) *Parent Power*, London, Routledge and Kegan Paul; BROOKSBANK, K. and REVELL, J. (1981) *School Governors*, Harlow, Councils and Education Press; SALLIS, JOAN (1977) *School Managers and Governors: Taylor and After*, London, Ward Lock; STONE, JUDITH and TAYLOR, FELICITY (1976) *The Parent's Schoolbook*, Harmondsworth, Penguin; WRAGG, E.C. and PARTINGTON J.A. (1980) *A Handbook for School Governors*, London, Methuen. The dates of some of these works remind us that the current was flowing strongly well before the 1980 legislation.

132 Contrast the NUT's initial reaction to Taylor (section 5.6 above) with their constructive statement of 1982 on 'Home-school relations: primary and middle schools' (duplicated).

133 For different approaches to a considerable literature see GAY, BRENDA

(1981) 'Accountability in education: A review of the literature and research in the United Kingdom', *Westminster Studies in Education*, 4, pp. 29–43; ELLIOTT, JOHN, *et al.*, (1981) *School Accountability: The SSRC Cambridge Accountability Project*, London, Grant McIntyre; MCCORMICK, ROBERT (Ed.) (1982) *Calling Education to Account*, London, Heinemann/Open University Press.

134 For an admirably clear account, see BROWN, PETER J.B. and FERGUSON, STEPHEN S. (1982) 'Schools and population change in Liverpool', in GOULD, W.T.S. and HODGKISS A.G. (Eds), *The Resources of Merseyside*, Liverpool, Liverpool University Press, pp. 177–90.

135 In the account that follows I am dependent on various local informants, for whose assistance I am very grateful. I thought it better not to name them as what follows is clearly my own interpretation of a complex sequence of events which is still unfolding. To unravel the whole story would be a demanding but fascinating case-study which would require exhaustive interviewing and study of council minutes, the local press, etc.

136 Press release, 28 March 1983, reproduced in *LASPA News Extra*, No. 11, Spring 1983 (duplicated).

137 This description is based on successive evaluations of the programme between 1979 and 1983, carried out by Dr John Davis. For a brief description see DAVIS, JOHN (1982) 'A parent support programme', *Remedial Education*, 17/2, pp. 57–60; and for a head teacher's account, DAVIES, ELSA (1982) 'Parents help make school policy', *Where*, 183, pp. 7–9.

138 MULLEN, GILL (1983) 'Token governors?', *Where*, 188, pp. 13–14. Gill Mullen is the part-time worker mentioned earlier in connection with LASPA.

139 Since this was written, an important government Green Paper has been published (DEPARTMENT OF EDUCATION AND SCIENCE AND WELSH OFFICE, *Parental Influence at School: A New Framework for School Government in England and Wales*, London, HMSO, May 1984). The Government declared its intention to legislate for a majority of elected parent representatives on governing bodies, and for a clarification of the functions of governing bodies. For characteristic reactions (almost all in varying degrees hostile to the proposals) see ANON, 'Parents in the majority — early responses', *Where* 200, 1984, 4–5 and ACE 'Parental influence at school', *ACE BULLETIN*, 1984, 1, 4–5. The new proposals do not invalidate the basic argument in this chapter as the redefinition of functions proposed is unspecific and the question of the locus of power is not addressed. For an important recent study of governing bodies in the early 1980s, see KOGAN, Maurice *et al.*, *School Governing Bodies*, London, Heinemann, 1984.

140 See section 1.2. The quotation is from PATEMAN, CAROLE (1970) *Participation and Democratic Theory*, London, Cambridge University Press, p. 68.

6 *Conclusions*

6.1 The Emergence of Parent Participation: A General Summary

Chapters 2, 3, 4 and 5 (principally in sections 2.2 and 2.3, 3.2 and 3.3, 4.2 and 4.4 and 5.4–5.6) portray how four Western European countries achieved legal recognition of the parent interest in the management of education. The basic question asked was: 'why did governments choose to legislate for consultative and participatory mechanisms whose rationale and utility were far from clear?' In each case, the proponents of the parent cause turned out to have values and objectives quite distinct from those entertained by the governments or other authorities which eventually accepted at least part of their plans. Enthusiasts for some form of legal recognition of parents in their relationship to the school system tended to be

— idealistic (their views on the parent issue were often only part of a wider world-view of a democratic, libertarian or progressive tinge);
— non-political, or at least oriented towards schools rather than politics (the most extreme example being a sizeable parent movement in England and Wales which over eighty years failed even to formulate any plans for political recognition);
— persevering, in circumstances which offered little encouragement;
— heterogeneous (often incorporating persons of different and even contradictory aims, and always a latent clash of interest between an idealist leadership and a membership more preoccupied with a particular school and even a particular child);
— middle-class, particularly in leadership, with substantial teacher input.

Governments had little difficulty in ignoring 'movements' of this description. When in due course the thinking of such movements was absorbed into the rhetoric and decision-making of governments, this change was due less to the size of the parent movement, or its lobbying skills, or to any new formulation of its case, than to felt needs on the government side.

Parent participation as a reform measure was attractive to governments because it appeared to be

— relatively cheap and capable of rapid implementation;
— consensual (or at least combined a variety of interests behind a smokescreen of democratic and participatory ideals);
— diversionary (providing complicated but not very significant activity for groups or individuals of potentially oppositional character);
— administratively advantageous (certain messy or controversial problems could be removed from the overcrowded central agenda and resolved at lower levels).

These advantages were perceived by governments only at moments when the problems of other sectors of the body politic seemed more than usually intractable. Sometimes those problems were sharply focused by actual political breakdown (Germany 1945, France 1968). At other times the problems were more diffuse — for example, the sustained economic slump of the 1970s and 1980s, which fuelled concern for the continued viability of liberal democracies and seems to have generated a readiness to experiment with limited forms of participatory activity.

Because the driving force behind such experiments lay with threatened governments rather than idealistic minorities, the arrangements for parent participation were invariably

— complex and legalistic (contrast the 'school soviets' of revolutionary Germany (1918–19) or the French school action committees (summer 1968) with the legal arrangements which replaced them);
— partial (in two senses: reflecting only parts of the more radical plans on which they were based, and also leaving gaps in the hierarchy of communication and control so that ultimately power was reserved to the traditional bureaucratic and political apparatuses).

This account of the emergence of parent participation does not mean that individual actors necessarily had a very clear idea of what they were doing, nor that legislators and administrators cynically manipulated other people's ideals in knowing pursuit of the interests of the ruling class. Although some actors undoubtedly were cynical, their awareness (or lack of it) as individuals is incidental to the overall interpretation of these four cases.

6.2 The Development of Parent Participation: A General Summary

The preceding summary of the emergence of parent participation suggests that the overriding motivation on the government side was 'legitimation'. Preoccupations of other groups — notably parent associations and political groups which were not part of government — were more diverse and often contradictory. Indeed that very diversity was one of the factors which made parent participation as a policy acceptable to governments. Divergent views could be monitored and to some degree contained within the formal framework of liberal consultation, guaranteed and consolidated through various forms of electoral process. Seated on the same committees as teachers, parents could sometimes be seen as diluting the impact of groups such as teacher unions which had some potential 'clout'.

Once the structures of participation are erected, the central question becomes: 'do these "legitimation" aims remain dominant as the machinery evolves?' The answers to this question are harder to formulate than those to the 'why?' question about the origins' of parent participation. This is partly because in three of the four cases presented (France, Italy, England and Wales) the new structures are so recent that there has been little time for clear trends and generally agreed evaluations to emerge; partly because of the great complexity of interactions going on within the new structures and the paucity of research in the area; partly because of the inherent difficulty of deciding unambiguously that any particular aim or class of aims is becoming more or less important.

While judgments cannot be definitive, two conflicting movements seem to be in process. The first is in the direction of *clarification of central control*, a growing realization of who ultimately has the whip hand and controls the purse-strings. This happens as parents and others explore the limits of the participatory system, and run up against problems (teachers' professional autonomy, bureaucratic procedures, financial constraints, legal and constitutional provisions). This exploration process is often painful. As conflicts occur, both sides may be learning, but the process can be disappointing and frustrating to idealists holding lofty views of the possibilities of participation. From this exploration or testing flows much of the disillusion of many parent activists in the four countries studied. To some extent disillusion represents a necessary recognition of the primacy of the general electoral process in any democratic state, but for many there is also a more complex and disturbing discovery of the legitimation aspect of 'pseudo-participation'.

This exploration process may be accompanied on the side of politicans and the bureaucracy by attempts to devise more elaborate participatory machinery — partly to meet the demands of parent activists as they test the original structures and find them wanting, but also to secure their own purposes. These purposes, initially often unformulated or incoherent, acquire clarity as the exploration process unfolds. Changes occur only within the limits already set. Some observers and participants evaluate such changes very negatively. They consider that as parent participation assists central bureaucracies to clarify their aims and perfect their machinery of professional control, it actually reduces parents to dupes who simply go through the motions of consultation and participation.

Against this negative evaluation must be balanced countervailing tendencies towards *a more liberal distribution of authority round the system*. The existence of committees at lower levels than the central bureaucracy, and especially at school level, gives scope for some *dispersion of authority and decision-making* to the periphery. The motivations for this movement are diverse. At the lowest level, commit-tees originally set up for reasons which may have had little to do with educational ideas or administrative efficiency have to be given some-thing to do: e.g., the vetting of accounts. Although to begin with such tasks are almost always meaningless, they feed into the bureaucracy the idea that their central task may be simplified if parts of it can be de-volved. Perhaps certain features of administration or decision-making can be handled more flexibly and economically at points closer to the actual work. For politicians, controversial issues can sometimes be defused by passing them to lower levels of the system: thus sex education in France[1] or corporal punishment in England and Wales[2] are in effect delegated to parents. The mere existence of formal participatory machinery enables this process to be organized in a decent and legitimate way (even though the solution adopted by authority is not collective at all, but relies on the judgment of individual parents). The existence of committees with parents and others sitting on them tends to attract business and to contribute to the idea of school autonomy. The more centralized and bureaucratic the education system, the more potentially important this aspect of parent participation is. For good or ill, it may trigger off a sequence of events which originally were not intended at all. As schools achieve a margin of autonomy, however small, they tend to become different or more obviously unequal; parents are therefore led to think in terms of choice; choice of school affecting one's own child produces emotion; emotion invests the process of parent participation with greater reality and importance; etc. In the long term this ratchet mechanism may have a much greater importance than now appears, and considerable curricular implications. This is particularly true of centralized nations like France and Italy. Measures such as the allocation of 10 per cent of curriculum time for school decision in France[3] or the approval of textbooks in Italy[4] may turn out to be growth points partly because of the scope they offer for parental interest.

More generally, the introduction of an electoral process tends to generate a *spread of awareness*. Increasingly parents become aware of themselves as an interest group. If they join the minority which attempts to operate the new structures, they meet teachers and administrators in novel circumstances and pick up information about the working of the overall system. That information will be passed on, often informally. Particularly if (as in France and Italy) the electoral process is national and happens at a certain fixed time in the year, the media regularly focus on education. Parent associations are encouraged, and have concrete objectives to work towards. As they grow, their own newsletters and magazines become fuller and more useful, and even commercial publishers (as in Italy) may see the potential of the parent market. Thus, whatever its origins, any system of parent participation rapidly constitutes a large and complex information network. However small the minorities actively concerned locally, they represent nationally a considerable body of people. The very existence of such a network, however large or small, makes it increasingly difficult to maintain the secrecy traditionally associated with bureaucratic power. Any system of parent participation represents a permanent leakage of information from bureaucrats and professionals towards lay persons. Again in the long term that may be a potent factor in achieving change: changes in *attitude* from politicians, administrators, teachers and parents, and even in the long term changes in *policy*.

It seems possible also that the growth of parent awareness through these information networks will promote parent activity (e.g., the growth of parent associations attached to schools or the more or less spontaneous crystallization of local campaigns on educational issues), which may in turn endow the formal processes of parent participation with more vigour and dynamism. West Germany (particularly those *Länder* with more elaborate systems of parent participation, such as Hessen or Hamburg) gives some evidence of this; one is very conscious in speaking to the well-informed and energetic parent leaders of such *Länder* that they see themselves as legitimized by large and lively movements. But West Germany also provides much evidence of controversies (such as those centring on comprehensive reorganization) switching rapidly from the 'participatory' track into the political system proper. One of the main issues to watch over the next decade will be this co-existence of participatory and political channels. Will a *modus vivendi* be arrived at which will allocate certain questions to one channel, and other questions to the other? Will the necessary primacy of the political channel produce a state of permanent demoralization and frustration in the participatory channel?

Whatever replies will be forthcoming, their meanings may differ quite sharply. On the one hand we have the classic 'Napoleonic' democracies, France and Italy, administratively centralized and politically polarized, with interest-groups (including those representing parents) falling more or less neatly into one or other of two great ideological camps. In such circumstances any real transfer of power from the centre to the periphery (e.g., to school or district councils) will tend to be seen as the transfer of power over schools to one or other of the ideological alternatives. It will, therefore, be resisted or fought for in those terms even though the rhetoric may be the less obviously politicized language of democracy, participation, liberty, etc. In urban areas in particular, decentralization, however timid and uncertain, may thus for the first time produce acknowledged differentiation between state-financed schools. Such differences highlight issues of parental choice which hitherto have been dormant or disguised on the continent, though well-rehearsed in England and Wales.

Italy and France constitute one clearly defined educational and political tradition. For all their differences, England and Wales and West Germany fall into a second category, as the table of 'parameters of similarity and difference' (section 1.4, Table 1) indicates. These are both polities in which politically uncommitted interest-groups (including parent groups) are seen as feeding into the party system which then *aggregates* such inputs to achieve some sort of national view. In such circumstances, transfer of power from the centre (London or *Land* capitals like Wiesbaden or Munich) to participatory councils at the periphery has different consequences from those obtaining in France and Italy. It indicates that a problem has been defined as *'non-political'* — a label which may mean 'embarrassing and insoluble' (as with sex education) or 'unimportant' (not worth the consumption of parliamentary time and energy). Indeed, when (as in England and Wales) schools already enjoy some degree of control over their syllabuses and other practices, the outcome of increased parental influence might not be greater differentiation between schools but a greater similarity. Collective parent opinion might curb the eccentricities of individual head teachers, and ensure a steady approximation towards some lowest common denominator likely to command approval from the largest proportion of parents.

Even four cases show the difficulty of making neat predictions. Any particular school council or parents' committee is the product of many general and historical forces as well as of particular personalities and local circumstances. The sort of evidence presented in Chapters 2–5 is more appropriate to reflection on general theories of the relationship between education and society, such as those briefly described in Chapter 1, than to detailed prophecy, and it is to that discussion that we now turn.

6.3 The Emergence of Parent Participation: Which Paradigm Provides the Better Fit?

In each of the four cases presented, it has been suggested that the 'reformist' theory sketched in section 1.3 offers a less adequate account of the *emergence* of parent participation than the 'general crisis' theory. There appeared to be strong evidence in each country that the new structures were set up more to meet various short-term needs of the political apparatus than to implement long-term idealistic plans. In addition, it appeared that favourable circumstances for 'learning' participation (as in England and Wales) did *not* lead to spontaneous demands for formal parent involvement with schools. In general terms Habermas's idea of a 'legitimation crisis' was supported. So, sometimes, were some of his more detailed speculations about the educational scene: for example, it was apparent in both the Federal Republic and in England and Wales that a shift towards the reorganization of secondary education produced pressures within the system to seek legitimation from parent groups through forms of consultation involving parent opinion, so that indeed 'administrative planning produced a universal pressure for legitimation in a sphere that was once distinguished precisely by its power of self-legitimation.'[5] In this model parent participation becomes a by-product of central *control*, which is itself a product of central elites' perception that traditional forms of education must be *changed*. In reality, however, the planning of legitimation is less coherent and conscious than it seems when presented in a compressed general theory like Habermas's. The links are not just with 'educational planning, especially curriculum planning',[6] but more generally with the economy and the political system. For example, almost irrespective of specifically educational problems, the economic crisis of the seventies seems to have produced in all four countries an unfocused casting around for superficially progressive innovations of a devolutionary or participatory character.[7] Behind the immediate economic stimulus there may have lain other problems inherent in the nature of the state: what Crozier has characterized as 'the bureaucratic crisis':

> . . . far from making it more powerful, the need to take more and more decisions makes the modern state more feeble . . . . Politicians and administrators have found it easier and more practical to embrace complexity. They tend to accommodate to it, and even to use it as a useful smoke-screen. It is possible to give access to more groups and demands without having to say No, and one can maintain and extend one's own liberty of action; or, to phrase it in a more hostile way, one's own irresponsibility.[8]

Whatever the precise weighting to be attached to these components of crisis, it seems to be generally true that parent participation cannot be viewed in isolation as a purely, or even primarily, educational phenomenon. It emerged as only one facet of a general movement of which other manifestations were regionalism in France and Italy, 'co-determination' legislation in the Federal Republic, and the reorganization of local government and the 'devolution' debate in the United Kingdom. The conceptual links between these phenomena and parent participation are far from clear: what connects them is that they all represent attempts to rationalize *and* democratize administration and decision-making while remaining within the constraints of the *status quo*.

The 'general crisis' theory seems to provide an adequate working model of the origins or emergence of parent *participation* in the formal legal sense. It does not at first sight explain parent *awareness* or parent *activity*, both of which usually antedate it, whether over a long period of considerable activity (as in England and Wales) or over a short period of restricted activity (as in Italy).

Parent awareness and parent activity may fit more easily into an account based on the 'reformist' paradigm. It seems reasonable to expect a gradual extension of awareness and activity as a small nucleus of activists gradually infects more and more people. This was, for example, the assumption behind the Italian experimentation of the 1950s. It failed to 'snowball' because of the hostility of the social and political environment. However, the English and Welsh example is even more interesting. The reluctance over almost a century to view the parent's relationship to the school in a collective way surely flows essentially from a dominant ideology, which defines the problems of schooling as susceptible only to individualistic and 'non-political' solutions. The parent movement is assumed to be concerned primarily or exclusively with helping parents to help their children. It is, therefore, not interested in parent participation as defined in Chapter 1, and has no real dynamic for growth beyond the organizing zeal of idealistic leaderships. Gramsci might have seen it as a characteristic institution of 'hegemony', with the PNEU as a type, transmitting the ideology of the ruling classes to the 'subaltern classes'. 'In Gramsci's formulation, hegemonic direction is by moral and intellectual persuasion rather than control by the police, the military, or the coercive power of the law: "rule by intellectual and moral hegemony is the form of power which gives stability and founds power on wide-ranging consent and acquiescence".[9] In this perspective it is no accident that both parent associations unrecognized in law and the legal structures of parent participation are dominated by ruling elites. Apparently unintentional malfunctions systematically guarantee that information, and therefore persuasion, flows from the top downwards. As Popkewitz notes in the American context: 'Our very notion of participation assumes characteristics not common of working-class communities. Often, the poor work long and arduous hours. A parent coming to a school conference may have to lose pay needed to support the family. At the end of the day, physical exhaustion and the immediate needs of the family make participation exceedingly difficult.'[10]

If this sort of interpretation is found persuasive, then the importance of concepts like 'crisis' and 'legitimation' is not limited to the emergence of parent participation in the narrower sense, but has to be extended to parent awareness and parent activity as well as to the development of parent participation itself. The 'reformist' paradigm carries the enquiry only a certain way along the road. It provides an adequate account of the explicit rationale of parent activity, awareness and participation, and of some important aspects of its day-to-day operations, but not of its deeper social purposes.

6.4 The Development of Parent Participation: Which Paradigm Provides the Better Fit?

It was argued in section 1.3 that if legitimation was a dominant concern in the setting up of structures of parent participation, then this would probably continue to be so during the ensuing phase in which these structures begin to operate and evolve: '. . . aim (ii) (legitimacy) will retain its supremacy: aim (i) (responsiveness) will be limited to its bureaucratic or efficiency aspects ("pseudo-" or "partial participation", with information flow largely from client to bureaucracy), and the aims of personal development and the overcoming of alienation will receive little or no attention in reality, however useful they may be in rhetoric.'[11] With one significant exception, to be discussed below, this is as useful a generalization as can be expected at this stage of the development of parent participation. 'The general crisis paradigm would lead to an expectation of *stasis.*'[12] Here the most telling examples are those West German *Länder* which have elaborated mechanisms of parent participation over considerable periods. Although they have been modified and tinkered with (for example, to adjust to the *Zeitgeist* of the late sixties), no widespread desire has been shown for parents to take over substantial new responsibilites. Hessian parents achieved in 1957 a position of theoretical legal veto over curriculum change, but when substantial changes were proposed fifteen years later, two things became apparent. Firstly, 'professional parents' had become almost part of the educational bureaucracy (the legitimation process really had worked!). Secondly, as soon as educational policy became controversial it moved out of the 'participation' track and into conventional political channels.

The French, Italian and English and Welsh examples are more recent and therefore more difficult to evaluate over time, but nothing suggests any fundamental difference in principle from Hessen or Hamburg. Certainly none of the four examples offers any real support for the gradual downgrading of the legitimacy aim and its replacement by a greater concern even for pragmatic 'responsiveness'. If parents (or more usually parents operating through mixed committees of which parents are only one element) take on bits of decision-making, they do so very much on conditions set by the existing system. Either they validate decisions already reached by professionals (as in most class council decisions about promotions), or they have referred to them more or less embarrassing value-laden decisions for which the central state machinery would rather not have responsibility.

All this suggests that in development as well as in origins the general crisis theory is the more satisfactory, describing as it does 'a legitimation process that elicits generalized motives — that is, diffuse mass loyalty — but avoids participation.'[13] However, the adequacy of the summary quoted above needs to be questioned at one point. It indicates, correctly, that in Pateman's terms we are dealing with 'pseudo-participation' or 'partial participation', then goes on to equate that with 'information flow largely from client to bureaucracy'. This phrase surely misrepresents the complexity of interests and information flows channelled through (and to some extent created by) systems of parent participation. On the one hand, bureaucracies (administrators and teachers) have conflicting interests. Secrecy is for them an important weapon of professional control. Yet at the same time many of them can see that dialogue with parents and others may help them to make sensible adjustments to changing social realities ('responsiveness') and may also defuse ill-informed criticism and rally support for the school. On the other hand, parents wish to feed their views into the bureaucratic machine and *be heard* — but in order to be heard they need information and advice from the machine itself so that they may choose the sort of issues on which some 'give' is possible, and present their cases in appropriate ways.

When this symbiotic relationship is combined with the view of participatory systems as large information networks, then the potential of such systems for producing change seems greater than when one views them in terms of their own basic rhetoric, that is, as variations on workplace democracy. In fact all four systems display a mismatch between their expressed purposes (which are political but elusively so, because of a reluctance to express obvious political limitations too crudely) and the observed reality (where the political impact comes less from direct political action within the structures than from the increased availability of information which the structures provide).

In terms of models of development, this suggests that the 'general crisis' theory is adequate only up to a certain point. It provides a general overarching account of how parent participation evolves from its legitimation origins. Such an account highlights the limits set by the political system as a whole. It needs, however, to be supplemented by a model stressing the potential of the new machinery as a network of channels, encouraging the flow of information, both 'upward' and 'downward'. Seen in that light, parent participation may develop more dynamically and interestingly, and have a greater impact on education than many 'professional parents' presently think. Also it may not be necessary to jettison the 'reformist' theory because it cannot illuminate the political realities underlying parent participation. There may indeed be a gradual collective learning process going on. As information networks, structures of parent participation are more or less ramshackle and inefficient, with many gaps and blockages. If more modest aims are admitted, there seems no reason why improvements of a generally 'liberal' character should not gradually occur. Such an evolution need not be a mere diversion from harsh political realities if through it people become more aware of the distinction between major educational change involving conflict over values and requiring political resolution, and minor incremental adjustments which can usefully be worked out and legitimated through systems of parent participation.

This would suggest that the answers to the simple question posed at the end of section 1.2 (Are people's attitudes and opinions likely to change as a result of the new structures?) may not be as totally negative as some of the evidence collected in the early stages of the functioning of the new systems suggests. Even so, the verdict must for the moment remain 'Not proven'.

We can now turn briefly to another broad question, posed originally in section 1.3. It related particularly to the emergence of parent participation. Was the appearance of these innovations at roughly the same time merely coincidental, or was it suggestive of 'some more general forces in action in western society at large'?

The evidence suggests two possible, and apparently conflicting, answers. One would divide the four cases presented into three categories. The first category would be Germany where in most *Länder* some form of parent participation can be traced back to the immediate post-war period, building in turn on local traditions reaching back into the last century, though interrupted after 1933. The second would be France and Italy where in each case the present structures originated in the complex of attitudes and events loosely labelled as '1968'. The third would be England and Wales, where the structures consecrated by the 1980 Act not only appeared later in time than their European counterparts, but could be traced back through quite distinct administrative, political and educational traditions. Thus each of these three strands could be seen as evolving independently, and the fact that much innovation occurred between 1968 and 1980 was in a sense merely an interesting coincidence.

A second interpretation would lay less stress on the precise moment of legislative birth of parent participation, and more on interaction over time between education systems and political systems. It would also lay greater weight on parent awareness and parent activity, recognizing that the significant change is a general recognition by the public (and hence by the media and politicians) that parents constitute some sort of separate group, whose views have to be considered and formed. The achievement of legal status may follow from that recognition, but may also precede it. For example, it might be argued that in Hessen the structures erected in the 1940s had no real significance till the late 1950s, and that that is still true of England and Wales, where the 1980 parent governor is still an oddly isolated creation, with little organic relationship either with the schools or with the wider parent movement.

The dangers of subjective interpretation are considerable, but this second interpretation may in the long term — say, looking back from the year 2000 — be more productive. If parent participation is linked to a society's deep and rather obscure needs for 'legitimation', one would expect those needs to be broadly similar in four liberal democracies which resemble each other in various important ways (see section 1.4, Table 1). The problem is that of standing back far enough to see the patterns and connections. Obviously, the evolution of legitimation structures will proceed at different rates and in different styles because of different histories and traditions. These four case studies have furnished ample evidence of such differences. Yet surely there is something *similar* in the four national experiences presented, and surely that similarity is somehow focused on the decade running from the late sixties to the late seventies. Over that period we see three factors:

(i) *traditional* elites striving to restrain control of

(ii) politics in the grip of *unfavourable political and economic circumstances* and producing

(iii) a series of *attempts at modernization through administrative devolution and the redrawing of traditional boundaries.*

If these categories fit West Germany slightly less well than the other three countries, the reason lies partly in the huge post-1945 shake-up, which affected an unusually clear division of powers and launched a radically modernized economy in which the problems of 'de-industrialization' were felt somewhat later than elsewhere. Even there, however, the seventies saw a widespread consolidation of small local government units into larger ones and a preoccupation with 'co-determination' structures in industry. The suggestion is that the implantation and remodelling of structures of parent participation falls into a wider pattern, and could normally be expected to occur amid various attempts made in other sectors of the state to streamline and rationalize the machinery of decision-making and administration. Parent participation in education is very far from a purely educational matter.

239

6.5   Future Lines of Enquiry

> To be able to explicate the ways in which our knowledge is
> limited and the reasons for that limitation is to have raised the
> level of our knowledge.[14]

The specification of those limitations is an important aspect of this study,
which has not claimed to be more than 'an attempt to *begin* a process of
reflexion' (section 1.1). No 'definitive' study is at present possible. The
topic is too large and covers too many sub-areas which have hardly been
researched at all.

Most obviously, there has been almost no serious *historical* enquiry
into parent movements over the years preceding the legal requirement
of parent participation. It is true that such enquiries may present
difficulties. Parent associations are often small local groups which
flourish for a spell then die, leaving little in the way of records. Yet
because the movements mentioned in the historical parts of Chapters
2–5 needed to communicate in order to survive, most of them began to
publish some sort of printed newsletter or magazine at quite an early
period. Where such newsletters can be combined with an association's
archive or committee minutes, or with the procedures of oral history (for
many of the pioneers are still alive), there exist ample data for in-depth
study.

If educational historians have overlooked such materials, it is
presumably because their interest has not been perceived. That interest
lies less in the parent movement itself than in the movement's
connections with other groups and trends: teacher unions and other
teacher groups, the progressive movement in education; the move
towards comprehensive secondary schooling; the political system and its
evolution; etc. Researchers who wish to move beyond compilation and
cast some light on the significance of parent activity will need to place
their enquiry in a wider context.

Two recent studies, one English and the other French, have
explored in a historical perspective the state's evolving relationship with
the family. For France, Donzelot goes back to the *ancien régime*.[15] He
describes 'the transition from a government of families to a government
through the family. The family no longer served to identify an interlocutor completely apart from the established powers, a force of the same
nature as itself; it became a relay, an obligatory or voluntary support for
social imperatives ....'[16] This approach informs the only principled
account of the evolution of parent associations in France, though the
stress is more on the *Ecole des Parents* than the more politicized

associations highlighted in Chapter 2 above.[17] For England, David[18] argues 'that the family and the education system are used in concert to sustain and reproduce the social and economic *status quo*. Specifically they maintain existing relations within the family and social relations within the economy — which has sometimes been called the sexual and social division of labour.'[19] In support of this thesis David presents a historical narrative from the nineteenth century onwards. She stresses mainly initiatives and attitudes on the government side, and devotes correspondingly little attention to where the ideas came from or to parent groups as such.[20]

The emphasis placed by these two authors on the family is largely absent from the present work because of its focus on participation. What is striking, though, is that in spite of considerable difference in period and national background, in ideology and conceptualization, Donzelot, David and this present study seem to view the central triangle of relationships (state, school, family) rather similarly. To read sections 1 and 2 of this chapter in conjunction with Donzelot's chapter on 'Government through the family'[21] or David's on 'Reasserting parental rights to achieve enonomic efficiency'[22] is to see three people looking at a complex but unitary problem from different angles.[23]

This suggests that sensitive historical enquiry in all four countries studied here should not stop at the opening-up of unexplored areas, nor the replication or elaboration of the highly preliminary studies reported in Chapters 2–5, but should press on to reformulate and refine the connections between parents and other forces and factors. In time, such enquiries should be able to offer a firmer base for interpretation of how the parent movement fits into wider patterns of influence and ideology.

Such historical research should contribute to, and in turn be fed by, more sophisticated attempts to conceptualize the *process* of parent participation. It has been suggested above that almost irrespective of the expressed intentions of participatory systems, any machinery of elected representatives and committees constitutes an information network. Such networks may be quite capricious in their effects. They may encourage or discourage particular flows of information or particular styles of relationship between the various actors.

A model of participation such as that evolved by Pateman (with her three types of participation)[24] lays stress on decision-making. In so doing, it corresponds well to the preoccupations of the vanguard of the parent movement and to the rhetoric of the late 1960s, as adopted and adapted by governments. It is, however, open to misinterpretation if it encourages a view of the participatory process which judges it principally according to the decisions emerging *from* the 'black box', and thus leads to neglect of the theoretical link between participation and learning: participation develops and fosters the very qualities necessary for it; the more individuals participate the better able they become to do so.'[25] Some variation of systems analysis should help to produce a more differentiated view of the process actually going on *within* the 'black box'. It might register more subtle changes in communication and attitude and produce a less dismissive evaluation of the impact of 'professional parents'. In time, it should also build up a stock of data which would assist informed judgments of the wider possibilities of participatory democracy. What Pateman observes of industry is also true of parent participation:

> The major difficulty in a discussion of the empirical possibilities
> of democratizing industrial authority structures is that we do not
> have sufficient information on a participatory system that con
> tains opportunities for participation at both the higher and lower
> levels to test some of the arguments of the participatory theory
> of democracy satisfactorily.[26]

A useful step in the direction of a more differentiated view of process has been taken by Macbeth *et al.* in their study of school councils in Scotland.[27] Although they do not formally adopt a systems approach, their detailed breakdown of purposes and functions allows them at least to discuss process, which they describe as 'human and dynamic', affecting 'attitudes, inter-personal relationships and co-operation or otherwise with the planned procedures.'[28] However, the relative brevity of their project and the recency of the councils studied (they had existed only for four years when their report was written) ruled out detailed case-studies over time; and it is these which are necessary to give a lively impression of the dynamics of the new machinery, and of its relationships to other parts of the educational, political and social systems. In their discussion Macbeth *et al.* drew interestingly on international experience, although their primary focus was Scotland. Their conceptual framework would certainly be adaptable to any attempt to open up the 'black box' and illuminate it by international comparison. The main problem would be to define terms in ways sufficiently precise to be useful, but sufficiently general to apply in different cultures and different 'systemic contexts'. This is exactly the problem encountered in section 1.2, in which a breakdown of the aims of parent participation was attempted. It raises the question of how useful the definitions advanced in Chapter 1 have proved in practice. The terms defined there fall broadly into two categories: those which can be used in a 'liberal' analysis (such as those of Pennock, Pateman or

Macbeth *et al.*), and those attached to some variation of legitimation theory.

In the first category, the central term is 'parent participation' itself. The narrow definition advanced in section 1.5, turning on the idea of 'legal requirement' has proved useful in structuring the studies round a basic distinction between origins and development. It has thus provided an objective point of reference in a topic where aspirations and idealistic rhetoric tend to dominate discussion. It needs, however, to be supplemented by terms such as parent activity and parent awareness (5.8). These have been discussed in Chapter 5, but not formally defined. They might be characterized as follows:

Parent activity. Associational activity organized by or for parents whose children attend school. Its purposes may be quite diverse, but its main defining element is negative: it has *no* official or legal status in the eyes of the state, and therefore, in the eyes of schools which are state institutions.

Parent awareness. The recognition that parents whose children attend school constitute a recognizable group within society. That recognition need not be universal: it may be limited to parents alone or to a section of parents. It usually carries with it the additional value loading that parents are in some sense an *interest* group, whose opinions *ought* to be taken into account in some way. It frequently incorporates a tension between *collective* views of the parent interest (in which parents are seen as a group whose views need to be balanced against those of professionals) and *individualistic* views (in which parents' interests are assumed to be primarily in the progress and welfare of their own children).

The notion of parent activity is more closely connected to *democratic involvement* (defined in section 1.5) than is parent participation. A commonsense observation arising from all four cases would be that the intensity and nature of parent activity in any given society reflects the level and style of general interest-group activity: less in Italy, more in England and Wales, centralized in France, related to the *Land* in the Federal Republic, etc. One would hypothesize that levels of parent activity could be predicted from indicators of 'democratic involvement' such as those proposed by Almond and Verba,[29] but that parent participation would correlate with other factors, as suggested in sections 6.3 and 6.4.

The four broad aims of participation derived from Pennock and presented at the beginning of 1.2 have been useful in organizing and evaluating the various complex evolutions described in the four case-studies, and in pointing up the gaps between aspiration and reality which characterize all of them. Admittedly, they are rather blunt instruments of analysis; but for that very reason they are probably more applicable to cross-national comparison than Macbeth *et al.*'s more delicate conceptualization.[30]

Two points need to be made about the four aims. Firstly, the case-studies have highlighted aims (i) and (ii) ('responsiveness' and 'legitimacy') and have devoted relatively little attention to aims (iii) and (iv) ('personal development' and 'overcoming alienation'). This reflects the perspective of this book which has been on the emergence of parent participation in *society*, rather than on the meaning of parent participation for *individuals*. Parent activists in all four countries are often people of high ideals and a strong sense of civic commitment. In talking to them, one often has the sense of meeting people for whom parent participation has been both a vehicle for and an instrument of their 'personal development' as citizens and as individuals. Yet the structures described in Chapters 2–5 were not set up for that individual purpose, which is rarely mentioned in the rhetoric. Even the more collective aspect of 'overcoming alienation' appears rather infrequently in the justifications of the new structures. The relative neglect of these two aspects of parent participation does not mean that these aims are meaningless. It does mean that to highlight them would call for a different study and different techniques.

The second point about the four aims is that their 'bluntness' and generality, though advantageous in some ways, make them poor instruments for sorting out *types* of participation. This was attempted in a schematic way in Table 4 (section 1.5). Perhaps in a very general sense the French system could be regarded as falling into column 1 ('legitimacy') and the English and Welsh system into column 2 ('responsiveness'). However, certain features of parent participation make such schemas or typologies rather unprofitable. The complex arrangements described in Chapters 2–5 attempt to cover *all* the aims listed. Indeed, it has been argued that one of the features of parent participation which makes it attractive as an innovation is its imprecision and its all-inclusiveness. Also, the reality of parent participation is of a complex and dynamic *process*, subject to a wide variety of external pressures. Typologies are more likely to emerge either through descriptions of *structural* features,[31] or through 'types of participatory *action*'.[32]

Macbeth *et al.*'s fourfold scheme (deciding, ensuring, advising and communicating) has been useful at various points in the case-studies. It seems to cover in a broad way almost everything that participatory councils and committees might be expected to do, and seems capable of development for purposes of cross-national comparison. Such a scheme is likely to be particularly important in studies concentrating on process and development.

The remaining terms defined in Chapter 1 relate more closely to 'legitimation' and the 'general crisis' theory. As this has already been discussed as a whole in sections 6.3 and 6.4, there seems little point in reconsidering the notion of legitimation itself. Two subordinate terms originally defined in 1.5 do, however, call for brief remark:

(i) *Ruling elite.* As predicted in Chapter 1, this has proved a somewhat slippery term in the sense that the boundaries of the elite, the precise limitations of its membership, are never clear. It has, on the other hand, been more revealing than 'government', even if governments (or governments plus bureaucracy) have often been the main interlocutors of organized parents and the providers and guarantors of structures of parent participation. Given the importance of middle-class elements in parent participation, it is arguable that the new structures represent an attempt by ruling elites to make more people on the fringes of the elite feel *as if* they belonged to it. It would further be argued that in liberal democracies the ruling elite is necessarily an elusive term because it is in the interests of such elites to blur the distinctions between themselves and the mass of the 'ruled'. In such a perspective, parent participation would appear as one technique among many for blurring the boundaries, thus affecting the perceptions of important minorities about power relations in society.

(ii) *Threat to ruling elite.* Once the idea of a ruling elite is accepted, the idea of 'threat' follows. It has at times to be interpreted somewhat elastically: e.g., in the discussion of the British crisis in sections 5.5 and 5.6. Readers will have different views as to whether the interpretation is strained.

Historical research into parent movements and the refinement of hypotheses, models and concepts should eventually lead to a more complete and accurate picture of parent participation and a more assured consensus as to its meaning. It seems probable that firmly-based generalization can be achieved only through comparison. Such comparative enquiries should learn from this one (i) that comparison is usually more easily and rapidly achieved by teams than by a one-man band, and (ii) that a clearer initial hypothesis should enable relevant cases to be selected consciously, rather than allowed to accrete almost by chance, as described in section 1.4.

For example, interesting linked studies could be done of systems of parent participation in countries which resemble each other in certain defined ways. In this book, France and Italy constitute a pair whose similarities and differences might well repay closer study. Scotland might usefully be compared with England and Wales: separate systems, but considerable intercommunication and some cultural pressure from the south upon its northern neighbour. An intriguing contrast could be drawn between the two German republics, starting from a common point in 1945, but finishing up with systems of parent representation which differ quite sharply in spirit and purpose.[33] In view of the importance of Soviet influence on the German Democratic Republic, a study of the growth and development of Soviet structures for encouraging parent involvement could be added to form a stimulating triple comparison. Parent participation in the United States appears to have a very different tradition from any of the Western European countries described in this book — so much so that a historical study might call into question some of the assumptions which underlie this book.[34] Rather than embarking upon an 'oppositional' study (USA: UK, USA: USSR), it might initially be more thought-provoking to compare certain American states with some of the Canadian provinces; some of the historical and geographical circumstances might be very similar, while the cultural presuppositions (British or French) might differ substantially.[35] If such cultural features could be shown to have a recognizable impact upon structures of parent participation, that might assist the researcher to disentangle the perennial issues from the accidents of history and geography. Scandinavia provides another testing ground of nations which resemble each other in many ways because of a certain common history, but differ in others.[36]

The possibilities are very great, but such studies need careful conceptualization and careful organization if they are to illuminate generalizations about the central themes of parent participation and how parents relate to schools and society at large. Nor should it be forgotten that there is an even wider context, that of the nature and future of democratic institutions. In that context, criteria beyond administrative efficiency or educational relevance may have to be taken into account. As Pateman observes in her discussion of workplace democracy: '. . . even if some inefficiency did result from the introduction of democratic decision-making in industry, whether or not this would provide a conclusive argument for its abandonment, would depend on the weight given to the other results that could also be expected to accrue; the human results which the theorists of participatory democracy regarded as of primary significance.'[37] It is in that perspective that the aims of 'personal development' and 'overcoming alienation' would move more strongly into the foreground.

6.6 Implications for Policy Development

The most obvious lesson to be drawn from an international study of this kind is that straightforward 'borrowing' is unlikely to be successful. The structures of parent participation are intimately connected with differing structures of educational government and administration, and with deep-rooted national attitudes and traditions. Holmes' scepticism about 'universal solutions' applies very obviously to parent participation: 'Most of these policies, far from being induced as Jullien hoped they would be from facts and observations, have been derived from ideologies, hopes, expectations, that is, from models of education conceived in terms of what a few men and women think "ought to be the case".'[38] No recipe can be distilled from all this complex norm-bound activity and identified as 'the best' or 'the most advanced'. The inspirations one may seek from looking at other nations' solutions to their problems will be of a very general kind. English and Welsh observers of some West German systems may for example ask themselves why in their structures parent representation at class or LEA level has been neglected, or French parents, impressed by informal parent-teacher interaction in some English and Welsh schools, may question the formal character of their class council meetings. They may then *within their own traditions* begin to work towards improvements. In so doing, they will need to work as it were *with the grain* of their local 'norms'.

Equally obviously, the lessons to be learnt will depend on the objectives desired. An administrator anxious to retain maximum power and control over the educational process will note the importance of 'divide and rule' fragmentation of committees, of not defining the functions of such committees, of keeping information leakage to a minimum, etc. However, it is assumed that most interested readers feel at least vaguely benevolent towards the idea of parent participation. Like most of the people described in this book, they have not thought very much or very clearly about these new structures; but having acquired them almost absent-mindedly, they would like to make them as useful and productive as possible.

The most important general advice to give to such persons is, 'Be realistic'. Each of the four case-studies has spelt out the stark limitations upon 'parent power'. Those limitations, which are essentially political and economic, exist irrespective of whether one sees them within some legitimation model or not. If the machinery of parent participation is not to be constantly paralyzed by confrontation and misunderstanding, and by the disillusion of those who are most needed to make it work, then all parties (politicians, administrators, teachers as well as parents) need to be more explicit and honest about what *cannot* be achieved by the new structures. This may be difficult, because parent participation was usually set up almost *in order* to deceive and confuse, to promise more than it could deliver. However, if a greater realism cannot be achieved, the structures described in this book will become what their more virulent critics say they already are: cosmetic, time-wasting, and eventually fossilized.

Realism will be discouraging unless accompanied by something positive. Implicit in the analysis summarized in sections 6.1 and 6.2 is the importance of communication. A concerted effort to improve communication in and between all parts of the system has several advantages. It is positive. It is achievable. It can be undertaken gradually step by step. It is acceptable even to people who may be sceptical of the wider implications of parent participation. It is a necessary precondition for any advances in other aspects of participatory action: advising, ensuring and deciding. Finally, it is a policy which up to a point can be pursued by some actors even though others refuse to cooperate. For example, a parent group can begin by reviewing its own internal methods of acquiring and disseminating information. Are its newsletters and reviews as effective as they should be? Do they communicate with the right people? Should there be a more positive policy for liaison with the press? Has the group adequate access to the sort of information it would like to have? If not, why not? If the answer lies in the area of political or administrative control, in what ways should that machinery be altered? Thus the group moves towards constructive criticism and negotiation — negotiation which, so long as it highlights the information issue, has a good chance of attracting wide support, including support within the political and administrative hierarchies.

It will be objected that to pursue communication as a prime objective of parent participation is to overlook the realities of parent participation as a contributor to legitimation of the political *status quo*: 'Community action points not to deficiencies in the mode of production, but in the products: the goods or services.'[39] Individuals must make their own judgments. It does not, however, seem inherently implausible that if pursued over a longish period (perhaps a generation) a policy of greater communication and openness about educational decisions *at all levels* among politicans, administrators, teachers and parents may be more subversive of existing power relationships than is often supposed.

Habermas himself points out that 'the procurement of legitimation is self-defeating as soon as the mode of procurement is seen through.'[40] It is often assumed that the crisis of western societies, and the corresponding draining away of legitimacy, will be, or should be, sudden and revolutionary: the May events in France would be paradigmatic. But 'seeing through' legitimation may equally well be a process of gradual social learning. Nicholas's study of English education in a comparative context points out that continuance of the present system requires that '... most people must as far as possible be kept ignorant about the educational system, so that those who know its terminology, and how it actually works, can continue to use it to their best advantage.'[41] He goes on to argue for clarity about 'our existing ground rules', and stresses the importance of 'new ground rules' if change is to be effected. Interestingly, and arguing from a quite different starting point, Crozier uses almost the same phrases: 'We must find new rules for a completely different social game. A new model of contradictory values will emerge in due time.'[42]

At a more concrete level or policy each of the four sets of actors involved in formulating education policy in democratic societies (politicians, administrators, teachers and parents) has to make decisions which ultimately affect the welfare of children. The more openness there is about such decisions, and the more information about the constraints upon them, then the less fear, suspicion, defensiveness and misunderstanding there will be — and the more likelihood of *all* parties eventually being able to participate in processes of advising, ensuring and deciding. The end product may be education systems which are more variegated and adaptable, and better supported by the communities they serve,[43] than is common at present. That result may be achieved more easily by aiming first for better communication than by 'going for broke' at too early a stage and aiming directly for 'participation as deciding'.

6.7 Final Remarks

Viewed in this wider context, the very existence of the 'professional parent' calls for a *prise de position*. The breathless activist evoked in the first paragraph of this book is not just an individual working out his or her needs for 'personal development', or anxious simply to improve the lot of his or her child. 'Professional parents' are the product of political and social innovation. Are they dupes of a decadent neo-liberalism anxiously trying to paper over widening cracks in the ramshackle edifice of late capitalism? Or are they the harbingers of a new civic responsibility, the firstfruits of a popular democracy in which bits of power will be devolved to those most directly interested in exercising them?

Or is it not an 'either/or' question at all? Will it be possible to recognize the constraints imposed upon 'pseudo-participatory' innovations such as 'professional parents', *while at the same time* using such devices to move towards something better? Can 'professional parents' re-model the imperfect sub-system at their disposal to clarify what 'something better' would be and to begin to erode the constraints within which they work? Can the 'reformist' and 'general crisis' theories be married in a sort of dialectic?

On present evidence one can only guess at the answers to such questions. The working-out of these answers will happen through events and people, and through what the people think about the events. It will also be long-term and probably painful. I hope at least that this book has established that one of the indicators to watch in judging the direction and extent of that evolution will be 'the professional parent'.

Notes

1 BEATTIE, NICHOLAS (1976) 'Sex education in France: A case study in curriculum change', *Comparative Education*, 12/2, pp. 115–28.
2 Faced with a ruling from the European Court of Human Rights, the Secretary of State for Education and Science announced that the government would allow parents to determine whether or not their children should be liable to beating (see *Guardian*, 29 July 1983; also ANON. (1983) 'Corporal punishment', *Education*, 162/5, p. 78).
3 See section 2.4. By the end of the 1970s this had evolved into various kinds of project work, under the general label of *Projets d'actions éducatives* and enjoined by ministerial circular. See VERS L'EDUCATION NOUVELLE, (1981) *Ouvrir l'École: Projets d'Action Éducatives*, Paris, Centres d'Entraînement aux Méthodes d'Education active; LESELBAUM, NELLY (1982) 'Le travail autonome: Premier essai d'évaluation d'une innovation pédagogique', *Revue Française de Pédagogie*, 59, pp. 9–23.
4 BEATTIE, NICHOLAS (1981) 'Sacred monster: Textbooks in the Italian educational system', *British Journal of Educational Studies*, 29/3, pp. 218–35.
5 HABERMAS, JÜRGEN (1976) *Legitimation Crisis*, trans. by T.M. MCCARTHY, London, Heinemann, p. 71.
6 *Ibid.*
7 Cf. HABERMAS, *op. cit.*, p. 93: 'Economic crises are shifted into the political system through the reactive-avoidance activity of the government in such a way that supplies of legitimation can compensate for deficits in rationality

and extensions of organizational rationality can compensate for those legitimation deficits that do appear.'

8 CROZIER, MICHEL (1980) 'La crise bureaucratique', *Revue Française d'Administration Publique*, 15, pp. 593–604; here, pp. 595. Cf. a British civil servant quoted by Beer: '. . . as the scope of the Government's involvement in the life of the country gets wider and wider, the more the Government has to rely on the willingness of people who are not its employees to do what it wants done . . .' (BEER, SAMUEL H. (1982) *Britain against Itself: The Political Contradictions of Collectivism*, London, Faber and Faber, p. 14)

9 ENTWISTLE, HAROLD (1979) *Antonio Gramsci: Conservative Schooling for Radical Politics*, London, Routledge and Kegan Paul, p. 12.

10 POPKEWITZ, T.S. (1979) 'Schools and the symbolic uses of community participation', in GRANT, CARL A. (Ed.), *Community Participation in Education*, Boston, Mass., Allyn and Bacon, pp. 203–22; here, pp. 206–7.

11 Section 1.3.

12 Section 1.3.

13 HABERMAS, *op. cit.*, p. 36.

14 ALMOND, GABRIEL A. and VERBA, SIDNEY, (1963) *The Civic Culture: Political Attitudes and Democracy in Five Nations*, Princeton, N.J., Princeton University Press, p. 76.

15 DONZELOT, JACQUES (1979) *The Policing of Families*, London, Hutchinson (original French version *La Police des Familles*, Paris, Editions de Minuit, 1977).

16 *Ibid.*, p. 92.

17 For the discussion of parent associations, see *ibid.*, pp. 199–217.

18 DAVID, MIRIAM E. (1980) *The State, the Family and Education*, London, Routledge and Kegan Paul.

19 *Ibid.*, p. 1.

20 See *ibid.*, p. 246: 'I have not been able to cover adequately all the origins of these educational policy developments . . . that would require another book and one in which the frame of reference was very different.'

21 DONZELOT, *op. cit.*, pp. 48–95

22 DAVID, *op. cit.*, pp. 185–211.

23 Habermas provides a wider and more abstract background — see, for example his discussion of 'socio-cultural crisis' in HABERMAS, *op. cit.*, pp. 48 ff., or his remarks on the competition between schools and families (*Ibid.*, p. 72).

24 PATEMAN, CAROLE (1970) *Participation and Democratic Theory*, London, Cambridge University Press.

25 *Ibid.*, pp. 43–4.

26 *Ibid.*, pp. 106–7

27 MACBETH, ALASTAIR et al. (1980) *Scottish School Councils: Policy-Making, Participation or Irrelevance?* Edinburgh, HMSO.

28 *Ibid.*, p. 82.

29 See, for example, ALMOND and VERBA, *op. cit.*, Chs 6 ('The obligation to

participate') and 7 ('The sense of civic competence').

30 MACBETH *et al.*, *op. cit.*, especially Ch. 2 ('Purposes for school councils').

31 Cf. *ibid.*, pp. 90 ff., where 'eight models of school council' are described.

32 *Ibid.*, pp. 23–4.

33 For the German Democratic Republic, see KUNATH, PAUL (1959–60) 'Historische Skizze über die Entwicklung der Zusammenarbeit zwischen Schule und Elternhaus in der D.D.R. von 1945–1959', *Wissenschaftliche Zeitschift der Deutschen Hochschule fur Körperkultur und Sport, Leipzig*, 2, pp. 9–22.

34 For example, the secondary curriculum in the USA seems to have been less stable and traditional than in Western Europe, so one of the functions of parent participation in the USA may be that of controlling and legitimating the distribution of knowledge — a function which is only beginning to appear in Western Europe. See APPLE, M.W., and FRANKLIN B.M. (1979) 'Curricular history and social control', in GRANT, CARL A. (Ed.), *Community Participation in Education*, Boston, Mass., Allyn and Bacon, pp. 177–201. For a general introduction to the US scene, see JENNINGS, R.E. (1981) 'School advisory councils in America: Frustration and failure', in BARON, GEORGE (Ed.), *The Politics of School Government*, Oxford, Pergamon, pp. 23–51; BRIDGE, R.G. '*Parent Participation in school innovations*', in MANN, DALE (Ed.) (1978) *Making Change Happen?* New York and London, Teachers College Press, pp. 101–19, is also thought-provoking.

35 For a useful introduction to the Canadian scene, highlighting Quebec, see LUCAS, B.G., and LUSTHAUS C.S., (1981) 'Public involvement in school governance in Canada', in BARON, *op. cit.*, pp. 53–79.

36 Lauglo has attempted an initial comparison between Sweden, Norway and Denmark which tries to relate forms of participation to differing national histories (LAUGLO, JON, (1981) 'Participatory committees and contrasting administrative styles in Scandinavian school governance', in BARON, *op. cit.*, pp. 251–78.)

37 PATEMAN, *op. cit.*, p. 108.

38 HOLMES, BRIAN (1981) *Comparative Education: Some Considerations of Method*, London, George Allen and Unwin, p. 69. CROZIER (*op. cit.*, p. 601) makes similar comments, adding that no industrialist would expect to invest with such paucity of information and such superficiality of basic knowledge as are frequent in 'reforms of human systems'.

39 COCKBURN, CYNTHIA (1977) *The Local State: Management of Cities and People*, London, Pluto Press, p. 160. Although not specifically related to education, Cockburn's Chapter 6 ('The new terrain of class struggle') is a useful statement of various pitfalls which more or less liberal activism presents for someone committed to a class analysis of social problems.

40 HABERMAS, *op. cit.*, p. 70.

41 NICHOLAS, E.J. (1983) *Issues in Education: A Comparative Analysis*, London Harper and Row, p. 223.

42 CROZIER, *op. cit.*, p. 597.

43 This is what Fenwick and McBride describe as 'negotiated consensus'. They point out that in order to survive in a changing environment, any complex institution with multiple goals must negotiate 'some reduction in the areas of overt conflict' (FENWICK, KEITH and MCBRIDE, PETER (1981) *The Government of Education in Britain*, Oxford, Martin Robertson, p. 141).

Glossary of Foreign and Technical Words and Phrases, Acronyms and Abbreviations

Note: The purpose of this glossary is not to provide a dictionary of definitive and exhaustive descriptions, but to give just enough information for the reader to steer by. The location of the first appearance of each item is given (chapter, section, page), so that the reader who wishes to follow up an item in greater depth can place it in context and where appropriate study its subsequent development. The section on England and Wales is written with the European or American reader in mind.

France

Après-mai (2.4, 40)	The period after the events of May and June 1968.
Association d'Éducation populaire (AEP) (2.2, 34)	Popular education association: the body legally responsible for an individual Catholic school. The AEP began in its present form in 1946. It is usually closely associated with the APEL, or school parents' association, and consists mainly of parents.
Association de Parents d'Élèves (APEL) (2.2, 34)	Parents' association. The phrase is usually used for a school-based association.
Association socio-éducative (2.3, 39)	Socio-educational association — formed in a secondary school to promote and supervise various extra-curricular activities.
Autonomes (2.4, 41)	Supporters of the 'Union nationale des associations autonomes de parents d'élèves'.
Centre d'Études et de Documentation (2.2, 32)	Study and documentation centre. Associated with the Jesuits. Generally took a progressive or 'conciliar' line on educational questions, which were its main concern: openness of the Catholic community to the secular world, etc.

255

Class council (2.5, 45)	A meeting of teachers, parent and pupil delegates, and other personnel, to discuss progress and promotions of a secondary school class.
Collège (2.2, 30)	Lower secondary school, notionally for 11- to 15-year-olds. The word was appropriated for that purpose in the first half of the 1960s. Before then, it usually meant a boarding school, often of religious character.
Collège d'enseignement secondaire (CES) (2.2, 35)	A lower secondary school, non-selective, notionally for 11–15-year-olds. More recently known simply as a 'collège'.
Comité d'action lycéen (CAL) (2.3, 36–7)	*Lycée* action committee — more or less informal body, associated particularly with 1968.
Comité de Liaison des Associations pédagogiques (2.2, 33)	Liaison committee for educational associations — a grouping of associations of a 'progressive' character.
Confédération syndicale des Familles (2.4, 41)	Trade union confederation of families. A grouping of organizations of a broadly left-wing character which attempts to promote policies favourable to working-class people with children.
Confédération syndicale du Cadre de Vie (2.4, 41)	Trade union confederation on the framework of living — roughly, a consumerist association with strong left-wing connections. Campaigns against government measures likely to disadvantage the working classes.
Conseil d'administration (2.3, 37)	Management council.
Conseil d'école (2.4, 42)	School council at primary level (1969–77).
Conseil d'établissement (2.5, 44)	The 'umbrella' council for secondary schools ('lycees' and 'collèges').
Conseil supérieur de l'enseignement public (2.2, 30)	Supreme council of public education — a consultative body at national level with representation from a wide variety of interested associations.
Département (2.5, 46)	For administrative purposes, France is divided into ninety-five 'departments' or administrative sub-units, each headed by a 'prefect' responsible to the Minister of the Interior.
Discipline council (2.5, 45)	A formal committee of the secondary school council, with the task of considering serious breaches of school discipline.
Ecole de parents (2.6, 52)	Sometimes used as shorthand for the national *Ecole des parents et des éducateurs*, sometimes

	used to designate local 'schools for parents', which organize courses, conferences, lectures, etc.
Ecole des Parents et des Educateurs (2.4, 40)	School for parents and educators — a body concerned with promoting parent education, with the stress on health education, sex education, good relationships in family life, etc.
Ecole élémentaire (2.5, 44)	Primary school. Historically, the elementary school was an 'all-through' school, non-selective in character, and thus provided a separate 'proletarian' track distinct from the more bourgeois 'lycée'.
Ecole maternelle (2.5, 44)	Nursery school.
Ecole unique (2.2, 30)	Comprehensive school. The phrase is used more to denote an aspiration than an actual existing institution.
Evénements (2.4, 44)	The events, i.e., those of May–June 1968, when for a time the Fifth Republic seemed about to collapse.
Fédération Andrieu (2.6, 48)	Shorthand, since 1980, for the 'Fédération des Conseils de parents d'élèves'.
Fédération Cornec (2.2, 30)	Shorthand for the 'Federation des Conseils de parents d'élèves'. The most common way of referring to this federation, at least until 1980, when President Cornec retired.
Fédération des Conseils de Parents d'Elèves (FCPE) (2.2, 30)	Federation of parents' councils. The official designation of the 'Federation Cornec'. The main left-wing parents' federation. Teachers were closely involved until 1968. Jean Cornec presided over the federation for a quarter of a century. After his retirement in 1980 the federation gradually became known as the 'Fédération Andrieu'.
Fédération des Parents d'Elèves de l'Enseignement public (FPEEP or PEEP) (2.2, 30)	Federation of parents of pupils in public education. The modern name of the 'Fédération des parents d'élèves des lycées et collèges'. Sometimes referred to in this book as the moderate-right parents' federation.
Fédération des Parents d'Elèves des Lycées et Collèges (2.2, 30)	Federation of parents of children in academic secondary schools — sometimes referred to in this book as the moderate-right parents' federation. This is the original label of what later became the 'Fédération des parents d'élèves de l'enseignement public'.

257

Fédération Lagarde (2.5, 47)	Shorthand for the 'Fédération des parents d'élèves de l'enseignement public'.
Foyer des élèves (2.3, 39)	Centre or club for pupils, responsible for promotion and supervision of various extra-curricular activities in secondary schools.
Laïcité (2.1, 28)	Secularism.
Left-wing parents' federation (2.4, 40)	Shorthand for the 'Fédération des Conseils de parents d'élèves'.
Ligue française de l'Enseignement (2.2, 31)	French league for education. Groups a number of associations interested in maintaining and promoting secularism. Has deep historical roots.
Loi-cadre (2.3, 37)	Framework law — a law setting broad aims and structures.
Loi Debré (2.2, 31)	The law of 31 December 1959 which set up 'contracts of association' between private schools and the French state, thus facilitating the provision of public subsidy to private schools.
Loi Haby (2.5, 44)	The Education Act of 11, July 1975 which attempted to provide a new basis for the French school system.
Lycée (2.2, 30)	Upper secondary school, notionally for 15-to 18-year-olds. The *lycée* in that form began to emerge only in the late 1960s. Before then it had denoted an academic secondary school, often with an attached preparatory section, so that the word carries distinct 'selective' or 'grammar school' connotations.
Lycée federation (2.2, 31)	Shorthand for the 'Fédération des parents d'élèves de l'enseignement public'.
Maire (2.5, 45)	Mayor — the elected head of local government at the level of the commune.
Moderate-right federation (2.2, 34)	Shorthand for 'Fédération des parents d'eleves de l'enseignement public'.
Parents' committee (2.5, 45)	A separate committee of parents, set up from 1977 in nursery and primary schools. In practice remained a dead letter, as parents normally meet with teachers in the joint 'conseil d'école'.
PEEP (2.6, 49)	Shorthand for 'Fédération des parents d'élèves de l'enseignement public'.
Péri et postscolaire (2.4, 43)	Roughly, extra-curricular and support activities; i.e., matters other than the delivery of formal teaching within the timetable.

Standing Committee (2.5, 46)	The committee which carried responsibility for school business between meetings of the 'conseil d'administration'.
Syndicat National des Instituteurs (SNI) (2.2, 31)	National union of primary school teachers — strong affiliations to the Left, especially the Communist Party. Large and powerful.
Teachers' council (2.5, 45)	In secondary schools this is (since the new arrangements of 1977) a meeting of all staff who teach a particular class. In nursery and primary schools it is a meeting of all the teaching staff of a school.
Union nationale des Associations autonomes de Parents d'Elèves (UNAAPE) (2.4, 41)	National union of autonomous parent associations — a right-wing federation formed in reaction to the events of May–June 1968.
Union nationale des Associations de Parents d'Elèves (UNAPEL) (2.2, 30)	National union of parent associations — restricted to Catholic schools.

Italy

Assemblea (3.3, 77)	An open meeting of interested parties to conduct, control and legitimize some more or less public activity.
Associazione Italiana Genitori (AGe) (3.3, 76)	Italian parents' association — the first national association, of a broadly right-wing character.
Bocciatura (3.3, 74)	The 'repeating' system, whereby failing students are required to repeat a whole year's courses before being allowed to move on up the system.
Centro Didattico Nazionale per i rapporti scuola-famiglia (from 1963: e per l'orientamento scolastico) (3.2, 69)	National didactic centre for school-family relations (from 1963: and for educational guidance). A study centre in Rome funded by the Ministry of National Education.
Centro Iniziativa Democratica Insegnanti (CIDI) (3.3, 76)	Centre for a democratic initiative among teachers — a grouping of teachers of a broadly progressive and left-wing kind.
Centro Operativo tra Genitori per l'Iniziativa Democratica e	Parents' working centre for the democratic and antifascist initiative in school — a parents' grouping of a broadly left-wing character. Later

Antifascista nella Scuola (COGIDAS) (3.3, 76)	evolved into the CGD.
Christian Democracy (3.1, 67)	The main political grouping on the Right, continuously in power in Italy since the late 1940s. A collection of varied and often competing tendencies and trends, rather than a unitary party with a clear doctrine.
Commune (3.3, 77)	The basic unit of local government, ranging from a tiny village to a large town.
Consiglio di circolo (3.4, 81)	The school council of an elementary school.
Consiglio di istituto (3.4, 81)	The school council of a middle or upper secondary school.
Consiglio d'interclasse (3.4, 81)	A council, considering mainly matters of progress and promotion, and serving two or more classes of a single grade working in one school building.
Cooperazione Educativa (3.2, 72)	The journal of the MCE.
Coordinamento Genitore Democratici (CGD) (3.4, 85)	Grouping of democratic parents. Emerged from COGIDAS in 1976 — a heterogeneous grouping of more or less left-wing local groups.
DC (3.1, 67)	Democrazia Cristiana, Christian Democracy.
Decreti Delegati (3.3, 80)	The decrees, legitimated by Law 477, which in 1974 specified the structures of the new participatory system.
Discipline Council (3.4, 82)	A committee to which serious breaches of school discipline are referred. It can order suspensions of pupils, etc.
District (distretto) (3.5, 90)	A zone grouping the entire range of schools up to the age of 18 and catering for a population between one and two hundred thousand.
District council (3.5, 93)	The council created by the *Decreti Delegati* to supervise and monitor educational activity within a school district.
Elementary school (3.3, 80)	The basic first or primary school, notionally for 6- to 11-year-olds,
Genitori (3.2, 70)	'Parents' — the first Italian parent review, quite strongly associated with Catholic views.
Genitori e Scuola (3.4, 86)	'Parents and School' — a Catholic parents' review.
Gestione sociale (3.3, 79)	'Social management'. The exact meaning of the phrase is unclear, but it indicates a style of management distinct from the traditional

centralized bureaucratic style, and intended in some way to involve 'social forces', groups or communities which hitherto had been excluded from the administration of state institutions.

Giornale dei Genitori (3.2, 70)	'Parents' Newspaper' — associated from its inception with the Left.
Giunta esecutiva (3.4, 81–2)	The executive committee, responsible for the conduct of school business between meetings of the school council.
Historic compromise (3.6, 96)	An informal agreement, of particular importance during the 1970s, between DC and PCI which promoted a certain tolerance and give-and-take, and permitted the achievement of various modernizing reforms which the DC had long resisted.
Law 477 (3.3, 79)	The Act of 30 July 1973 which laid down the broad principles of new participatory structures in school government.
Liceo (3.3, 74)	Upper secondary school, roughly for 14- to 18-year-olds. There are various specialist types — scientific, classical, commercial, etc.
Liste confederali (3.4, 84)	'Confederation voting lists' — groupings of left-wing candidates.
Liste unitarie (3.4, 84)	'Solidarity voting lists' — groupings of left-wing candidates.
Mezzogiorno (3.1, 66)	The south — usually taken to mean regions south of Rome: Abruzzi, Basilicata, Calabria, Campania, Molise, Puglia, Sicily: used more loosely as a synonym for poverty and backwardness.
Middle School (3.3, 80)	The 'scuola media inferiore', a comprehensive middle school accepting pupils at about 11 years of age, and keeping them up to the age when compulsory schooling finishes (14).
Misasi committee (3.3, 79)	An optional consultative committee attached to some middle and upper schools after 1971.
Movimento Cooperazione Educativa (MCE) (3.2, 71)	Movement for cooperative education — an association of progressive teachers, with connexions with the Left generally.
National Council of Public Instruction (3.5, 90)	A central consultative body with wide representation from various interest groups and associations.
North (3.3, 76)	Usually regarded as comprising the following regions: Piedmont, Lombardy, Veneto, Liguria,

	Trentino-Alto Adige, Friuli-Venezia, Giulia, Valle d'Aosta. It includes the most economically successful parts of Italy, especially the 'golden triangle' — Turin-Milan-Genoa.
Organi collegiali (3.4, 89)	'The collegiate bodies' — shorthand for the participatory structures established by the *Decreti Delegati*.
Patronato scolastico (3.2, 69)	A school-based association of charitable character aimed largely at subsidizing the poorer scholars of a particular school.
PCI (3.1, 67)	Partito Comunista Italiano, the Italian Communist party — the main opposition on the Left, and more broadly based and heterogeneous than the tiny groups of communists in northern Europe.
Plesso (3.4, 81)	A school building — usually one site of a multi-site school.
Province (3.1, 66)	A unit of administration between region and commune, comparable with a French *département*; Italy contains ninety-four provinces.
Provincial council (3.5, 90)	The consultative body created by the *Decreti Delegati* to monitor education within a province.
Provveditorato (3.5, 91)	The office of the provincial education officer, or 'Provveditore'.
Provveditore (3.5, 90)	The representative of the Minister of Public Instruction at provincial level: his basic duty is to ensure that central decisions are carried out.
Quartiere (3.6, 98)	A town district.
Region (3.5, 91)	The Italian constitution states that Italy is a regional republic, though with the exception of a few peripheral areas the region had no real existence until the early seventies. The region is an intermediate area between Rome and the province. Powers are delegated to it from the centre and exercised by an elected assembly. Most of the regions correspond to historically distinct units: Tuscany, Piedmont, etc.
Riforma della Scuola (3.2, 70)	The most serious education review of the PCI and widely read outside party circles.
Scuola e Città (3.2, 72)	An important journal of educational theory and discussion. Although not narrowly party-based, it represents to some extent the socialist strand in Italian educational thought.

Sistema anglosassone (3.4, 82)	The 'Anglo-Saxon' system of administration. In Italian usage its main feature is that it differs from the traditional centralized system. The assumption is made that British and North American practices are rather similar, and more democratic, organic and efficient than their Italian counterparts.
Sistema napoleonico (3.4, 82)	The 'Napoleonic', or traditional Italian system of administration, centralized, hierarchical and bureaucratic.
Social forces (3.5, 93)	Groups in society distinct from teachers and parents who have an interest in the aims and functioning of schools. In practice, this means trade unions, cultural associations, chambers of commerce, local political bodies and the like.
Socialist (3.2, 70)	The Italian Socialist party (PSI) is much smaller and less powerful than its main competitor of the Left, the PCI. Its influence has, however, been considerable. It represents the acceptable, or democratic face of socialism, and is available in the formation of coalitions, both to Right and Left.
Spazi (3.4, 93)	Spaces — the possibilities offered by the new participatory structures for ordinary citizens to take initiatives and make their influence felt.
Tempo pieno (3.6, 100)	Whole-day school, with which is associated an opening up of the curriculum and a willingness to view the child as a social being, rather than as an empty pot into which the school pours information.
Tuttoscuola (3.4, 86)	'Everything about School' — a commercially produced parents' monthly of a loose centre-right complexion.
Upper secondary school (3.3, 80)	'Liceo', or 'scuola media superiore', notionally for 14- to 18-year-olds.
Vatican Council (3.3, 77)	The Council of the Catholic Church throughout the world, which between 1962 and 1965 initiated many measures intended to modernize the practices and structures of the church.
Voto (3.3, 74)	The formal grade given, often publicly, by Italian teachers and forming a central part of the school assessment system.

German Federal Republic

Additive Gesamtschule (4.8, 139)	Multilateral comprehensive school — A form in which the traditional three tracks or streams are separated for most teaching.
Basic Law (4.2, 109)	The *Grundgesetz* — the constitution of the Federal Republic, promulgated in 1949.
Bayerische Elternverband (BEV) (4.3, 120)	The Bavarian parents' association.
Bildungsbürokratie (4.4, 129)	Educational bureaucracy.
Bildungsrat (4.6, 131)	Educational council — a body at federal level attempting to coordinate the educational policies of the *Länder*.
Bildungsweg (4.4, 127)	Educational track or ladder.
Bürgerschaft (4.2, 110)	City parliament — a historic term still used in Hamburg.
Burgomaster (4.2, 108)	Mayor or executive head of a city or town — in Germany this is a paid functionary, sometimes elected by popular vote, sometimes chosen by a town council.
CDU (4.2, 109)	Christlich-Demokratische Union — the Christian Democratic Union, a broadly-based centre-right party which dominated the federal political stage until the mid-sixties.
CSU (4.2, 114)	Christian Social Union, the Bavarian equivalent of the CDU. The Christian Democratic block in the Bonn parliament is technically a CDU/CSU Coalition, and as the CSU tends to be somewhat to the right of the CDU, the connection is sometimes stressful.
Einheitsschule (4.8, 143)	Comprehensive school. The word (which literally means 'unity school') is associated with the first comprehensives erected by radical left-wing governments in the 1920s. In the fifties and sixties the term was replaced by the less tainted *Gesamtschule* (literally 'together school').
Elternbeirat (4.3, 119)	Parents' consultative council (Bavaria) — attached to individual schools.
Elternkammer (4.2, 113)	Parents' assembly or chamber.
Elternrat (4.2, 110)	Parents' council.

Elternsprecher (4.3, 124)	Parent spokesperson, representing under Bavarian legislation the parents of children in a class.
FDP (4.2, 113)	Freie Demokratische Partei, the Free Democratic Party, sometimes known as 'the Liberals' — a party of the Centre, smaller than the CDU and the SPD, but important in the formation of local and national coalitions.
Förderstufe (4.5, 129)	A two-year cycle of studies, common to all pupils entering a secondary school (10–12). The Hessian term for what elsewhere is known as the *Orientierungsstufe*.
Gemeinschaftsschule (4.3, 121)	Literally, community school — used to refer to schools which were previously confessional but which are now administered directly by the *Land*, so that provision for all religious groups can be guaranteed.
Genossenschaft (4.3, 116)	Cooperative, or more generally, any collective or community group assuming formal responsibility for some public activity or enterprise.
Gesamtschule (4.5, 131)	Comprehensive school.
Gewerkschaft Erziehung und Wissenschaft (GEW) (4.8, 141)	The education and science union — the main general teachers' union (not restricted to one region or one type of school). Tends to be more left-oriented than, for example, the *Philologenverband*.
Grand Coalition (4.3, 115)	A government formed by the two main parties, with the FDP in opposition (1966–9).
Grundgesetz (4.6, 134)	The Basic Law — the constitution of the Federal Republic, promulgated in 1949.
Grundschule (4.3, 121)	The basic, or primary school (normally 6–10; 6–12 in the city states).
Gymnasium (4.2, 112)	The academic secondary school — traditionally with a strong classical tradition, and controlling entry to the university. However, for many years there have been different types of *Gymnasium* offering different types of curriculum, and the *Gymnasium* now recruits from a broader band of society than a generation ago.
Hauptschule (4.3, 121)	Non-selective secondary school.
Integrierte Gesamtschule (4.8, 139)	Integrated comprehensive school — the more radical form of West German comprehensive, with some stress on mixed-ability grouping (especially with the younger age-groups) and differentiation

	through setting rather than streaming into three separate tracks for all subjects.
Kooperative Schule (4.8, 140)	Cooperative school — a variation on the *additive Gesamtschule*, with three separate tracks kept largely separate.
Kreis (4.2, 113)	District — normally a *Land* is split into a number of 'Kreise'. These are quite large sub-units of local administration — 316 of them in 1976, with an average population of 160,000.
Kultusminister (4.9, 147)	The minister of education in a *Land* government.
Land (plural:Länder) (4.1, 107)	State, in the sense of one of the constituent parts of the West German Federal Republic. Constitutionally, the primary responsibility for education lies with the states, not with the federal government, whose function is restricted to coordination, planning, research, etc.
Landeselternschaft der Bayerischen Realschulen (4.3, 120)	the *Land* parent body for Bavarian *Realschulen*.
Landeselternvereinigung der Gymnasien in Bayern (LEV) (4.3, 119)	The *Land* parents' association for academic secondary schools in Bavaria.
Landesschulbeirat (4.2, 114)	*Land* school consultative council.
Landtag (4.4, 127)	The *Land* Diet or Parliament.
Lehrerkammer (4.2, 113)	Teachers' assembly or chamber.
Mitbestimmung (4.4, 127)	Joint decision — the label used for forms of participatory involvement in decision-making which are seen as more radically democratic than *Mitwirkung* or *Mitverwaltung*. A common catchphrase, especially in the late sixties and seventies.
Mitverwaltung (4.4, 127)	Joint administration.
Mitwirkung (4.4, 127)	Joint operation.
NRW (4.8, 137)	North Rhine-Westphalia — the most populous West German *Land*.
Orientierungsstufe (4.8, 140)	A two-year cycle of studies, common to all pupils entering a secondary school (10–12).
Parents' circle (4.2, 110)	Informal groups of SPD inspiration to support individual schools and promote parent education.
Personalwesen (4.4, 127)	A legal term — that aspect of public administration

	which concerns the appointment and management of staff.
Philologenverband (4.3, 119)	The professional association of teachers in academic secondary schools; tends to be conservative in its views.
Rat (plural : Räte) (4.2, 110)	Council — sometimes used in the more restricted sense of 'soviet'.
Realschule (4.3, 120)	Intermediate secondary school — selective, but not so narrowly university-oriented as the *Gymnasium*, and catering for a large middle band of ability and aspiration.
Reformpädagogik (4.2, 109)	Progressive education. The term evokes particularly the education reformers of the first thirty years of the twentieth century.
Reich (4.2, 110)	The unified German state which was created in 1871, became a republic after 1918, incorporated Austria and other areas under Hitler, and ceased to have any real existence after 1945.
Schulaufsichtsbehörde (4.4, 128)	Literally, authority with oversight of schools — the administrative office with responsibility for a given area. Similar to the *Schulbehörde*.
Schulbehörde (4.2, 111)	The school authority — the controlling body at executive level. Dependent in principle on the *Land* and its laws and regulations, though its area of responsibility may be more local. Similar to the *Schulaufsichtsbehörde*.
Schulbeirat (4.2, 109)	School consultative council — or, when it covers a *Land* or other large area, a schools consultative council.
Die Schulfamilie (4.3, 119)	'The School Family' — journal of the LEV.
Schulforum (4.3, 122)	School forum — a consultative committee with mixed representation attached to individual Bavarian schools.
Schuljugendwalter (4.2, 111)	Parent adviser, literally a ruler or manager of school youth — a Nazi term.
Schulkonferenz (4.8, 138)	School conference — a consultative governing body with mixed representation (North Rhine-Westphalia).
Schulpflegschaft (4.2, 114)	School consultative council — i.e., without executive powers.
Schulwesen (4.4, 127)	A legal term — that aspect of public administration

	which concerns the planning, construction and closure of schools.
Schulzentrum (4.8, 140)	A form of organization in which separate schools are grouped on one campus, and there is some interchange of staff.
Senat (4.3, 118)	The *Land* government — a term used only in the city-states of Hamburg, Bremen and Berlin.
SPD (4.2, 109)	Sozialdemokratische Partei Deutschlands — the Social Democratic Party of Germany. The main centre-left party in the Federal Republic, it traces its history back into the nineteenth century.
Stufenbezogen (4.8, 139)	Horizontally organized, as opposed to the vertically organized selective or tripartite system.
Verwaltungsordnung (4.2, 113)	Executive order.
Volk (4.2, 111)	People, especially the common people — used by the Nazis to mean the German people, as opposed to Jews and other 'aliens'.
Volksbegehren (4.8, 142)	Peoples' petition — a provision of the NRW constitution allowing direct popular intervention in the parliamentary process.
Volksentscheid (4.8, 142)	Referendum.
Volksschule (4.3, 120)	Elementary school — the non-selective sector of the West German tripartite system. Historically, the term refers to an all-through school, particularly in rural areas. The all-through *Volksschule*, covering the whole compulsory age-range, had by the late 1960s generally been replaced by a separate primary or basic school (*Grundschule*) and a non-selective secondary school (*Hauptschule*); the old term lingered on in casual usage.
Volksschulgesetz (4.3, 120)	Elementary School Act.

England and Wales

Advisory Centre for Education (ACE) (5.3, 173)	An advisory service for education consumers — i.e., parents. Subscribers received *Where*, and could also request personal advice. ACE made various attempts to make its services available

beyond the middle classes who were its original supporters and principal users.

Articles of government (5.4, 185)

These have meaning only in conjunction with the instruments of government. They are a document specifying the functions and responsibilities of the governors of a particular school.

Association of Assistant Mistresses (AAM) (5.6, 202)

A teachers' association, originally for teachers in girls' grammar schools; amalgamated in the 1970s with its male counterpart, mainly in order to comply with equal opportunities legislation.

Board of Education (5.1, 162)

The central government committee formally responsible for the oversight and conduct of education in England and Wales from 1900 to 1944. Its President was in effect the Minister of Education. The Board was succeeded by the Ministry of Education, subsequently renamed the Department of Education and Science.

Cash limits (5.5, 189)

A system under which, by manipulating the rate support grant and setting conditions for its payment, the government can control the level of local expenditure.

Circular 10/65 (5.4, 177)

A circular, issued by the Secretary of State in 1065, requesting all LEAs to prepare and submit to him plans to phase out selective education in the areas for which they were responsible.

City council (5.7, 208)

The elected 'parliament' of a city.

College of education (5.4, 208)

Usually known prior to the sixties as a teacher training college. In the seventies their curriculum diversified, and they were again renamed as colleges or institutes of higher education.

Community school (5.5, 179)

A vague term, which usually implies that a school will make efforts to relate more closely to its surrounding clientele by opening up sports halls and other facilities, by encouraging parental involvement, even by opening classes to local adults. This usually requires some element of extra expenditure for improved staffing, specialist outreach workers. etc.

Comprehensive school (5.4, 191)

A non-selective secondary school catering for all abilities. The exact form of organization could differ considerably, both internally and externally; Circular 10/65 specified six basic types, including

	the possibility of two types of middle school and of separate sixth-form provision. The most frequent type catered for children from 11 to 18.
Confederation for the Advancement of State Education (CASE) (5.3, 173)	A national organization coordinating local groups; it was at local level that the main activity took place and income was generated, so that 'National CASE' always had a difficult task of coordination and credibility.
Conservative party (5.5, 188)	The main party of the Centre-Right and Right.
County sector (5.7, 209)	Schools maintained by the LEA directly, i.e., without any voluntary (usually church) intervention or control. The LEA is also reponsible for church schools, but certain powers are reserved to the church authorities, so that for an LEA to impose its will in matters such as reorganization can be somewhat more cumbersome and uncertain than in the 'county' or 'state' sector.
Department of Education and Science (DES) (5.1, 162)	Formerly the Ministry of Education. Has the oversight of the education system in England only, though before 1970 Wales was also included in its brief. Does not actually run schools or appoint teachers, but has a much greater influence than this fact may suggest to observers from the Continent of Europe, through its powers to inspect, approve examinations and teacher qualifications, etc. Since the mid-1970s it has taken a more active role than previously.
Education Act, 1902 (5.4, 181)	This Act of Parliament replaced the existing patchwork of school boards of various types by a consistent system of local councils with dependent local education committees. It also inaugurated a coherent policy of LEA provision of secondary education.
Education Act, 1944 (5.1, 161)	The Act of Parliament which set up the Ministry of Education and which forms the broad constitutional framework within which the school system has evolved since 1944. It delineates relationships and responsibilities, rather than types of school or details of curriculum (apart from religious education).
Educational Priority Area (EPA) (5.4, 181)	An area of particular deprivation and educational difficulty, identified as such in order to justify additional resources.

Further education (5.4, 179)	A rather loose term, usually denoting formal post-compulsory education outside the A-level based school/university/institute of higher education sector — substantially but not exclusively education of a vocational or technical character.
Governing body (5.4, 198)	A group of persons who meet from time to time to carry out their rather ill-defined task of overseeing the 'general conduct and curriculum' of a particular school.
Governor (5.2, 166)	Member of the governing body of a school — secondary school up to the 1980 Act, after which the term was used also for primary schools. Until recently, almost all governors were appointed by LEAs or churches, but during the 1970s an element of election was introduced by some LEAs and for a proportion of governors this was consolidated in the 1980 Act.
Grammar school (5.4, 183)	The main form of LEA provided selective secondary schooling. After 1944 fees were not paid, and selection was typically by test (the '11 plus'). The age-range was 11 to 18, and in most places it centered to 20–25 per cent of the age group.
Home and School Council (5.2, 170)	A national grouping of regional councils of PTAs, 1930–51. A body of the same title was formed in 1967 by ACE, CASE and NCPTA, and acts largely as a publishing body.
Inspectorate (5.4, 180)	The corps of Her Majesty's Inspectors (HMIs) whose function within the system is to act as the eyes and ears of the DES, and to exercise influence indirectly by the publication of reports, the running of in-service courses, etc.
Instruments of government (5.5, 191)	The constituting document of a governing body which specifies its members, how they are elected and how business is conducted.
Labour party (5.5, 189)	The main party of the Centre-Left and Left, with strong historical ties with the trade union movement; this is still the party's major source of finance.
Liberal party (5.5, 191)	The main party of the Centre. Because of the first-past-the-post voting system, its representation in parliament is much less than its voting strength in the country.

Local Education Authority (LEA) (5.1, 162)	An English or Welsh LEA run by a committee appointed by a local council, and consisting mainly of its elected councillors, is responsible for the overall conduct of the education system in that area. It is ultimately subordinate to the directives of the Secretary of State for Education and Science (or the Secretary of State for Wales), but within those limitations has discretion to organize schools as it thinks best. It determines levels of resourcing and local school structures. It appoints and pays teachers in its schools, and commands a substantial administrative machine.
Local education committee (5.4, 178)	A committee of a local council, which has the responsibility for running schools in that area. It consists of a majority of councillors elected in local elections to the council, and usually has some appointed membership from churches, teacher unions, etc. It can be overruled by the elected council from which it derives its legitimacy and to which it submits its decisions.
Local government (5.5, 188)	The network of elected councils responsible for education and other locally organized services in their areas. The system differs in principle from the West German federal state in that the Westminster parliament is supreme and can pass any law it chooses affecting the present powers of local government. Local government is financed partly from local property taxes ('rates'), partly by central government, which currently provides over 60 per cent of local government income.
Manager (5.2, 166)	A member of the managing board of an elementary or primary school. The 1980 Act removed the difference in nomenclature between primary managers and secondary governors. Until recently almost all managers were appointed by LEAs or churches, but during the 1970s an element of election was introduced by some LEAs and for a proportion of managers (now called governors) this was consolidated in the 1980 Act.
Metropolitan county (5.5, 188)	The 1973 reorganization of local government established two different structures, one for densely populated urban areas, and one for more rural parts. The former comprised metropolitan counties with general responsibilities for planning and coordination of services, but not for education,

and metropolitan districts which were LEAs and had responsibility for schools. A metropolitan county contains within its borders several districts, some of which may be known more usually as 'cities' or 'boroughs'.

National Association of Governors and Managers (NAGM) (5.4, 183)

Founded in 1970 — a pressure group for a more coherent policy on school government.

National Education Association (NEA) (5.4, 179)

A national association of parents and others who disapproved of comprehensive education, or thought that comprehensive schools were compatible with the retention of selective schools.

National Federation of Parent-Teacher Associations (5.2, 172)

A national coordinating body for PTAs, founded in 1957. In practice a large number of PTAs are not affiliated.

National Union of Teachers (NUT) (5.6, 201)

The largest teacher union, with heavy representation from primary school teachers. Mildly leftish, but only in relation to some of the teacher associations with which, particularly in secondary schools, it competes for members.

New Education Fellowship (NEF) (5.2, 171)

Founded in 1921 to promote the kind of child-centred education typified in a number of pioneering progressive schools. Still survives as the World Education Fellowship.

Parents' Association (PA) (5.2, 169)

A body similar in objects and character to a PTA, but organized by parents alone, with teachers attending by invitation, not by right.

Parents' National Education Union (PNEU) (5.2, 167)

Founded by Charlotte Mason to propagate through parents her views of education and how families should interact with it.

Parent-teacher association (PTA) (5.2, 169)

An association linking parents and teachers of a particular school. Sometimes all parents and teachers are automatically members, sometimes it is necessary to join and pay a subscription. Such associations usually organize fund-raising and social activities; the extent to which they also engage with educational issues varies.

Plowden Committee (5.3, 173)

Appointed in 1963 to report on the future of primary education. Its report, published in 1967, was seen as a confirmation of 'progressive' methods in primary schools.

Public examination board (5.1, 162)

The certificates of the General Certificate of Education (Ordinary and Advanced levels) which are the main publicly recognized school

	examinations, are granted by a number of semi-public boards, usually with strong university representation, and independent of central and local government. They are maintained largely by fee income.
Rate support grant (5.5, 189)	The element of central government subvention in local government finance; currently over 60 per cent of the total.
School board (5.2, 166)	A body elected locally to run schools in some areas (1870–1902).
Secondary modern school (5.4, 184)	The main non-selective secondary school, running from 11 to the end of compulsory schooling (successively 14, 15 and 16 years of age), sometimes with a 'top end' of stayers-on; normally catered for 75–80 per cent of the age-group.
Secretary of State (5.4, 184)	The Minister of Education — responsible since 1970 only for schools in England; the chain of communication with Wales goes through the Welsh Office.
Social priority school (5.7, 210)	The recently adopted label for what used to be known as 'EPA' schools. The change of name reflects a change in the criteria for identifying deprivation.
Society of Education Officers (5.6, 201)	The association of local civil servants responsible for the day-to-day administration of the education service.
Zoning (5.4, 184)	Schools normally serve a defined catchment zone. However, zone boundaries can be altered or interpreted more or less tightly; the less tightly they are observed, the more scope there is for parental choice. Thus, the placing and interpretation of zones can become a matter of importance to parents ambitious for their child to attend a particular secondary school, and can also be manipulated by LEAs to secure or deflect changes in the character of schools.

Index

Note: To facilitate reference to the case study material in this volume all relevant entries have been made under country headings.